BEARING WITNESS
TO CRIME AND SOCIAL JUSTICE

SUNY series in Deviance and Social Control
Ronald A. Farrell, editor

BEARING WITNESS
TO CRIME AND SOCIAL JUSTICE

Richard Quinney

STATE UNIVERSITY OF NEW YORK PRESS

Published by
State University of New York Press, Albany

© 2000 State University of New York

Printed in the United States of America

For information, address State University of New York Press,
90 State Street, Suite 700, Albany, NY 12207

Production by Diane Ganeles
Marketing by Patrick Durocher

Library of Congress Cataloging-in-Publication Data

Quinney, Richard.
    Bearing witness to crime and social justice / Richard Quinney.
        p. cm. — (SUNY series in deviance and social control)
    Includes bibliographical references and index.
    ISBN 0-7914-4759-6 (alk. paper) — ISBN 0-7914-4760-X (pbk. : alk. paper)
        1. Critical criminology. 2. Crime. 3. Social justice. I. Title. II. Series.

HV6019.Q56 2000
364—dc21
                                                                    00-020270

10 9 8 7 6 5 4 3 2 1

*With gratitude and thanks to
the sociologists and criminologists
I have known and worked with
over the last forty years.*

Contents

Preface

We are all witnesses to the life of our times. We are witnesses in one way or another to the joys and the sorrows of being human in a particular time and place. We are witnesses to the sufferings around us and within us. And at times we are moved by conscience to observe and report these sufferings. "This thing I'm telling you about, I saw with my own eyes," reports a woman who witnessed a mass killing a century ago. Such witnessing comes out of awareness, and is an act of conscience. If actions more physical in nature follow, they do so because there has been awareness and there has been witnessing.

As criminologists, especially, we are in a position to observe the human sufferings of our times. We have devoted much of our lives to observing these sufferings. The subject of our attention, crime, is by definition that of suffering. Crime is the window through which we understand the world that produces crime. We soon realize that there can be no decrease in crime without the ending of suffering. The primary object of our attention is thus suffering rather than crime. We are students of suffering, and we bear witness to suffering.

One's biography as a criminologist could be traced as a journey in witnessing. In the book that follows, I have gathered what symbolically may be regarded as the signs along the way. Forty years of travel are marked by the signs of witnessing to crime and social justice. Retrospectively, after the fact, we pause and review the journey, knowing that there was more struggle than the repose of reflection might suggest—the existentials of one's own life, to be sure, but in larger scope the times, the divisions and conflicts, the changes, the struggles of millions of people. As witness and participant, I am part of this. A critical criminology is one product of this life.

My purpose in gathering these writings into one book—these writings that are as much personal essays as they are theoretical treatises and philosophical texts—is to present the development of a particular criminology. This criminology, a critical criminology, developed in the course of my association with many other criminologists. Critical criminology has been a collective effort of witnessing to crime and the emergence of the criminal justice system. Gathered here, with minor revisions, are the artifacts of one social theorist who is trying to make sense of the world, who is bearing witness to the sufferings in the world, and who is hoping at the same time for a better world.

When I began graduate school in 1956, the dominant stance in the social sciences—in sociology in particular—was the acceptance of existing social conditions. Perhaps because of my background, on the edge of two worlds, town and country, I became an observer and critic of the status quo. Some of this background I would later allude to in articles, and I would discuss more fully in my autobiographical books *Journey to a Far Place* and *For the Time Being*. Enough to say here that as I studied sociology I became greatly interested in the social problems endemic to the country. Asking, of course, Why? And how could things be different? The United States, in the midst of the cold war, seemed to be driven more by class, conflict, and inequality than the consensus suggested in the prevailing social theory and national ideology. I thus pursued a class and conflict theory as I began to write and to teach in a series of colleges and universities.

Clearly, what was defined as crime was a product of the economic and political life of the country. Criminal laws were constructed to protect special interests and to maintain a specific social and moral order. This understanding of law and order was evident in the turmoils of the time: the civil rights movement for racial equality, the protests against the war in Vietnam, and the revolts within the universities. At the same time, there was emerging a legal apparatus, called the criminal justice system, to control threatening behavior and to preserve the established order. Critical criminology developed with an awareness of these events and conditions. By many names—radical, Marxist, progressive—a critical criminology was created to understand and to change the direction of the country.

My own travels through the 1960s, the 1970s, the 1980s, and the 1990s were marked by a progression of ways of thinking and acting: from the social constructionist perspective to phenomenology, from phenomenology to Marxist and critical philosophy, from Marxist and critical philosophy to liberation theology, from liberation theology to Buddhism and existentialism. And then to a more ethnographic and personal mode of thinking and being. It is necessary to note that in all of these travels nothing was rejected or deleted from the previous stages; rather, each new stage of development incorporated what had preceded it. Each change was motivated by the need to understand crime in another or more complex way, in a way excluded from a former understanding. Each stage incorporated the changes that were taking place in my personal life. There was to be no separation between life and theory, between witnessing and writing.

The progression of my thinking in criminology is contained in the ten essays making up Part I of this book. These essays are followed by a group of three essays that offer a context for my work.

I begin the book with a presentation of the meaning of the concept of crime and a history of the study of crime, titled simply "Crime: Phenomenon, Problem, and Subject of Study." After moving to New York City in the mid-1960s, I immersed myself in the literature of criminology. This study provided a grounding for my further work in the field.

In the preface to my book *The Social Reality of Crime*, published in 1970, I stated that my purpose was to provide a reorientation to the study of crime. It was my intention to create a new theoretical perspective for criminology, drawing from past criminology but informing the new perspective with the sensibility that was forming at the end of the 1960s. The second essay in the current book is the first chapter of *The Social Reality of Crime*. The propositions and the model for the social reality of crime are presented.

This is followed by the article "There's a Lot of Folks Grateful to the Lone Ranger," subtitled "With Some Notes on the Rise and Fall of American Criminology." Here I was investigating the cultural sources of criminology in the United States, and I was suggesting that baggage from the past needed to be thrown aside, although there was something in the character of the Lone Ranger that motivated us to be criminologists. "Hi yo Silver . . . away."

I left New York for a long sabbatical in North Carolina at the beginning of the 1970s. I resigned my tenured professorship at New York University to live and to write away from the confines of the university. I needed time for reflection and time to write about what was happening in the United States, as reflected in the criminal law and the emerging criminal justice system. I began my book *Critique of Legal Order* with a call for a critical understanding of crime and the legal system. With a critical Marxian philosophy, I suggested, we could demystify the existing social order and, at the same time, create a way of life that would move us beyond the exploitation and oppression of capitalism. The first chapter of *Critique of Legal Order*, which is the third essay in this book, traces the modes of understanding existing conditions, and offers a critical theory of crime control in American society. I observed that only with the making of a socialist society would there be a world without crime.

During the mid-1970s, I moved to the New England city of Providence, Rhode Island. I began working on a book that was about Providence and about my life there, and about the reconstruction of social and moral order. I turned my attention to the study of theology, especially the theology of Paul Tillich, and brought my current thinking to criminology in an article titled "The Production of a Marxist Criminology," reproduced here as the fifth essay. I pursued the thesis that we all are at the same time products of our culture and creators of it. I quoted Marx's concise statement that people make their own history "but they do not make it just as they please; they do not make it under circumstances chosen by themselves, but under circumstances directly encountered, given and transmitted from the past." My argument was, as it continues to be, that criminology is a cultural production that shares the character of such other productions as philosophy, religion, and art. The criminologist is engaged in a cultural practice that interprets and gives meaning to the existing society. Our productions are located in the class relations of the existing society, and our critical understandings are part of the struggle for a better society. The objective in knowing the world critically is to change it. Criminology is to be more than a reflection of the world; it is part of the process through which the world is transformed. I close the essay with a quotation from Paul Tillich: "The most intimate motions within the depths of our souls are not completely our own. For they belong also to our friends, to mankind, to the universe, and to the Ground of all being, the aim of our life."

At the end of the 1970s, I published my book *Class, State, and Crime*. My purpose was to provide a structural interpretation of the current developments in crime and criminal justice. When I revised the book for a second edition, published in 1980, I incorporated my thoughts on a socialist theology. I argued that our whole being, personal and collective, is defined by the historically specific goals and demands of advanced capitalism. The social and moral problems of contemporary society are the result of capitalist development and the secularization of ultimate concerns. In the book before us, I present the first two chapters of *Class, State, and Crime*. The first, titled here "The Prophetic Meaning of Social Justice," is about the roots of justice found in both Marxism and the Judeo-Christian tradition. The rise of criminal justice is analyzed in relation to the struggle for social justice. In the second chapter of *Class, State, and Crime*, the seventh essay in this book, I present a theory of crime and the development of capitalism. The criminal justice system is an integral part of the capitalist state. Crime results from domination and repression and from accommodation and resistance. The solution to crime and to social injustice is ultimately in a transformation that is fundamentally socialist.

The time came for me to return to my homeland in the Midwest. In 1983 I moved back to the Midwest. I would teach sociology for the next fifteen years at Northern Illinois University. Upon being given the Edwin H. Sutherland award for contributions to criminological theory, I presented my thoughts on being a criminologist—a criminologist who is also living a daily life that includes keeping a journal and carrying a camera to photograph the landscape. My song of choice was "On the Road Again" by Willie Nelson. Along the way, I was beginning to see criminology as the making of myths that necessarily have consequences in the social worlds that we create. Criminology—as part of the making of myths—is as much art as it is science. We are the makers of myths, and because of this, we must take great care in what we think and what we do. And there was the awareness of the passing of time: "Gee, ain't it funny how time just slips away."

One's personal life cannot be separated from mental productions—at least I have found this to be true in my life and work. Each life is a spiritual journey. Add to this a sense that absolute reality is beyond human conception, that all that exists is transient, and that human existence is characterized by suffering. With all of this you have the makings of a special kind of criminology. By the end of the 1980s, I placed these thoughts and experiences into my criminology. The essay titled "The Way of Peace: On Crime, Suffering, and Service" presents this criminology—a criminology which assumes that crime is suffering and that crime will be ended only with the ending of suffering, only when there is peace. This is a peacemaking criminology, a nonviolent criminology of compassion and service, which seeks to eliminate crime by lessening the suffering in ourselves and in the world.

The tenth essay in this book—"Criminology as Moral Philosophy, Criminologist as Witness"—is in large part a review of my development in the field of criminology with the advantage of hindsight. The organizing idea is that whatever we may be doing as criminologists, we are engaged in a moral enterprise. Our underlying questions are always: How are we human beings to live? Who are we, and of what are we capable? And how could things be different? Whether or not we are educated as moral philosophers, and whatever the nature of our criminology, we operate with an implicit moral philosophy and we are constantly engaged in the construction of moral philosophy. The essay also contains the realization that as criminologists—in addition to the other things we are doing—we are witnessing to our times. We are witnesses to suffering, to violence in its many forms, to hatred and greed, to inequality and injustice, and to the possibilities of peace and social justice. Witnessing is an active vocation that is grounded in a particular moral stance toward human existence.

Part II contains three essays that furnish an underlying context for my work in criminology. "Journey to a Far Place: the Way of Autobiographical Reflection" shows how one's life course—my own in this case—affects intellectual life. The search for home has been a driving force throughout my adult life. Another force, as presented in the next essay, has been the constant wonderment about what reality is. My questioning of the conventional scientific enterprise has come out of this query. As an existentialist, I share the humane concerns of Albert Camus: How are we to find meaning in a universe devoid of inherent meaning? Our revolt is to live a life of human inquiry and responsibility. This is an affirmation of our human existence.

Finally, the last essay in the book brings into criminology one of the perennial stories of Buddhist thought and practice—the allegory of oxherding. Crime is viewed as a koan in the Zen tradition, as a question that takes us beyond linear thought. As criminologists we become part of the larger reality—beyond the ego-self. The question of crime is now inseparable from who we are; our study of crime is simultaneously a study of ourselves. We and the criminal are one and the same. Returning to the source, mountains are mountains and rivers are rivers. With open heart and open mind, we enter the marketplace with helping hands.

∝∞

The Judeo-Christian tradition is filled with directives and observations on witnessing. Whatever our faith and practice, we are a part of this tradition. In the Ten Commandments, we are told not to bear false witness against our neighbor. The Commandment is repeated by Jesus in the New Testament. John the Baptist came as a witness to testify to the light, the light that was coming into the world. Paul, in his letter to the Romans, writes of the conscience that bears witness. Traditions from the East, outside of the Judeo-Christian tradition—Taoism, Hinduism, Buddhism—make us aware of doing what is correct, in the here and now. Secular literature, as well as contemporary journalism, is replete with the act of bearing witness. Alexander Pushkin has the monk Primen speaking by the lamplight:

> Not in vain
> Hath God appointed me for many years
> A witness, teaching me the art of letters;
> A day will come when some laborious monk
> Will bring to light my zealous, nameless toil,
> Kindle, as I, his lamp, and from the parchment
> Shaking the dust of ages will transcribe
> My true narrations.

We—observers and participants in this life—cannot do other than bear witness. Keeping watch, recording our observations, understanding, but most of all bearing witness to the only life we know.

Part I. Witnessing

ONE

―――――

Crime:
Phenomenon, Problem, and Subject of Study

Crime is first a state of mind. Any discussion of crime necessarily begins with this assumption. Apart from a subjective
assumption, crime has no meaning as objective phenomenon, social
problem, or subject of study. In order for the phenomenon of crime
to exist there must be the construct of crime. The construct must
then be associated with specific social behaviors. The association of
construct and behavior constitutes the social problem. Inquiry into
crime and the crime problem presupposes prior social definitions.

Creation of Crime: Phenomenon and Problem

There is no crime without declaration. That is, some person or
body of persons through established procedures creates the concept
of crime. This means, first, that the concept of crime originates in
the formulations of criminal law and, second, that the concept is
imposed on persons and their alleged behaviors. The crime phenomenon thus exists because of the creation of the concept of crime by
means of the criminal law, its enforcement, and its administration.

Once conduct has been defined as criminal through law and
through legal action—that is, once there is the phenomenon of
crime—the phenomenon may be defined as a social problem. It is at
this point that crime differs in concept from other human behaviors
and conditions that may be defined as social problems. According to
the traditional definition of social problems (Frank, 1925; Waller,

―――――

Original source: Chapter 7 in Erwin O. Smigel (ed.), *Handbook on the
Study of Social Problems*. Chicago: Rand-McNally, 1971.

1936; Fuller, 1938), a social problem is any behavior or condition that a fairly large number of persons wishes to remove or change. In discussing social problems in general, Fuller and Myers (1941) proposed the following conceptualization:

> A social problem is a condition which is defined by a considerable number of persons as a deviation from some social norm which they cherish. Every social problem thus consists of an objective condition and a subjective definition. The objective condition is a verifiable situation which can be checked as to existence and magnitude (proportions) by impartial and trained observers, e.g., the state of our national defense, trends in the birth rate, unemployment, etc. The subjective definition is the awareness of certain individuals that the condition is a threat to certain cherished values (Fuller & Myers, 1941:32).

The Fuller and Myers conceptualization does not satisfactorily extend to crime because of the insistence that an objective condition exists prior to the subjective defining of a social problem. Clearly, crime is a subjective construct which categorizes human behavior. Only after such a construct has been formulated and imposed by select members of society can it be said that the phenomenon of crime exists in any objective sense. Other behaviors, unlike crime, may exist without a formal legal definition. But crime occurs only when constructs are created through the efforts of designated definers.

Furthermore, in the case of crime as a social problem, in comparison to other social problems, there is no need to question who defines the problem or how many persons must be involved in the conduct for it to reach a magnitude that it is defined as a social problem. The identification of crime as a social problem is inherent in the criminal law and accompanying legal action. The social act of creating crime is an indication that the conduct that is being so defined is regarded as a social problem by those who are engaged in the formulation, enforcement, and administration of the criminal law—that is, by the ruling class. Thus, when crime is studied as a social problem, both the phenomenon and the problem are objective only when they have first been defined in the society as crime.

Theoretical Perspectives in Criminology:
A Chronology of the Study of Crime

The history of the study of crime as phenomenon and problem could be written as a progression from an absolute conception of crime to a relativistic one. Early studies and writings tended to rely upon the observer's absolute standard of what constituted crime and the crime problem. Only in very recent years has the society's legal definition been used as the standard for the study of the crime phenomenon. Today the study of crime has been expanded to include the study of (1) the defining of persons and behaviors as criminal, (2) the development of persons and behaviors defined as criminal, and (3) the social reactions to criminally defined phenomena. Until this time, the study of crime (ambiguously referred to as criminology) was narrowly construed as the study of 'criminals' and their behavior.

In the course of reviewing the history of the study of crime, one can find continuities on a general level; however, on a more specific level, one is impressed by the lack of continuity and of accumulated growth. No linearity can readily be found that leads to criminology's present position. The study of crime has been characterized by a number of divergent theoretical orientations, orientations which have existed in relative isolation from one another. Even within particular theoretical orientations, accumulation of knowledge has not occurred according to common expectation. A great deal of material in the history of criminology has not become obsolete but has merely been misplaced, ignored, or forgotten. Much research that appeared when other ideas prevailed has been neglected and thus has failed to become part of the utilized and accumulated knowledge of criminology.

The development of criminology may be reviewed in terms of various time periods and according to the major theoretical perspectives of the periods. Five periods may be delimited in the development of criminology: (1) early criminological thought, (2) nineteenth-century sociological criminology, (3) nineteenth-century biological criminology, (4) twentieth-century eclectic criminology, and (5) twentieth-century sociological criminology.

Early Criminological Thought

While it may be correct to date the beginnings of modern criminology in the first half of the nineteenth century, crime has been a topic of speculative thought for centuries. Most noted social philosophers usually have found it necessary to make observations about crime. The early social philosophers including Plato, Aristotle, Thomas Aquinas, and Thomas More found a discussion of crime necessary for their observations on human beings, society, and the ideal condition of humankind.

While much of the writing of the early social philosophers was focused on the relation of crime to factors in the temporal world, it was common to attribute crime to the influence of powers outside of this world. Supernatural explanations of crime were commonplace in popular thought. These demonological explanations (Vold, 1958:5–6) can be found in various forms. In primitive and preliterate animism, there was the belief that evil spirits cause crime. According to Hebrew and Christian traditions, crime was the will of God. During the Middle Ages, demons and devils were thought to be responsible for crime and other deviant acts. The ideas of 'sin' and 'moral defect' occupied popular thought and much of the writing of the sixteenth, seventeenth, eighteenth, and early nineteenth centuries. The criminal was viewed in some way as having an improper relation to other-worldly principles and powers.

The writers of the eighteenth-century Enlightenment mark the beginning of a naturalistic approach to criminal behavior. In their philosophy, the explanations of human behavior were to be found in human beings themselves, not in supernatural forces. When they devoted their attention to crime, it was primarily in respect to the relation of the offender to the criminal law. Among the French were Montesquieu, who in 1748 in *Esprit des Lois* considered criminal justice at length; Voltaire, who expressed opposition to the arbitrariness of justice; and Marat, who in 1780 criticized legislation in his *Plan de legislation criminelle*. French socialists, especially Fourier and Enfantin, also gave considerable attention to crime. A number of English utopian writers, anarchists, and socialists also observed and criticized the administration of the criminal law in relation to social conditions.

Perhaps the most important ideas in criminological thought prior to the nineteenth century are found in what is commonly referred to as the 'classical school.' The classical school in criminology represents the culmination of eighteenth-century humanitarian rationalism which preceded the application of scientific methods to the study of human behavior. Guided by the assumption of human beings' ability to reason and control their own destinies, the classical writers directed their attention to the relation of citizens to the legal structure of the state. In reaction to contemporary legal practices, these writers protested against the inconsistencies and injustices of the criminal law and its administration, proposing reforms that were more in keeping with their conception of humankind. The publication of *Dei delitti e elle pene* by Beccaria in 1764 (translated in 1767 as *Essay on Crimes and Punishment*) provided the focus for the adherents of the classical school, which included such writers as Bentham, Blackstone, Romilly, Feuerbach, and Peel. A concern for justice and the reformation of the criminal law characterized the main body of thought of these writers.

Nineteenth-Century Sociological Criminology

Modern criminology has been dated by Bonger (1936:47) as beginning in the 1830s with the study of crime as a social phenomenon. Before individualistic theories came into vogue, explanations of crime were largely in terms of factors in the social environment. The origins of the sociological study of crime were in part the result of the rise of the social sciences. The collection of criminal statistics in a number of European countries provided early criminologists with a great source of material on crime and gave direction to research.

EUROPEAN CRIMINOLOGY

During the early and middle nineteenth century, a number of scholars from continental European countries gathered and analyzed crime statistics (de Quirós, 1911; Sorokin, 1928). Alexander Oettingin of Germany, one of the pioneers in the analysis of crime statistics, devoted considerable attention to problems of measuring crime in his *Moralstatistik*. In Belgium, statisticians such as Edouard Ducpétiaux and Adolphe Quételet studied the social nature of crime as reflected in crime statistics. Using ecological maps, A. M. Guerry, in charge of judicial statistics for Paris, analyzed rates of crime against the person and against property for the regions of France. A number of Italian socialists, especially Colajanni, Loria, Turati, Prampolini, and Zoria, were also active in making observations about crime as a social phenomenon.

During this period two journals were instrumental in providing a source of publication for European studies of the social aspects of crime. In 1836, Lacassagne established the *Archives de L'Anthropologie Criminelle*, and in 1896 Durkheim founded *L'Annee Sociologique*. Other members of the early sociological school of criminology created the International Criminological Association.

In England, roughly between 1830 and 1860, there was a great deal of interest in the geographical distribution of crime (Levin & Lindesmith, 1937; Lindesmith & Levin, 1937). Influenced by the impact of social change brought about by industrialization and the growth of cities, several English writers turned their attention to the social problems, especially crime, provoked by these changes. In 1839, Rawson W. Rawson published a paper on "An Inquiry into the Statistics of Crime in England and Wales" in the *Journal of the Statistical Society of London*. In the same journal, Joseph Fletcher, Rawson's successor as Honorary Secretary of the Statistical Society of London, reported on rates of crime in relation to social characteristics of the countries of England and Wales. Fletcher refuted theories of crime based on poverty, ignorance, and density of population. He proposed instead a theory that explained crime as a profession in which persons receive training in prisons, jails, and certain kinds of neighborhoods.

Henry Mayhew, one of the founders of *Punch*, made detailed ecological analyses of crime in London. In a book entitled *Those Who Will Not*, Mayhew noted the location of the offenses and residence of the offenders for various types of crimes. John Glyde, in an examination of the relation between population density and crime, published an article in 1856 on "The Localities of Crime in Suffolk," based on an analysis of the records of persons waiting trial. In his *Irish Facts and Wakefield Figures*, John T. Burt in 1863 suggested that habitual crime is the result of "criminal classes already existing" and that "crime is reproductive."

As one reviewer (Morris, 1958) of these early works concludes, such studies cannot be classed with the ecological studies of the twentieth century because of their lack of a specific body of theory and hypotheses. Yet, these works have been unduly ignored by contemporary criminologists. These early English ecological studies were, unfortunately, to be eclipsed by the individualistic theories of the biological positivists.

In addition to the studies already noted, several monumental works that related in one way or another to social conditions and crime were published during the nineteenth century in England. At the beginning of the century (1806), Patrick Colquhoun, a magistrate for the counties of Middlesex, Surrey, Kent, and Essex, published the seventh edition ("corrected and considerably enlarged") of *Treatise on the Police of the Metropolis*. As indicated by the subtitle of the book—"Containing a Detail of the Various Crimes and Misdemeanors By which Public Property and Security are, at present, Injured and Endangered: and Suggested Remedies for their Prevention"—Colquhoun devoted attention to a discussion of various forms of criminal behavior. The book contained little direct empirical evidence to support bold arguments. The primary purpose of the book was to criticize existing criminal law, punishment, and police procedures.

Toward the end of the century, Luke O. Pike (1873–1876) published in two volumes *A History of Crime in England*, subtitled "Illustrating the Changes in the Laws in the Progress of Civilization; Written From the Public Records and Other Contemporary Evidence." The book is an impressive work of scholarship, extensively documented and, for the criminologist, a source of descriptive material on crime over a great period of time, including material on the reactions to crime. Crime is discussed by Pike as being relative to changing criminal laws.

Another notable contribution to the study of social conditions and social life, including crime, is the monumental multiple-volume work of Charles Booth, *Life and Labour of the People of London* (1892–1897). Although first published as a two-volume work in 1889 and 1891, Booth's book was expanded in subsequent editions to include nine volumes in one edition and seventeen volumes in another. Booth was a merchant, ship owner, and manufacturer who, while benefiting from industrialization, was concerned about the changes in social conditions brought about by industrialization. Like others of his station, Booth apparently felt a moral obligation to improve society. As his biographers, the Simeys, observe: "Booth appears to be a true Victorian in so far as he acclaimed the positive values of industrial and commercial enterprise, but sought at the same time to devise methods of combating the evils that had resulted from it" (Simey & Simey, 1960:4). Booth was a practical man who believed that social policy should be guided by facts, and he set out to gather the facts. What resulted was essentially an application of scientific inquiry to the understanding of social problems. As the Simeys (1960:3) have noted, "Objectivity and obligation were fused together by him into a new system of thought and inquiry." Booth's potential influence on British sociology was apparently diminished because of continuing confidence in deductive reasoning in academic circles. This delay in the application of scientific methods to the study of social problems influenced the character of sociology in England until recent times.

AMERICAN REFORMISM AND THE STUDY OF CRIME

There was the tendency in American popular thought during the nineteenth century to equate crime with sin, pauperism, and immorality. Even when crime was recognized as a distinct phenomenon, it was usually regarded as an ill that had no place in social life and therefore certainly had to be eliminated. Crime was one of those conditions that fell within the domain of nineteenth-century reformism.

From the beginning of the century, reformism, shaped by the Enlightenment, Romanticism, humanitarianism, the principle of democracy, and the religious idea of community, created an awareness of social problems. Various behaviors and conditions became defined as problems not fitting the American ideal. Crusades, movements, and organizations flourished in the attempt to attack such evils as intemperance, slavery, poverty, mental illness, idleness, defective education, war, and discrimination against women. Criminal and penal codes were rewritten in an attempt to achieve a more humane and rational justice. Specific agitation for prison reform resulted in new concepts of imprisonment.

Reform efforts by no means went unchallenged. The teachings of classical, laissez-faire, individualistic economics and the eventual popularity of conservative social Darwinism were counterthemes for any attempt at reform and social planning. Yet many persons in positions of responsibility and authority were impressed with the need for more adequate knowledge to guide their endeavors, especially in charitable and philanthropic work, and to supply them with rational grounds for implementation. The social science movement in the second half of the century was stimulated to a great extent by such a need. The conception of social science as a systematic body of knowledge for the purpose of reform became an important part of the American academic community (House, 1936:331–337). In the colleges and universities, newly established social science departments designed courses on the basis of specific social problems, criminology being one of the first sociology courses offered in the curriculum. Thus, the study of crime became at an early time an integral part of academic sociology, providing the groundwork for the developments of the early twentieth century.

Outside of the academic world, crime received study as a social phenomenon by a number of persons engaged in prison and welfare work. In a study of these writers, Guillot (1943) documents that a sociological criminology flourished in the United States during the Civil War and post-Civil War period. In evaluating the work of these writers, Guillot comments:

> Their efforts may seem naive to the criminologist of today, but there was a groping toward objectivity. Students obtained their

data at first hand, they recorded and analyzed what they saw with their own eyes, and they put their common sense to work in a quantitative framework (Guillot, 1943:21).

The writers of the period between 1860 and 1885 viewed crime as a product of 'disharmony' in the operation of social forces, 'constituents,' or institutions of society. "When these institutions were not soundly constructed, or when their functions were not realized competently and responsibly, and when the patterns of behavior characteristic of groups of people differed from predominating standards, crime was a natural consequence" (Guillot, 1943:172). In explaining crime in terms of social conditions, most of the writers assumed that the operation of any one factor could only partially explain the phenomenon of crime. While they pointed to associations, they believed that a multiplicity of social causes operated to produce crime. Of the many factors considered, drinking, lack of a trade education, desire for luxuries, poverty, oblivion of religious and moral principles, idleness, abnormal family relations, bad company, and civilization in general, provided the most popular explanations of criminal behavior.

Crime in the growing city became a problem and focus of attention for several writers in the last half of the nineteenth century. Charles Loring Brace, who devoted his life to the organization of charities, believed that the causes of crime lie in the way of life of a significant segment of the urban population. In his fascinating book *The Dangerous Classes of New York* (subtitled "And Twenty Years Among Them"), Brace (1872) described in considerable detail the life conditions of numerous groups in New York with whom he worked as secretary of the Children's Aid Society.

Another commentator on urban crime was the journalist Edward Crapsey (1872). In *The Nether Side of New York* (subtitled "Or the Vice, Crime and Poverty of the Great Metropolis"), Crapsey, in one of the first empirical studies of crime, utilized police department records, coroners' records, interviews with officials, and the records of courts, public meetings, and various agencies. He then described and analyzed types of crime, modes of operation, and the location of crime in New York. His underlying theory was that crime had developed in the city because of the lack of community integration and because of the corruption that permeated the political structure. He stated his position as follows:

With its middle classes in large part self-exiled, its laboring population being brutalized in tenements, and its citizens of the high-

est class indifferent to the commonweal, New York drifted from
bad to worse, and became the prey of professional thieves, ruffi-
ans, and political jugglers. The municipal government shared in
the vices of the people, and New York became a city paralyzed in
the hands of its rulers (Crapsey, 1872:9).

The religious temper of the latter part of the nineteenth century, especially as found in the social gospel movement, was
attuned to the crime problem. The social gospel movement was an
outgrowth of a reaction within Protestantism to the perils attributed to the new industrial capitalism and to the failure of the
church to grapple with social conditions. At the turn of the century
a number of religious leaders, such as Washington Gladden in
Applied Christianity and Walter Rauschenbusch in *Christianity
and the Social Order*, argued for a religion that would adjust Christianity to the problems of this world and create a kingdom of God
on earth—or so they hoped. The social gospel movement helped to
revolutionize attitudes toward social problems and to affirm
humanitarianism. One of the outgrowths of the movement was the
development of urban neighborhood programs and settlement
houses. Religious and humanitarian indignation over social ills was
expressed to the public through such popular books as *In His Steps*
by Charles M. Sheldon and *If Christ Came to Chicago* by W. T.
Stead. Thus, a combination of social, religious, and political movements, including the social gospel, humanitarianism, pre-muckrak-
ing thought, reform Darwinism, and emerging progressivism,
joined to focus critical public and intellectual attention on crime as
a social problem, as a condition that was not appropriate to the
American character.

The use of the environmental theory of crime and delinquency
provided a rationale for correctional reform which was brought to
public attention by the publication in 1884 of Peter Altgeld's *Our
Penal Machinery and Its Victims*. Altgeld's passionate argument
that poverty lay at the bottom of most crime and delinquency
received wide attention. Altgeld, a wealthy reformer and aspiring
politician, sent copies of the book to every legislator, judge, warden,
minister, teacher, lecturer, and social worker he could find. In
Ashtabula, Ohio, the book came to the attention of a young county
lawyer, Clarence Darrow. Throughout his illustrious career, Darrow
defended clients and pursued justice on the basis of the environmental argument. Speaking to an audience of offenders at the Cook
County jail, Darrow (quoted in Goldman, 1952:96) pushed environ-

mentalism to its limits: "There is no such thing as crime as the word is generally understood. If every man, woman and child in the world had a chance to make a decent, fair, honest living, there would be no jails and no lawyers and no courts."

Academic criminology in the United States, however, was to be influenced only minimally, and at most only indirectly, by the ideas on crime which emanated from several sources in America during the nineteenth century. Sociological criminology in twentieth-century America was more affected by the new social science, European positivism, and the criminological writings of European thinkers than by the leads provided by the nineteenth-century reformers, prison administrators, humanitarians, and socially conscious writers in the United States. Nor was nineteenth-century American sociological criminology influenced by the contemporary sociological study of crime in Europe.

Nineteenth-Century Biological and Positivistic Criminology

The beginning of modern study of crime is usually dated (see Barnes, 1931; Kinberg, 1935; Radzinowicz, 1962) from the work of the Italian physician Cesare Lombroso (1876; translated 1911a) and his immediate followers, Raffaele Garofalo (1885; translated 1914) and Enrico Ferri (1881; translated 1917). This determination is based on the assumption that there were no efforts before the Italian criminologists to take the discussion of crime out of the realm of theology and metaphysics and into the objective description and analysis of crime as a natural phenomenon.

A reading of the history of criminology, however, shows that there was a scientific study of crime before the appearance of the Italian school and, furthermore, that the prior writings were more pertinent to the sociological study of crime than the work of the Italian writers. An extensive literature on the social aspects of crime as scientifically valid as the writings of the Italians was in existence before Lombroso began his work. There is, thus, a myth in criminology that Lombroso is the founder of scientific criminology. What Lombroso and his followers actually did, as Lindesmith and Levin have noted, was to change the conception of crime and the focus of attention, not necessarily to make the study of crime more scientific or objective. "For centuries the criminal had been regarded as a human being living in society: Lombroso's contribution seems to have been to have inaugurated the study of the criminal as an animal or as a physical organism" (Lindesmith & Levin,

1937:664). In studying the individual criminal, the criminal apart from the social setting, the Lombrosians turned attention away from the perspective of crime as a social phenomenon.

The Italian criminologists are usually regarded as the founders of the 'positive school' of criminology. Although *positive* is used to identify these criminologists, the distinction must not be confused with the substantive theories of the writers. The theoretical orientation of the Italian criminologists was for the most part substantively biological. Their approach to the study of crime was positivistic in that they utilized, or attempted to utilize, the point of view and methodology of the natural sciences. Methodologically, then, the positive school of criminology is in contrast to the speculative approach of the classical school. The two schools also differ in their general theoretical orientations. While the classical school emphasized the idea of choice between right and wrong, the positive school emphasized the determinism of conduct outside of human will. Apart from these elementary differences, it is not particularly useful to review nineteenth-century developments in criminology according to the concept of positivism. In a sense, all of modern criminology is positivistic in method and basic formulation, and the sociological criminology of the nineteenth century is as positivistic as the biological criminology of the Lombrosians. Most students of crime are in some sense positivistic.

In addition to its biological orientation and positivistic emphasis, the Lombrosian school exerted a significant influence on the study of crime, an influence that is still found in much of European criminology today. Various concurrent factors undoubtedly helped to influence the acceptance of Lombroso's criminology, including (1) the prevailing prestige of the natural sciences, especially biology, which was central to Lombroso's theory; (2) the use of the terms *new* and *positive*, which gave distinction and excitement to the approach, capturing the spirit of the late nineteenth century; (3) the tradition in Europe of the idea of using physical features as indicators of character; (4) the eminence of the European physicians, psychiatrists, lawyers, and magistrates who accepted and perpetuated the ideas and methods of positivistic, biological criminology; and (5) the emphasis on individual inferiority, which supported nationalistic political structures. In other words, Lombrosian or biological criminology was accepted to a great extent for reasons usually regarded as contrary to the ideal image of scientific development.

Twentieth-Century Eclectic Criminology

The first decades of the twentieth century, especially in the United States, were marked by explanations of crime based either on a particular factor or a collection of diverse factors. Both kinds of explanation usually focused on characteristics of the individual. During this period the choice of factors was influenced to a great extent by professional controversies and attitudes toward the criminal. Dogmatic adherence to one point of view over others and the cultish pursuit of a particular viewpoint characterized the period. The controversy, however, was misguided because of the failure to recognize that the emphasis on a particular factor or collection of factors was a matter of methodological strategy.

Those criminologists who preferred the strategy of trying to explain criminal behavior in terms of a variety of factors, because of dissatisfaction with particularistic explanations, were faced with a unique problem. For them no theory was possible. Those who followed the multiple-factor approach failed in the formulation of criminological theory because they made no attempt to abstract factors to a common principle, to integrate factors into a theoretical scheme, or theoretically to relate multiple factors.

As in Europe, American writers in the nineteenth century were relating crime to individualistic factors. Propounded in the American writings of the nineteenth century were theories of criminal behavior based on phrenology, insanity, anatomy, physiology, heredity, feeblemindedness, personality, and mental degeneration (Fink, 1938). An especially noteworthy work was Richard Dugdale's *The Jukes* (1877), a study of a family whose history contained a large number of criminals. Dugdale, an inspector for the New York Prison Association, while supposedly presenting evidence on hereditary degeneracy, stressed the tentative nature of his work and indicated the likely importance of environmental factors.

The writings of the Italian positivists were translated for the American audience in the second decade of the twentieth century: Lombroso's *Crime, Its Causes and Remedies* (1911b), Garofalo's *Criminology* (1914), and Ferri's *Criminal Sociology* (1917). Their work, however, had been known to a number of American writers before the translations. Some had read the summary and interpretation of Lombroso and criminal anthropology which Havelock Ellis (1892) had prepared for English readers.

At the same time, Arthur MacDonald acknowledged the influence of Lombroso in his *Criminology* (1892). MacDonald, who had trained in theology in the United States and in medicine and psychiatry at various European universities, was employed by the U.S. Bureau of Education as "Specialist in Education as Related to the Abnormal and Weakling Classes." Included in MacDonald's book was a discussion of the physical-type criminal. But, like most other early American writers on crime, MacDonald found it necessary to broaden his scope to include psychological and social factors. Such writers, while acknowledging in some way the biological factors, were most impressed with the positivistic methodology of the Italian criminologists.

Lombroso indicated his approval of another American writer, August Drähms, by writing the introduction to Drähms's *The Criminal, His Personnel and Environment: A Scientific Study* (1900). Drähms, a resident chaplain of San Quentin State Prison, utilized criminal statistics to support a classification of criminals. Yet in spite of his biological orientation, Drähms regarded criminology as basically a social science: "Criminology is that department of social science that relates to the causes, nature, and treatment of crime with special reference to its individual exponents regarded from a psychological, physiological, and socialistic standpoint" (Drähms, 1900:1).

The continuing influence of Lombroso's substantive theory can be seen in a number of fairly recent post-Lombrosian developments in the United States. Notable are E. A. Hooton's *The American Criminal* (1939), in which he revives Lombrosian criminal anthropology in his research on the assumed biological inferiority of criminals; William H. Sheldon's *Varieties of Delinquent Youth* (1949), an investigation of somatotypes and constitutional inferiority; and the Gluecks' *Physique and Delinquency* (1956), a treatise on the physical characteristics of delinquents. Earlier there had been an attempt to explain criminal behavior in terms of the biological functioning of endocrine glands. For example, in *The New Criminology* (1928), Schlapp and Smith, primarily through reasoning by analogy, claimed that individuals suffering from endocrine disturbances were the typical born criminals.

Another post-Lombrosian development can be seen in the research attempting to relate criminal behavior to heredity. As noted by Sutherland and Cressey (1966: 123–128), at least five types of methods have been used to reach the conclusion that criminality is hereditary: (1) by comparing criminals with the "savage," as in the work of Hooton (1939); (2) by tracing family trees, as in A. H. Estabrook's *The Jukes in 1915* (1916); (3) by determining

Mendelian ratios in family trees, as in the study of family histories of German prisoners by Carl Rath (cited in Sutherland, 1947:84); (4) by establishing statistical associations between crimes of parents and of offspring, as found in Charles Goring's *The English Convict* (1913); and (5) by comparing identical and fraternal twins, as found especially in Johannes Lange's *Crime and Destiny* (1930). Post-Lombrosian criminal anthropology also appears in the numerous multiple-factor approaches to criminality which include biological factors among the many other diverse factors.

For the most part, however, the development of criminology in the United States disregarded Lombroso's biological emphasis, although his positivism was accepted as essential to modern criminology. The translation of Gustav Aschaffenburg's *Crime and Its Repression* (1913) presented to American criminologists a severe criticism of Lombroso's biological theory. Using data collected in Germany, Aschaffenburg considered many individual and social factors as causes of crime.

Perhaps the most crucial blow to Lombrosian theory was the evidence presented by Charles Goring in his statistical study of 3,000 male convicts, published as *The English Convict* (1913). From the data collected as medical officer at Parkhurst Prison, Goring sought "to clear from the ground the remains of the old criminology, based upon conjecture, prejudice, and questionable observations," and "to found a new knowledge of the criminal upon facts scientifically acquired, and upon inferences scientifically verified: such facts and inferences yielding, by virtue of their own established accuracy, unimpeachable conclusions" (Goring, 1913:18). Goring did not intend to refute Lombroso's theory but rather, through newly developed statistical techniques, to rigorously test its validity. Goring concluded that there was not a born criminal type, as Lombroso had assumed; however, he maintained that criminals are nevertheless distinguishable from non-criminals. In rejecting inheritance as a cause of crime, Goring turned the attention of criminologists to the study of psychological characteristics, especially defective intelligence, as a cause of criminal behavior.

As intelligence testing came into vogue immediately before and after World War I, an increasing number of scholars began to apply intelligence tests to delinquents and criminals in an attempt to prove a causal relationship between crime and the notion of feeblemindedness or low intelligence. Henry H. Goddard (1914), an enthusiastic supporter of the notion of feeblemindedness as a cause of criminality, estimated in his book on feeblemindedness that over

50 percent of criminals were feebleminded. In a later work he concluded: "It is no longer to be denied that the greatest single cause of delinquency and crime is low grade mentality, much of it is within limits of feeblemindedness" (Goddard, 1920:74). With the publication of army data on intelligence testing and with a revision of the tests and their standards, the relationship between crime and intelligence was critically evaluated. A critical review by L. D. Zeleny (1933) and studies by H. M. Adler and M. R. Worthington (1925), Carl Murchison (1926), and Simon H. Tulchin (1939) led to the retraction of low intelligence as a causal explanation of criminal behavior.

Through the use of other tests and measures, however, attempts continued to be made to differentiate criminals from noncriminals. There were numerous efforts to differentiate criminals according to such psychological traits as emotional instability, aggressiveness, character, mechanical aptitude, immaturity, excitability, and so forth. For the sociologically oriented criminologist, the summary and critique by Schuessler and Cressey (1950) of 113 studies in which personality scores of delinquents and criminals were compared to scores of control groups provided the necessary evidence for the conclusion that criminality and personality are not causally related. Nevertheless, a notable recent effort to establish such a relation to delinquency is found in the use of the Minnesota Personality Inventory by S. R. Hathaway and Elio D. Monachesi (1953). But as Cressey has cautioned, whatever relationships may be found in such studies, "establishing statistically significant differences between criminals and noncriminals, even when the statistical techniques are adequate and the sample groups are truly representative, does not in itself lead to conclusions about crime causation" (Cressey, 1966:167).

Emphasis on a multitude of factors in the causation of crime was a reaction by criminologists to the practice of explaining crime in terms of one particular class of phenomena. The search for factors (or variables), their measurement, and their correlation with criminal behavior reflected the growing trend toward empiricism and quantification in the social sciences. The multiple-factor approach to theories of crime causation had, of course, been present in many of the writings before the beginning of this century. However, it was reaction to particularistic theories, especially the biological theories, that led many research scholars in the first half of the present century to insist that criminal behavior was a product of a large variety of factors and that the many factors possibly could never be organized into general propositions, because each criminal act was caused by a different set of factors.

One of the first empirical studies to employ the multiple-factor approach was William Healy's *The Individual Delinquent* (1915), in which a large variety and combination of factors were considered. The multiple-factor approach was also used in Cyril Burt's *The Young Delinquent* (1925). In this study, the percentage of causative importance attributed to each of the factors was considered. Burt's comment on crime causation was typical of the underlying assumption of the approach: "Crime is assignable to no single universal source, nor yet to two or three: it springs from a wide variety, and usually from a multiplicity, of alternative and converging influences" (Burt, 1925:575). The multiple-factor strategy is found today in the work of Sheldon and Eleanor Glueck. In their *Unraveling Juvenile Delinquency* (1950), the Gluecks report the results from a controlled comparison of 500 delinquent boys and 500 non-delinquent boys on a host of factors.

The most recent individualistic movement in the study of criminal behavior is found in the field of psychiatry. While various branches of psychiatry are concerned with the relation of mental illness to deviant social behavior, psychoanalytic psychiatry has developed the most elaborate explanations of criminal behavior. Following from the work of Freud, psychoanalytic psychiatrists, in their study of criminal cases, have related the criminal act to such concepts as innate impulse, mental conflict, and repression. In most of the psychoanalytic theories, crime represents a form of substitute behavior. However, all the psychoanalytic works (including Karpman, 1935; Lindner, 1944; Friedlander, 1947; Abrahamsen, 1952; Alexander & Staub, 1956) rest on questionable research procedures and upon a theory that is not subject to verification. There is also the problem of circularity in the psychoanalytic approach, psychopathy being suggested as a cause of criminal behavior, and criminal behavior, in turn, being used as an indicator of psychopathy. (For a critique of the psychoanalytic approach, see Hakeem, 1958.) In regard to the radical differences in approach between psychiatry and sociology, the pertinent question remains: Do the two approaches to the explanation of crime refer to different and distinct classes of phenomena?

Twentieth-Century Sociological Criminology

With the turn of the century, the study of crime as a social phenomenon became centered in the United States. The rapid changes taking place in American society provided the background for a social perspective on crime. As the history of criminology indicates, crime is one of those behaviors that scholars have had difficulty accepting as social. It has always been more convenient to view crime as an individual phenomenon, more convenient for purposes of study as well as for programs of treatment. To conceive of the criminal as a personal failure rather than as an indicator of societal conditions also gave support to—or certainly did not attack—the status quo.

Perhaps because of the dynamics of American society, the relation between social conditions and crime seemed obvious to American scholars. Urbanization, immigration, population growth, and social and geographical mobility were some of the dynamics which faced scholars at the beginning of the twentieth century. Since much of criminal behavior occurred among groups most affected by these changes, it was reasonable to investigate the social sources of crime. In addition, American criminology came to display a strong sociological emphasis because such a view "accords with the fundamentally optimistic American outlook on life in general, into which the thesis that crime is a product of remediable social forces would fit more naturally than insistence on the part played by endogenous factors" (Radzinowicz, 1962:119). Also important to the social conception of crime was the fact that crime was included in the sociological study of social problems. The study of crime has since shared in the general growth of a sociology.

While it is significant that the study of crime became located primarily within the sociological tradition, the social conception of crime was part of a new thought system which was developing at the beginning of the century in the United States. In what Morton White (1949) has documented as "the revolt against formalism," a style of thinking, a liberal social philosophy, developed at the turn of the century compounded of pragmatism, institutionalism, behaviorism, legal realism, economic determinism, and the "new history." Among those instrumental in the new intellectual pattern were John Dewey, who held that ideas are plans of action; Thorstein Veblen, who insisted upon the importance of studying the connections between economic institutions and other aspects of culture; Justice Oliver Wendell Holmes, who rejected the view that law is an abstract entity; Charles A. Beard, who looked for the underlying economic forces that determine the acceleration of social life; and James Harvey Robinson, who represented the view that an understanding of history is essential for explaining the present and controlling the future.

All of these emerging ideas had in common a *relativism* which suggested that ideas and events have meaning only in relation to context. It was this same relativism that made the study of crime in the United States different from previous and other contemporary efforts. Only when crime was viewed as relative, in respect to the criminal law and the behavior of the offender, could crime be truly studied as a social phenomenon. Relativism had implications both for the research approach to the study of crime and for the formulation of criminological theory. Only by freeing themselves from an absolute conception of the world could students of crime perceive crime as being a violation of one of a number of possible codes, with the behavior of the offender seen as a consequence of participation in one of several social worlds. Although the ideas of the social philosophers who reacted against nineteenth-century formalism no longer serve as reference points, relativism increasingly continues to influence the study of crime. Recent developments and current trends in criminology reflect the extreme extension of modern relativism.

A Struggling Sociological Criminology

The sociological study of crime proceeded at a painstaking pace in the United States during the first half of the century. Given the hindsight of today, the study of crime by early sociologists was filled with questionable assumptions and was not specifically concerned with the social. For example, one of the first supposedly sociological works on crime, Frances A. Kellor's *Experimental Sociology* (1901), was actually a study of physical differences (according to length of ears, average width of mouth, height of forehead, weight, nasal index, etc.) between women criminals and women students. In the introduction to the book, C. R. Henderson, one of the first members of the sociology department at the University of Chicago, gave expression to a social moralism that had not yet been tempered by relativism, while also showing the adventure the early sociologists must have felt in the new social science: "The university cannot neglect any phase of social life. As in astronomy the study of perturbations in the movements of known bodies leads to the discovery of new worlds, so in social science the investigation of evil brings us nearer to an understanding of the good and helps us on the path upward" (Kellor, 1901:ix–x).

Henderson himself wrote on crime and the related topics of the time in *An Introduction to the Study of Dependent, Defective, and Delinquent Classes* (1901). Much of the book was devoted to the organization of care for dependents. In the preface Henderson stated: "We seek the ethical basis of charity, the ideals of philanthropy, and the social mechanism for attaining in larger measure what ought to be done." Outside of the programmatic aspect of the book, Henderson suggested an early social psychology of crime which stressed the reaction of the person possessing inherited tendencies: "The causes of crime are factors of personality and of environment, and of the reaction of personality upon environment in the formation of habits and new nature. Personal nature is, at a given moment, the product of inherited tendencies, of acquired habits and character, and of the response to external circumstances" (Henderson, 1901: preface).

At the beginning of the twentieth century in the United States, criminology, like other areas of study, was affected by evolutionary theory, particularly social Darwinism. This theoretical orientation to crime is perhaps best displayed in *Crime and its Relation to Social Progress* (1902), written by Arthur C. Hall, a fellow in sociology at Columbia University. In the introduction to the book, Franklin H. Giddings, first professor of sociology at Columbia, set the tone by arguing that as civilization evolves it is necessary to define, through the criminal law, certain behaviors as criminal, and that "this process of connecting immoralities into positive crimes is one of the most powerful means by which society in the long run eliminates the socially unfit, and gives an advantage in the struggles for existence to the thoughtful, the considerate, the far-seeing, the compassionate; so lifting its members to higher planes of character and conduct" (Hall, 1902:xi). Hall, in viewing crime in relation to social progress, considered the criminal law itself as well as the behavior of the offender. To Hall, crime was "the branding by society of some forms of conduct as criminal." Crime was viewed as inevitable to social progress. Using a "natural law" conception as well as evolutionary theory, Hall wrote:

> Out of the teachings of natural law, which, whether we like it or not, whether we aid or oppose it, is driving the world forward to higher and higher planes of life, intelligence and mutual helpfulness, comes the idea of crime, and the necessity for the appearance of the criminal in every human community. Crime is an inevitable social evil, the dark side of the shield of human progress. The shifting processes of natural selection continue within the domain of social life, rejecting, through social pressure, both weaklings and workers of iniquity. Antisocial individuals, or malefactors,

result from the persistent tendency to variation, manifest in all life. They become criminals through processes of social selection, during which individuals refusing to live up to the social standard of right action are punished by the community, and their actions become known as crimes" (Hall, 1902:376).

One of the most significant events in the development of criminology during the first decade of this century was the establishment in June 1908 of the American Institute of Criminal Law and Criminology by the faculty of law at Northwestern University to celebrate the first fifty years of the University. The Institute represents the formal recognition of American criminology. In addition to the founding of a journal for the communication of ideas in criminology, known today as the *Journal of Criminal Law, Criminology and Police Science*, the Institute initiated the Modern Criminal Science Series. In the course of the series, the writings of European criminologists were translated and introduced to American readers. Included in the series were the writings of Gross, de Quirós, Ferri, Saleilles, Lombroso, Tarde, Bonger, Garofalo, and Aschaffenburg. An international bibliography was published (Wigmore, 1909), introducing American criminologists to an extensive list of writings in criminology and criminal law. The editor was John H. Wigmore, dean of the Northwestern University law faculty, who was instrumental in initiating the Modern Criminal Science Series.

Extremely important in the development of sociological criminology was the translation of Gabriel Tarde's *Penal Philosophy* (1912) and William A. Bonger's *Criminality and Economic Conditions* (1916). In setting forth a sociological conception of crime, as well as attempting to reconcile moral responsibility with determinism, Tarde attacked Lombroso's theory of an anthropological criminal type. Bonger's use of statistics and his analysis in terms of the economic structure of society also contributed to sociological criminology, although his economic determinism found few adherents in the United States.

Maurice Parmelee, perhaps more than any other person at the beginning of the century, brought about the union of sociology and criminology. In his *Principles of Anthropology and Sociology in Their Relations to Criminal Procedure* (1908), while at places drawing favorably upon Lombroso's theory, Parmelee suggested a sociological criminology. Later, in the first American attempt at a comprehensive exposition of criminological knowledge, Parmelee in his *Criminology* (1918) discussed the social sources of crime. Yet he found it necessary to devote attention to evolution, the physical environment, "criminal traits," and the "organic basis of criminality." Parmelee's work nevertheless marks the beginning in the United States of a transition from a general, eclectic study of crime to a sociological level of explanation.

UNIVERSITY OF CHICAGO SOCIOLOGY AND CRIMINOLOGY

A truly sociological criminology was achieved during the 1920s and 1930s at the University of Chicago. Albion W. Small, as founder and head of the first sociology department to be established as an independent unit anywhere in the world, gathered a distinguished group of colleagues at the University of Chicago. Persons with great ability and scope established a sociological tradition that had as one of its principal concerns the study of crime. That criminal behavior is similar to any other social behavior became the underlying theme in the sociological study of crime.

Two early concepts to come from the Chicago school were 'social disorganization' and 'the four wishes.' In what is regarded as the first American empirical study in sociology, *The Polish Peasant in Europe and America* (1927), W. I. Thomas and Florian Znaniecki defined the concept of social disorganization as a "decrease of the influence of existing social rules of behavior upon individual members of the group." As employed by Thomas and Znaniecki, the concept was a useful tool to describe the condition of the groups they were studying. But the concept became unwieldy when it was later used by criminologists to explain crime. In terms of the social disorganization concept, crime became an indicator of the condition of social disorganization and, in a circular fashion, disorganization became an explanation of crime. Also, as used in the hands of others, social disorganization implied a social absolutism that regarded only one system as being the standard by which all behavior was evaluated. Thomas and Znaniecki were to a certain extent relativistic, as can be seen in their concept of the four wishes—response, recognition, security, and new experience. Utilizing the four wishes in *The Unadjusted Girl* (1923), Thomas indicated that the wishes, as the basis of motivation and behavior, can be satisfied in any number of ways. Whether the result is regarded as moral or not depends upon the meaning attached by others to the activity. To Thomas, the means of satisfying the wishes were merely functional alternatives.

The influence of Robert E. Park on early students of crime was considerable. Park, in collaboration with another University of

Chicago professor, E. W. Burgess, suggested the possibilities of the study of the spatial distribution of social phenomena within the city (Park, 1925). Students of Park and Burgess examined the proposition that various deviant behaviors may be associated with urban growth and ecological patterns. Frederick M. Thrasher, in his 1927 study of 1,313 gangs in Chicago, argued that groups of boys located in "interstitial areas" of the city, through participation in a particular way of life, would become transformed from slum groups into unified delinquent groups. Clifford R. Shaw and his collaborators, in a 1929 study of the distribution of delinquency rates, found (among other things) that delinquency was concentrated in deteriorated areas of the city and that these areas of high delinquency rates consistently had high rates despite population changes.

Through a number of case studies, including *The Jack-Roller* (1930), *Natural History of a Delinquent Career* (1931), and *Brothers in Crime* (1938), Shaw shifted his attention from physical factors in the environment to a consideration of the relationships of offenders with others. Slum youth were seen as participating in a culture in which delinquent behavior was prescribed. Thus, the distinctly sociological view, that criminally defined behavior patterns are acquired in a social and cultural setting, emerged among sociologists at the University of Chicago.

THE PERSON IN SOCIETY

In an early article entitled "The Study of the Delinquent as a Person," E. W. Burgess suggested that the individual delinquent could be studied sociologically as a "person" who is the product of social interaction with his or her fellows.

> Not only criminology, but all social problems, indeed the entire area of group behavior and social life, is being subjected to sociological description and analysis. The person is concerned in his interrelations with the social organization, with the family, the neighborhood, the community, and society. Explanations of his behavior are found in terms of human wishes and social attitudes, mobility and unrest, intimacy and status, social contacts and social interaction, conflict, accommodation and assimilation (Burgess, 1923:679).

In the hands of Burgess, the concept of the person in society was a sound statement of the sociopsychological explanation of offenders and their behavior. As used by others, however, the social psychology of crime became a conception cluttered by factors outside of interpersonal relations, as well as a perspective which included unwarranted value assumptions.

Partly because of the failure to understand the construction of theory, numerous students of crime have suggested that crime is a consequence of various factors interacting with the individual. All the early criminology textbooks (e.g., Parsons, 1926; Ettinger, 1932; Gault, 1932) were organized according to various factors that were supposedly associated with criminal behavior. The response to the complexity of crime thus tended to be the acceptance of a multiple-factor approach rather than the construction of theory in terms of a particular level of explanation. The conclusion reached by Ploscowe in a survey of the research and writing in criminology is typical of this response: "The soundest approach to the problem of the causation of crime therefore lies through a study of the individual criminal in relation to all the social and environmental factors which have an influence on his personality" (Ploscowe, 1931:17).

While still pursuing an early form of social psychology of the interaction of the person with factors in the environment, a number of criminologists offered theories of crime which included the assumption that the organization of society is not appropriate for the functioning of the individual. For example, one of the first statements of the interaction between the individual and an improper environment is found in John L. Gillin's *Criminology and Penology* (1926). In a well-written, erudite criminology textbook, Gillin conceived of a sociopsychological explanation of the criminal in the following way:

> Hence there is a conspiracy of conditions which account for his becoming a criminal—conditions in his own constitutional make-up, in his early social development, in his lack of training, in his poverty and in the surrounding social atmosphere, including habits, customs, ideals, beliefs, and practices. The social conditions around him set the stage on which each of these factors plays its part and release in his conduct the good or the evil in his nature. Thus, is the criminal made (Gillin, 1926:250–251).

In a not too different explanation of crime based on an unsophisticated psychology, Boris Brasol suggested in 1927 a "psychosocial interpretation" of crime. In noting that "social friction is the prime cause of crime," Brasol wrote that "between society as a whole and its individual member, there develops friction promoting the latter to violate certain traditions which have been produced and sanctioned by the community" (1927:28).

The thesis that crime results from problems in the interaction of the individual with society is found in Nathaniel F. Cantor's *Crime and Society* (1939), a popular textbook of its time. According to Cantor: "Criminal behavior, then, is in part symptomatic of the needs of the individuals which have been frustrated by their culture" (1939:399). He argued, further, that when the emotional stresses become too intense some individuals are unable to make "normal adjustments" and that this social maladjustment may take the form of criminal behavior. Similarly, noting that the criminal must be understood in reference to his community, associates, and culture, Arthur E. Wood and John B. Waite observed: "From this sociological view of things the criminal may be said to be *maladjusted* to his social environment" (1941:5). More recently, in the preface to his *Crime: Causes and Conditions*, Hans von Hentig noted: "Crime, being a pattern of social disorganization, has a multiplicity of causations that rest on defects and obstructions in the working order of society" (1947).

Thus, the conception of crime as a result of interaction between the person and society has taken several forms. The forms have differed from the social psychology which was developing among sociologists at the University of Chicago. Criminologists who utilized the person-society interaction perspective to crime either resorted to a multiple-factor approach, often employing factors outside of the interaction between person and society, or formulated their conceptions on questionable assumptions about the relation of the person to society and the nature of society. Often, in addition, the values of the observers determined the standards for appropriate social behavior.

CRITICISM OF THEORETICAL CRIMINOLOGY

The 1930s mark a period of turmoil and assessment in the development of criminology. As we have seen, a number of students of crime, dissatisfied with the various particularisms, turned to the multiple-factor approach. Other criminologists, such as Sutherland, sought to integrate the diverse facts associated with crime. Still others, such as N. F. Cantor in *Crime, Criminals and Criminal Justice* (1932a), attempted to critically examine the state of criminology and add "sound methods of inquiry." Others summarized the findings of criminology in little more than a descriptive form, as did Fred E. Haynes in his *Criminology* (1930). Some criminologists (e.g., Best, in 1930) unabashedly presented the findings of criminology without any theoretical perspective whatsoever, in the name of objectivity.

The beginning of the 1930s was characterized by an optimism brought about, in part at least, by the American acceptance of positivism. There was the belief that the causes of criminal behavior could be discovered if enough effort was devoted to the study of crime. Such optimism was soon questioned on the basis of a single report. In the early 1930s a foundation became interested in establishing an institute of criminology. Two Columbia University professors, Jerome Michael of the law school and Mortimer J. Adler of the philosophy department, were commissioned to examine the state of knowledge in criminology. Their report, published as *Crime, Law and Social Science* (1933), was highly critical of criminology. The conclusion reached in the review of past research on crime was typical of the tone of the whole book: "The absurdity of any attempt to draw etiological conclusions from the findings of criminological research is so patent as not to warrant further discussion." But despite the severe criticism, Michael and Adler recommended that an institute of criminology and of criminal justice be established. But their criticism had been so devastating that the foundation was left with little hope that an institute could improve criminology. Yet few criminologists were convinced of the diagnosis presented by Michael and Adler. A committee, consisting of a number of sociologists and criminologists appointed by the Social Science Research Council to review the report, submitted a contradictory conclusion on the status of criminology (Cohen, Lindesmith, & Schuessler, 1956:290).

Nevertheless, the Michael and Adler report did provide a point of reference for criminologists. A distinct contribution of the report was its focus on the importance of criminal law in defining the scope and boundaries of criminology, a point which is being rediscovered today by criminologists. The report also made some criminologists recognize that the criteria used by Michael and Adler to judge criminology represented only one view of science. In stating that "there is no scientific knowledge in the field of criminology," Michael and Adler could only reach such a dogmatic conclusion by basing their survey on (1) a misconception of the methodological theory of causation, (2) a natural science model of social science, and (3) a restricted sampling of research and writing in criminology. Given the criteria and sources of the report, the conclusions are not incorrect. But by using other criteria and by looking to other research in criminology, a report on criminology could have been much different. Nevertheless, *Crime, Law, and Social Science* provided criminologists with a guide that could be used as a basis for the further development of criminology.

CULTURE CONFLICT

Michael and Adler forcefully argued that the most precise and least ambiguous definition of crime is based on behavior that is defined as criminal in the criminal code. The formulation and administration of criminal law could conceivably provide a level of criminological explanations. A number of criminologists, sociologists, and anthropologists in the 1920s and 1930s presented evidence on the existence of norms in conflict with one another. The delinquency-area studies by Shaw indicated that urban areas with certain characteristics give rise to social attitudes that conflict with the norms of the law. In an early article, Sutherland wrote on the emergence of criminal law out of conflict between cultures. Criminal behavior, he noted, is itself

> a part of the process of conflict, of which law and punishment are other parts. . . . This process begins in the community before the law is enacted, and continues in the community and in the behavior of particular offenders after punishment is inflicted. This process seems to go on somewhat as follows: A certain group of people feel that one of their values—life, property, beauty of landscape, theological doctrine—is endangered by the behavior of others. If the group is politically influential, the value important, and the danger serious, they secure the enactment of a law and thus win the cooperation of the State in the effort to protect their value (Sutherland, 1929:41).

Thus, to carry the argument further, persons who are following the norms of a culture which prescribes ways of behaving that are in opposition to the norms embodied in the criminal law share the possibility of being defined as criminal.

The case for the analysis of crime according to culture conflict was most strongly presented in a monograph by Thorsten Sellin, *Culture Conflict and Crime* (1938). Noting the importance of criminal law to the study of crime, Sellin observed the operation of the law as follows:

> Among the various instrumentalities which social groups have evolved to secure conformity in the conduct of their members, the

criminal law occupies an important place, for its norms are bind-
ing upon all who live within the political boundaries of a state and
are enforced through the coercive power of the state. The criminal
law may be regarded as a part of the body of rules, which prohibit
specific forms of conduct and indicate punishments for violations.
The characteristic of these rules, the kind or type of conduct they
prohibit, the nature of the sanction attached to their violation, etc.
depend upon the character and interests of those groups in the
population which influence legislation. In some states, these
groups may comprise the majority, in others a minority, but the
social values which receive the protection of the criminal law are
ultimately those which are treasured by dominant interest groups
(Sellin, 1938:21).

For Sellin, culture conflict could arise in several different
ways, with each form of conflict being potentially related to crime.
In general terms, there is the conflict that develops with the growth
of a civilization, and the conflict that results from the contact
between the norms of divergent cultural codes. Sellin gave support
to his thesis by reviewing the research and findings on criminal
behavior among immigrants and second-generation Americans. In
all cases, crime was viewed as a matter of conflict between conduct
norms, with legal norms being one form of conduct norms.

The importance of conflict to the making of the individual
offender was vividly presented in a popular criminology textbook,
Crime and the Community (1938), by Frank Tannenbaum, professor
of Latin American history at Columbia University. Crime was
viewed as a matter of definition by the community and, therefore,
the offender as one who is in conflict with the community and who
continues in conflict (crime) as he accepts the community's definition
of him as a criminal. Tannenbaum referred to the process by which
the person becomes a criminal in the course of community reaction
as "the dramatization of evil." As a result of various forms of community reaction, the offender begins to conceive of himself as a criminal or delinquent and carries out the corresponding behavior.

The process of making the criminal, therefore, is a process of tag-
ging, defining, identifying, segregating, describing, emphasizing,
making conscious and self-conscious; it becomes a way of stimulating, suggesting, emphasizing, and evoking the very traits com-
plained of. If the theory of relation of response to stimulus has any
meaning, the entire process of dealing with the young delinquent
is mischievous in so far as it identifies him to himself or to the
environment as a delinquent person (Tannenbaum, 1938:17–18).

The cultural conflict perspective thus provided a framework for the analysis of both the creation of criminal definitions and the response of the individual to the application of these definitions.

DIFFERENTIAL ASSOCIATION

As a prelude to his theory of differential association, Edwin H. Sutherland, in a 1937 study of the professional thief, presented the view that criminals gradually learn the knowledge, skills, and motivation for engaging in criminal behavior. Two years later, in the revision of his popular criminology textbook, Sutherland attempted to offer an explanation of crime that would replace the multiple-factor approach and go beyond the simple enculturation explanation of crime. Thus was introduced Sutherland's theory of differential association.

The theory of differential association as finally developed contained the following, by now well-known, propositions:

1. Criminal behavior is learned.

2. Criminal behavior is learned in interaction with other persons in a process of communication.

3. The principal part of the learning of criminal behavior occurs within intimate personal groups.

4. When criminal behavior is learned, the learning includes (a) techniques of committing the crime, which are sometimes very complicated, sometimes very simple, and (b) the specific direction of motives, drives, rationalizations, and attitudes.

5. The specific direction of motives and drives is learned from definitions of the legal codes as favorable or unfavorable.

6. A person becomes delinquent because of an excess of definitions favorable to violation of law over definitions unfavorable to violation of law.

7. Differential associations may vary in frequency, duration, priority, and intensity.

8. The process of learning criminal behavior by association with criminal and anti-criminal patterns involves all of the mechanisms that are involved in any other learning.

9. While criminal behavior is an expression of general needs and values, it is not explained by those general needs and values since non-criminal behavior is an expression of the same needs and values (Sutherland, 1947:6–7).

Sutherland thus provided an integrating theory for criminology. The theory of differential association assumed that the many diverse factors and correlates of crime were important to the extent that they affected an individual's associations and learning experiences.

SOCIAL STRUCTURE AND ANOMIE

In 1938, Robert K. Merton published his now famous article, "Social Structure and Anomie." Elaborating upon Emile Durkheim's description of the emergence of aspiration and the breakdown in regulatory norms, Merton sought to account for the kinds and amounts of deviation in a society. The theory, nevertheless, was similar in some ways to criminological theories that had preceded it. Merton's emphasis on the breakdown of cultural structure, occurring particularly where there is a disjunction between goals and norms, is similar to the social disorganization theory in analyzing deviation from what is assumed to be a fairly homogeneous culture. Also, the social structure and anomie theory is a sophisticated version of the criminological theories which stated that crime was in some way a result of problems in the interaction between person and society, without the explicit assumption that deviant persons are maladjusted. According to Merton's theory, explanations of crime were to be sought in the social and cultural structure of society rather than in the individual. Merton's theory went beyond the others in suggesting that there are different ways in which individuals adapt to social and cultural conditions. The theory sought to explain both the behavior of individuals and the rates of forms of deviant behavior.

POST-WORLD WAR II DEVELOPMENTS

Theoretical developments in criminology during the post-World War II period have consisted primarily of an extension of the theoretical perspectives that were formulated at the end of the 1930s. Current efforts in the study of crime tend to be in reference to the perspectives of culture conflict (e.g. Vold, 1958; Quinney, 1964, 1970; Turk, 1966, 1969), differential association (e.g. Glaser, 1956; Reckless, Dinitz, & Kay, 1957; Short, 1957; Reiss & Rhodes, 1964; Burgess & Akers, 1966; DeFleur & Quinney, 1966), and social structure and anomie (e.g. Cohen, 1955; Cloward & Ohlin, 1960; Clinard, 1964).

Perhaps the most significant development in recent years has been the extension of the relativistic viewpoint to its logical extreme. As crime has come to be viewed as a construct imposed by some persons on others, new research problems and theoretical vistas have emerged. Underlying the current study of such topics as types of crime, sociology of criminal law, law enforcement, administration of justice, and social reaction to crime is the thesis that crime is a socially defined phenomenon and problem.

Current Issues in the Study of Crime

Unlike the study of some other social problems, then, the study of crime has been marked by a diversity of theoretical perspectives. Such diversity has been due to the fact that criminology claims the interest of several different academic and vocational fields (Wheeler, 1962:141). The very nature of criminology accounts to a considerable degree for its diversity.

With the increasing emphasis that is being placed on crime as a socially defined phenomenon, however, a common core of concerns is forming in the study of crime. To be certain, variations in the sociological perspective will continue in criminology. But there are a number of issues which underlie any theoretical perspective in the study of crime. These issues are in reference to (1) research methodology, (2) criminal statistics, (3) theoretical explanation, (4) comparative criminology, and (5) criminal definitions and criminal behavior. The future study of crime will be related to the positions taken in respect to these issues.

Research Methodology

Any given research may be considered as a process in which a "series of basic choices" are made in regard to the design and execution of the research (Riley, 1963). When research is thus conceived, a great variety of research designs are available to the criminologist. Concrete research in criminology actually consists of decisions regarding such matters as the nature of the research case, sampling, the sociotemporal context, sources of data, method of gathering data, measurement, and the method of handling relationships among properties. As the subject matter of criminology is redefined, the traditional methods of criminology must be superseded by research designs appropriate for new problems.

Other matters, of course, must be confronted in addition to research design and data collection. Criminological research as a process also includes the relating of the research findings to a body of theory. In all stages of the research, as well as in the analysis and interpretation of findings, there must be a bringing together of theory and research.

"RESEARCH METHODS" OF CRIMINOLOGY

Rather than considering research as a process, criminologists have commonly divided the complexities of research into a number of gross categories. These categories have been referred to as the "research methods" of criminology (see, for example, Taft & England, 1964:70–74; Sutherland & Cressey, 1966:65–73). Accordingly, the research methods usually listed for criminology include the following:

1. *Statistical study of crime rates in relation to other conditions.* Rates of arrest or conviction are correlated with specific social characteristics. An attempt is made to relate crime rates to characteristics of the population of the geographical areas in which the rates of crime occur (Bonger, 1916; Shaw, 1929).

2. *Statistical study of the traits of criminals.* A study of the frequency with which one or more personal or social traits are found among persons regarded as criminals. Often there is a comparison between the traits of criminals and non-criminals (Goring, 1913; Healy, 1915).

3. *The study of an individual case.* The object of study is the person in his or her social setting rather than the study of traits among a sample of offenders. A life history is constructed and the offender's "own story" may be prepared as a document for study (Shaw, 1930; Sutherland, 1937).

4. *The experimental method.* Under controlled conditions, hypotheses regarding the causes of crime and delinquency are tested. Analogous to the natural experiment in the physical and biological sciences, an attempt is made to observe the change in one group of persons, in comparison with a controlled group, as a result of the introduction of a stimulus of some kind (Powers & Witmer, 1951; Miller, 1962).

5. *Analytic induction.* The method involves the study of a number of individual cases. An initial hypothesis is formulated and altered if necessary as cases are encountered which do not substantiate the hypothesis. The final statement must encompass all of the cases (Lindesmith, 1947; Becker, 1953; Cressey, 1953).

6. *Study of the criminal in the natural setting.* Although there are many difficulties which have presupposed the use of this method, the study of criminals and their associates "in the open" can provide information about crime that cannot be obtained in any other way. In the use of this method, the investigator must be able to associate with offenders, gain their confidence, and somehow solve the problem of not exposing his or her own identity (Thrasher, 1927; Short & Strodtbeck, 1965; Polsky, 1967).

Any such presentation of research methods is necessarily simplistic and naive because of the fact that research is a *process* in which the procedures and techniques are only one aspect of the research design. Research methods are inextricably linked to the many decisions that must be made in the formulation and implementation of a research design. It makes more sense, therefore, to consider research methods in relation to research as a process. Furthermore, the research process is related to broader assumptions about ontology and epistemology. Assumptions about the nature of reality and the grounds of knowledge ultimately affect the accumulation of a body of knowledge.

Criminal Statistics

Criminal statistics collected by numerous agencies for various purposes have traditionally served as primary forms of data for criminological research. The use of these statistics has, at the same time, been a source of considerable controversy among criminologists. Much of the controversy has revolved around the issue of the collection of criminal statistics (e.g., see Beattie, 1955). But to criticize the existing criminal statistics and to advocate better and uniform crime reporting is to accept the assumption that official statistics can, in themselves, serve as indexes of the actual amount of crime. This, then, raises the issues of the appropriate use and meaning of criminal statistics.

USE OF CRIMINAL STATISTICS

Since most collections of criminal statistics have been gathered for purposes other than those explicitly intended in any particular criminological research, the appropriate use of criminal statistics by the criminologist is an important issue. Basically, all criminal statistics represent the operations of agencies which are charged with the administration of criminal law. Most criminologists, and the general public for that matter, have attempted to use criminal statistics as measures of the *actual amount of criminality* in any given geographical area or in the country as a whole.

When criminal statistics are used for the purpose of assessing the 'true' incidence of criminality, a number of valid criticisms may indeed be raised concerning the methods of collecting criminal statistics. Pessimistic appraisals such as the following have relevance *if* criminal statistics are used to indicate criminality:

> The general statistics of crime and criminals are probably the most unreliable and most difficult of all social statistics. It is impossible to determine with accuracy the amount of crime in any given jurisdiction at any particular time. Obviously a large proportion of the crimes committed go undetected, others are detected but not reported, others are reported but not officially recorded. Consequently any record of crimes, such as crimes known to the police, arrests, convictions, or commitments to prison, can be considered only as an "index" of the crimes committed. But these "indexes" of crime do not maintain a constant ratio with the true rate, whatever it may be (Sutherland & Cressey, 1966:27).

On the basis of such criticism, numerous suggestions and recommendations have been made to improve the collection of criminal statistics, especially to improve the procedures used in the *Uniform Crime Reports* (see Sellin, 1950; Pittman & Handy, 1962; Wolfgang, 1963; Wilkins, 1965; Lejins, 1966; Robison, 1966).

A principal difficulty in using available criminal statistics as indexes of criminality in the United States results from the lack of uniform reporting in the United States. Because of the political organization of the United States, each of the fifty states represents a separate political jurisdiction. Each state has its own constitutional provisions, penal codes, courts, criminal procedures, and systems of law enforcement. Furthermore, the administration of criminal law in each state is not centralized, but is instead a localized activity. These political facts create considerable variation in the recording of criminal offenses and thus prohibit the comparability of information on criminal offenses from state to state and from one locality to another within states.

Sellin pointed out some time ago that "the value of a crime rate for index purposes decreases as the distance from the crime itself in terms of procedure increases" (1931:346). That is, police records are more reliable measures of the actual incidence of criminal offenses than arrest statistics, arrest statistics are more reliable than court statistics, and court statistics are more reliable than prison statistics. The implication is that many offenses are 'lost' between arrest and prosecution. It is with an awareness of these facts that criminologists usually use the records of police rather than other sources to make inferences about the extent of criminality.

Perhaps the most critical drawback in using official criminal statistics as indicators of the incidence of criminality, even when 'offenses known to the police' are employed, is the unknown amount of criminality that never becomes a part of the public record. For various reasons many criminal offenses are never reported to the police, or when reported are not recorded by the police. Any given violation of the criminal law likely carries with it a certain probability that it will come to the attention of law enforcement agencies.

The existence of a considerable amount of 'hidden criminality' has been indicated in a number of studies. Wallerstein and Wyle (1947) found in a sample of New York residents that criminal behavior was much more widespread than was reflected in official criminal statistics. Ninety-one percent of their sample admitted that they had committed one or more offenses. In an examination of the extent to which official statistics measure juvenile delinquency, Robison (1936) found that about a third of the behavior problems known to New York City agencies did not become court cases. The juvenile offenses were known by certain authorities but were handled informally. Porterfield, in a 1946 study of delinquent acts committed during high school and college as reported by Texas college students, found that the college students had engaged in similar amounts and forms of delinquent behavior as had juveniles who were officially processed in court. The college students, because of their advantageous background, had not been referred to court for their illegal acts while the other juveniles had been officially handled. More recent investigations, using the self-reporting technique, continue to find that behaviors which may be defined as criminal or delinquent are much more common than official statistics suggest (see, for example, Short & Nye, 1958; Erickson & Empey, 1963; Akers, 1964; Voss, 1966).

There are many special forms of reported offenses that are not collected in the traditional sources of criminal statistics (see Schulman, 1966). Among these offenses are those that occur in commerce and industry, management-labor relations, union management, income tax reporting, and social security and public administration. These offenses are for the most part dealt with by state and federal regulatory agencies. The statistics in regard to these offenses, therefore, are in the files and reports of the respective agencies. Such criminal records seldom become a part of official criminal statistics. Reliance on the traditionally collected criminal statistics obscures the prevalence of these and other crimes. Official statistics in this instance serve better as indicators of the reaction of society to certain kinds of offenses than as measures of the amount of criminality in society.

MEANING OF CRIMINAL STATISTICS

The use of official criminal statistics as measures of the incidence of criminality is a questionable practice. Nevertheless, official criminal statistics continue to be used as indicators of criminality in society. On the basis of these statistics, the student of crime and the entire public is periodically reminded that the crime rate for the current year is higher than that of previous years. Once knowing that the crime rate is increasing, we are expected to experience collective alarm. The reader is not usually provided, however, with the additional information that there is uncertainty as to what the criminal statistics mean. They may mean only that law enforcement procedures change from year to year. Moreover, the crime rate may not reflect the actual amount of crime so much as it reflects the way police departments operate and change in their operations.

In other words, the wrong question is being asked of our criminal statistics. In the first place, official criminal statistics represent only a fraction of some unknown amount of criminality in any given geographical area. In this use of criminal statistics, there is much 'hidden criminality' and the statistics are 'dark figures.' Second, since most of human behavior can at some time be labeled as criminal by those with the authority to so label, the statistics reflect the policies and behaviors of the agencies engaged in the administration of criminal law.

Therefore, the conception of official criminal statistics must be broadened to include the process of labeling behavior as criminal. Rather than assuming that criminal statistics indicate only the *incidence of criminal behavior* in a population, it must be assumed that criminal statistics reflect differentials in the *administration of criminal law* as well (Newman, 1962; Kitsuse & Cicourel, 1963; Quinney, 1966). These two conceptions of criminal statistics should not necessarily be regarded as alternative and mutually exclusive. A third meaning of criminal statistics represents a combination of the first two conceptions, that is, criminal statistics reflect a mixture of the *incidence of criminality and the administration of criminal law*.

A fourth meaning, on a distinct conceptual level, is that criminal statistics are indicators of the socially recognized volume of crime. In this conception, official statistics are viewed as production figures from the standpoint of the society. Whether there is more or less 'actual' criminality, strict or lenient administration of criminal law, or some combination of criminality and inadequate administration is not the issue. The crucial question is why societies report, manufacture, or produce the volume of crime that they do (Cressey, 1957). This question is especially important in current criminological research. Ecological studies of crime, in particular, are beginning to be focused on the meaning of officially reported crime (Wilks, 1967). To the student of crime, the basic meaning of official criminal statistics is clear: they represent the volume of socially recognized crime in a given society, or in a specific jurisdiction, at a particular time.

Theoretical Explanation

The objective of much of the theoretical explanation in criminology has been to find the 'causes of crime.' The search for the causes of crime, sometimes referred to as criminal *etiology*, continues to be a principal concern of criminologists. The use of the concept of causation in the explanation of crime, however, is open to serious question.

A general acceptance of the notion of causation in criminology has been in large measure a result of the influence of a particular body of thought, i.e., positivism, with its own version found in the positivist school of criminology. The positivist school combined a substantive theory of behavior, based on the assumption of the determinism of behavior, with a particular methodology that was modeled after the natural sciences. The methodology was based on the assumption that phenomena could be divided into units, or variables, and that the variables could then be considered as being causally linked. The study of criminal behavior has, for the most part, been based on the methodological view that A is the cause of B.

A number of criminologists have on occasion, however, expressed concern with the positivistic concept of causation. It has been suggested (Cantor, 1932b), for example, that the concept of cause as used in the natural sciences cannot be applied in the same way in the social sciences. Others have suggested that the solution to the problems of causal analysis is to use the concept only in a very loose sense (Sellin, 1938:17–18; Lejins, 1951). Alternative concepts have been offered, such as "categoric risks" (Reckless, 1940) and "conditionality" (Bianchi, 1956). Another approach to the issue of causation has been to study the statistical relationship between variables, with statements of causality being made only when the variables are related in specified ways (Nowak, 1960).

The elaboration of the possible statistical relationships between two or more variables and an indication of their causal significance by no means solves the problems of causal analysis in the study of crime. In fact, a number of questions are raised in multivariate analysis. First, the concept of cause remains vague, referring to little more than a time ordering of variables. Second, the proximity of variables in time does not necessarily mean that phenomena are causally connected in any meaningful manner. Third, the analysis of variables assumes that phenomena can be meaningfully divided into units. Fourth, the selection of the specific variables is to a considerable extent arbitrary. Fifth, the number of variables selected is limited by the procedure of statistical manipulation itself. And sixth, the analysis of the statistical association between variables is based on the positivistic assumption that separable phenomena exist in the real world and that these phenomena are in reality mechanistically (and causally) connected. All of these assumptions are based on faith, that is, on an unverifiable notion of what the world is like and how human beings can comprehend that world.

Another problem in the use of the concept of causation in criminology arises in reference to the classic distinction made by John Stuart Mill between *necessary* and *sufficient* causes. This distinction asserts: X is a necessary condition for Y if Y *never occurs without the occurrence of X;* X is a sufficient condition for Y if Y *always occurs with the occurrence of X;* and X is both a necessary and sufficient condition for Y if Y *never occurs without the occurrence of X and always occurs with the occurrence of X.* The classic distinction between necessary and sufficient causes may be appropriate for the discussion of absolutes in the realm of logic, but in the realm of science exceptions to any generalizations are to be expected. For this reason, the scientist finds it necessary to view his data in terms of relative certainty, that is, in terms of *probability* statements. When probability reasoning is used, X and Y may be said to be causally related in spite of the fact that some Xs may occur without Ys and some Ys may occur without Xs. In other words, when the probability of concomitant variation is utilized, the classic distinction between necessary and sufficient causes loses its significance.

Acknowledging that in the world of science one rarely expects to find a single event or condition that is both necessary and sufficient to bring about another event, several methodologists in the social sciences have proposed that the scientist be interested instead in *contributory* conditions, *contingent* conditions, and *alternative* conditions (see Selltiz, Jahoda, Deutsch, & Cook, 1959). All of these forms of conditions operate to make the occurrence of an event probable, but not certain. Such a conception of conditions is more appropriate to causal reasoning in science than is the concept of necessary and sufficient causes, which is based on the logic of absolutes. The distinction between necessary and sufficient conditions will continue to have meaning for the explanation of specific and singular events but, for the study of the regularity of a collection of events, when 'universal laws' are sought, the distinction is inappropriate.

Nevertheless, it is interesting to note that the theory which has the greatest influence in criminology and currently provides the major orientation for criminologists is formulated in terms of necessary and sufficient causes. Sutherland's theory of differential association asserts that criminal behavior has as its necessary and sufficient conditions a set of criminal motivations, attitudes, and techniques, the learning of which takes place when there is exposure to criminal norms in excess of exposure to corresponding anti-criminal norms during symbolic interaction in primary groups. Sutherland's initial formulation in terms of necessary and sufficient causes was most likely a reaction to the doubtful attempts at the construction of theories of criminal behavior as found in the multiple-factor approach of the time. In spite of the passage of time, however, it is still suggested that the appropriate model for a theory of criminal behavior is based on the logic of necessary and sufficient causes: "Conditions which are said to cause crime should always be present when crime is present, and they should always be absent when crime is absent" (Sutherland & Cressey, 1966:77). The point that this statement misses is that scientific theories may be, or perhaps must be, formulated in other than the logic of necessary and sufficient conditions.

A CONCEPTION OF EXPLANATION

In the modern philosophy of science, causation is either omitted from the vocabulary or, when used, is given a special meaning (see Heisenberg, 1958; Bridgman, 1961; Nagel, 1961; Bunge, 1963). While one should not model the social sciences after the physical sciences as often has been done in reference to other matters, there is need for a reconsideration of a change in the use of the concept of causation in the social sciences. In reference to the study of crime, a conception of explanation may be proposed which considers ontology, epistemology, and methodological and substantive theory.

Ontology. The belief that knowledge is derived from sense experience and that no facts exist independent of our knowledge of them is the foundation of the idealist position. Accordingly, to state the extreme, there is no reality beyond man's conception of it. Or, to put it in more romantic terms, "Beauty is in the eye of the beholder."

The implications of this ontological position for a conception of causation is that any defined causal relationship has to be regarded as a construct of the observer, i.e., one way that the observer orders his observations. The role of constructs in the social sciences has been concisely outlined by Alfred Schutz:

> All our knowledge of the world, in commonsense as well as in scientific thinking, involves constructs, i.e., a set of abstractions, generalizations, formalizations, idealizations specific to the respective

level of thought organization. Strictly speaking, there are no such things as facts, pure and simple. All facts are from the outset facts selected from a universal context by the activities of our mind. They are, therefore, always interpreted facts, either facts looked at as detached from their context by an artificial abstraction or facts considered in their particular setting. In either case, they carry along their interpretational inner and outer horizon. This does not mean that, in daily life or in science, we are unable to grasp the reality of the world. It just means that we grasp merely certain aspects of it, namely, those which are relevant to us either for carrying on our business of living or from the point of view of a body of accepted rules of procedure of thinking called the method of science (Schutz, 1963:304).

Thus, whether causation actually exists in the real world is not the proper question; rather the question is whether causation as a construct is a useful way of expressing our understanding of our observations. This conception of causation is neatly expressed by Hanson in *Patterns of Discovery*: "Causes certainly are connected with effects; but this is because our theories connect them, not because the world is held together by cosmic glue" (1965:64). Who knows, events may actually be held together by imponderables, but this is beyond our comprehension and also is irrelevant to an understanding of the social world. In our scientific quest for some comprehension of the world that we experience, we may operate 'as if' causation existed as a fact in reality. In causative reasoning we must remember that causation is a construct and, as construct, is basically an activity of the observer.

Epistemology. Some of the confusion in the use of the concept of causation in the social sciences (as well as in the physical sciences) has been a result of the failure to distinguish between the philosophical issues of ontology and epistemology. Ontology refers to the theory of the nature of being, existence, and reality, while epistemology refers to the theory of the nature and grounds of knowledge. Suggested in any ontology is a view of what the real world is like. This view is, of course, related to how humans are to understand that world.

The ontological position presented thus far may be viewed as an 'agnostic ontology.' That is, we just cannot be certain of the nature of the real world, although we are always ready to entertain any suggestions. This ontological position is directly related to the nominalistic epistemological position. One cannot be certain about the nature of reality when it is held that our knowledge of 'reality' is a mental construction. The nominalistic position that I am suggesting for criminology dispenses with the question of an objective reality and of the ability of the observer to 'copy' it. There is no reason to believe in the objective existence of anything. Our concern is, rather, with the formulation of constructs that are meaningful for the purposes at hand.

Methodological and substantive theory. A problem that often arises in sociology (see Bierstedt, 1959) is that constructs become so familiar that we forget that they are nominal and begin to treat them as real. The danger of inadvertently turning constructs into descriptions of reality can be avoided if we explicitly distinguish between *methodological theory* and *substantive theory*. Methodological theory refers to the way in which scientific observers understand their controlled experiences. Substantive theory consists of propositions about the subject matter of the scientist's observations. Substantive theory is ontological in that there is an attempt to define the nature of existence, while methodological theory is epistemological in that questions are raised about the way in which the observer may gain knowledge.

Thus, in reference to causation, a distinction may be made between causation as a methodological construct and causation as a substantive construct. In the *methodological* sense, causation is a heuristic device that is used by scientists to order the world they experience. However, if causation is used in the social sciences as a *substantive* construct, the concept must be related to the nature of social phenomena. Since the world of social phenomena is one that has meaning for the human beings within it, the constructs of the social scientist have to be founded upon the *social reality* created by humanity. *Social causation* may thus be part of that reality. To that extent, social scientists may base their substantive descriptions and generalizations upon a substantive construct of causation.

Conclusions on explanation in criminology. Certainly there are other forms of explanation available to the sociologist when causal analysis is not appropriate for either methodological or substantive purposes. By no means, as has been indicated before, can explanation be equated with causal explanation (see Brown, 1963; Kaplan, 1964:327–369). Many of the important contributions in sociology have used empirical generalizations, probabilities, classification, *Verstehen* and phenomenological analysis, and developmental stages. In general, sociologists have been interested in social structure, the functioning of systems and their parts, regularities of behavior, patterns, and processes. All of these concerns may be pursued for the most part without the aid of cause-and-effect reasoning. It is obvious that there could be a science of human social behavior without the notion of causality.

Nevertheless, as social scientists we may conceive of a substantive causal process that is part of the social reality constructed by human beings. To the extent that human individuals define situations as members of society, that is, construct their world in relation to others, students of social life (criminologists included) may conceive of social causation as part of a social reality.

The general conclusions reached in respect to explanation and causation may be summarized as follows:

1. Causative reasoning in criminology has been based primarily on positivistic assumptions.

2. Social science has relied upon an outdated notion of causation rather than on the modern notions found in the philosophy of science.

3. Causal explanation is by no means the only form of explanation available to the scientist.

4. Causation as a methodological construct must be distinguished from causation as a substantive construct.

5. If causation is used in the social sciences as a substantive construct, the concept must be used in the special sense of social causation.

Comparative Criminology

Present theory and research in criminology tends to be confined to a limited range of phenomena. The present body of knowledge in criminology is derived primarily from observations of crime under selected social conditions. A comparative criminology, on the other hand, would deal with the wide range of variability of the crime phenomenon. Included in a comparative criminology would be a systematic consideration of the different types of societies in which crime occurs, the various legal systems of societies, the differing forms of criminally defined behavior, and variations in social reaction to crime.

Typology provides the means for the development of a comparative criminology. The principal function of typology is to order the diverse observations within a field of study (McKinney, 1966).

As abstractions, types necessarily deviate from concrete observations and accentuate a group of characteristics that are relevant to a particular analysis. The characteristics have empirical referents, although they cannot be experienced directly in this particular form. The abstracted characteristics are then combined into distinct configurations, patterns or types. Thus, a typology provides a framework in which concrete occurrences can be ordered, compared, and explained.

CONSTRUCTION OF TYPOLOGIES IN CRIMINOLOGY

Today criminologists agree that because the category of crime includes a diverse range of behaviors, attempts at explanation must be focused on *types* of crime. Criminologists are, therefore, giving more attention than ever before to the identification, description, and classification of the phenomena included in the concept of crime. Efforts are being made to construct types of crime which are subject to specific forms of explanation.

Students of crime have always, of course, found it necessary to some extent to construct and utilize classifications of crime. The oldest and still most commonly used form of classification is based on the *legal* category of crime. Accordingly, criminal behavior and criminals have been identified in terms of the legal titles designated in criminal statutes. One attempt to use legal titles in a typology of crime is found in the *Uniform Crime Reports*. However, because in the United States the legal titles of offenses differ from one state criminal code to another, the FBI in collecting criminal statistics has found it necessary to combine the varying legal titles into a number of categories. These categories of crime, as based on a synthesis of the legal titles, are utilized in the compilation of the official crime statistics.

There are various other ways in which legal titles may be used in the construction of typologies of crime. One possibility is to define types within specific legal categories. For example, burglars, depending upon their mode of operation, could be divided into housebreakers, safecrackers, professional burglars, and amateur burglars. Criminologists who favor the strategy of defining types within legal categories (Roebuck, 1967) claim that the procedure is desirable because official data concerned with criminal histories exist in terms of legal nomenclature and because the criminal code contains specific, operational definitions of criminal behavior.

Another possibility for using legal categories is to combine categories into types of crime. In a similar fashion, sociological types may cut across some of the behaviors included in a number of legal categories. Cressey (1953), for example, included within "criminal violation of financial trust" some of the behaviors officially handled as forgery, embezzlement, and larceny by bailee.

A novel departure from the traditional use of the legal labels of crime is found in the typological system devised by Sellin and Wolfgang (1964). Constructed as a method for the measurement of delinquency, their system ignores the generic labels used by the law and is based instead on police descriptions of events associated with the violating conduct of offenders, including information on the manner in which an offense is committed, the nature and degree of the harm caused by the offense, the kind of victimization involved, and other similar characteristics of the offense. While devising a scheme for the placement of offenses into categories independent of legal labels, but nevertheless giving attention to the legal processing of offenses, Sellin and Wolfgang have provided a method for the construction of sociologically meaningful offense categories.

In contrast to the various legal classifications that define the overt act are schemes based solely on personal attributes of the criminal. In this manner, offenders have been divided according to sex. Similarly, criminals have been categorized in terms of age. Several Italian criminologists of the positivistic school delimited types of offenders according to a collection of personal attributes. Lombroso, for example, stressed the physical aspects found in the "born criminal." Garofalo and Ferri noted the psychological anomalies of the criminal, e.g., the "lascivious" and "passionate" criminal. In a similar fashion, clinical psychologists and psychiatrists have attempted to classify criminals according to single personality traits or syndromes of traits. Such classifications have included criminals who are "immature," "hostile," "psychopathic," "antisocial," and "aggressive."

More recently, as crime has been increasingly studied as a social phenomenon, criminologists have constructed typologies in terms of the social context of crime. Mayhew and Moreau, two European criminologists of the last century, proposed types of crime based on the way in which crime is related to the activities of the criminal. They distinguished between the accidental offender who commits criminal acts as a result of unanticipated circumstances and the professional criminal who makes a living through criminal activity. Lindesmith and Dunham (1941), with an awareness of the Mayhew-Moreau distinctions, devised a continuum of criminal behavior ranging from the "individualized criminal" to the "social criminal." The criminal behaviors of the individualized criminal find little cultural support, the behaviors being engaged in for diverse personal reasons. The criminal behaviors of the social criminal, on the other hand, are prescribed and supported by group norms.

A number of criminologists have since stressed the *vocational* aspects of certain forms of crime. They have viewed criminal behavior as being a part of the offender's career. Reckless (1961), for example, has suggested three criminal careers: ordinary, organized, and professional. In a more elaborate fashion Gibbons (1965) has proposed a typology of criminals which consists of fifteen role-types. The types are characterized according to definitional and background dimensions. The resulting typology includes such criminal types as "semiprofessional property criminal," "automobile thief," "violent sex offender," and "narcotic addict."

Another approach to the construction of typologies of criminal behavior has been based on the construction of *criminal behavior systems* (Clinard & Quinney, 1967). The types of criminal behavior systems have varied according to such characteristics as the social roles of the offender, association with other criminals, group support of criminal behavior, and social reaction to criminal behavior. The types constructed in the typology consist of several criminal behavior systems: violent personal crime, occasional property crime, occupational crime, political crime, public order crime, conventional crime, organized crime, and professional crime.

In addition to the above typologies, a number of other criminologists have suggested typologies or have delineated particular types in their own research (see Clinard & Quinney, 1967). Since it is realized that the construction of typologies is necessary to the development of a scientific body of knowledge, a bridge which links unordered empirical data with theoretical explanation, such efforts will continue in the further development of criminology. The construction and use of typologies will modify the general theories in criminology. Also, the developing theories will require an alteration in typologies. The interaction of general criminological theory and criminal typology promises to be one of the most dynamic forces in the future study of crime.

TYPOLOGY FOR A COMPARATIVE CRIMINOLOGY

Criminal typologies differ considerably from one another according to the phenomena included within them. The phenomena included within a typology, in turn, depend upon the purpose for which the typology is intended. For example, if the purpose is the analysis of criminals, the emphasis will be on such matters as life histories of offenders, self-conceptions, attitudes, and social background factors. On the other hand, if the objective is a typology of criminal behavior, attention will be focused on such matters as the mode of operation, the overt criminal act, the situation in which the offense occurs, opportunities to commit crime, subcultural norms, relationships between offenders, and the structural aspects of the larger society.

Typologies in criminology have focused primarily on criminals and criminal behavior. Yet, criminology has as its object the study of the processes involved in defining persons and behavior as criminal and the social reactions to the criminally defined persons and behavior. Because legal definitions of behavior, actions of enforcement agencies, and public response influence what is regarded as crime, it is necessary to study the formulation and administration of criminal law and the social reactions to crime as well as the persons and behaviors that are defined as criminal.

There is the possibility of integrating the various phenomena associated with crime into a typology of crime. In such a manner, a typology could be constructed which would consider the conditions under which certain persons and behaviors in particular kinds of societies with certain kinds of legal systems become defined as criminal. Such a typology actually consists of the construction of several separate typologies, which may then be integrated into one general typology for the comparative study of crime. A comparative typology could be composed of such dimensions as societal types, legal systems, criminal behavior systems, and social reactions.

Criminal Definitions and Criminal Behavior

The final issue crucial to the study of crime involves a controversy between two schools of thought. On the one hand is the argument that the proper study of crime concentrates on offenders and their behavior. On the other hand is the conviction that criminology should be devoted primarily to how the label of crime is formulated and applied. In the development of criminology, students of crime have traditionally focused on how and why the person becomes a criminal to the almost total neglect of how persons become defined as criminal. The sociological study of criminal law—its formulation, enforcement, and administration—is thus a fairly recent development in criminology. The attention of a considerable number of criminologists is being devoted to such study.

While the controversy at present is especially heated, there is no reason that the two schools of thought should become deadlocked in polemics. The current interest in criminal definition is long overdue. It provides a welcome corrective to the excesses and absurdities that often resulted from the sole study of the offender. The two approaches of criminal definitions and criminal behavior actually complement one another. And there is the possibility that the two approaches may be combined or synthesized in various ways to provide new theoretical orientations to the study of crime (as in Matza, 1964).

The study of criminal definition has received stimulation from a number of sources. Several writers (e.g., Jeffery, 1956; Vold, 1958; Geis, 1959) have called for the sociological study of criminal law. The "labeling" approach to social deviance has been advocated by a number of sociologists (Erikson, 1962; Kitsuse, 1962; Becker, 1963).The study of social reactions to deviance and crime has been suggested and illustrated by others (Lemert, 1951; Clark & Gibbs, 1965; Rooney & Gibbons, 1966). In sociological jurisprudence such scholars as Pound (1943) have proposed theories of criminal law. Political scientists (such as Truman, 1951; Rosenblum, 1955; Key, 1958) have discussed the role of group interests in the formulation of public policy. In addition to these various writings there have been studies of the development of particular substantive criminal laws (Sutherland, 1950; Hall, 1952; Chambliss, 1964). There have also been studies of law enforcement (Banton, 1964; Piliavin & Briar, 1964; LaFave, 1965; Skolnick, 1966) and studies of the administration of justice (Sudnow, 1964; Newman, 1966; Blumberg, 1967).

All of these efforts are resulting in the rapid growth of a body of knowledge concerning the defining of behavior as criminal. The study of criminal definition is one of the most significant developments in the modern study of crime.

Public Reaction to Crime

As already indicated, the defining of behavior as criminal is at the same time an act of designating a condition as a social problem. The creating of a problem by public definition also signifies that something ought to be done about the problem. Consequently, some solution to a condition is always proposed or implied whenever conduct is defined as criminal.

The proposed and attempted solutions to the crime problem have been many and varied. A wide range of sanctions, punishments, and correctional programs have been utilized. Since the middle of the last century, such 'solutions' as imprisonment, parole, and probation have been used extensively in the United States. Within institutional settings individual offenders have been preached to, counseled, and treated. On the community level several kinds of programs have been attempted.

During this century, the trend in reaction to crime has been toward treatment rather than punishment. As a consequence, various correctional programs are currently involved in an organizational and ideological conflict reflecting the conflict between the punitive and treatment reactions (Ohlin, 1956:45–48; Sutherland & Cressey, 1966:365–384). Perhaps the key to understanding correctional programs can be found in the conservative ideology on which these programs are generally based. The programs tend to concentrate on custody, rehabilitation, or redirection of individuals rather than on the relation of offenders to more basic social conditions. According to Martin and Fitzpatrick (1964:37), "None of these efforts aims at social change conceived in broad terms. They take the side of discipline, law and order, and rehabilitation, but not of social reform." Only recently have a number of programs been instituted which go beyond the conservative ideology that has long dominated public reaction to crime.

The extent to which public reaction to crime has interested criminologists is indicated in the fact that most criminology textbooks devote half or more of their attention to crime control, prevention, and treatment (see, for example, Korn & McCorkle, 1959; Tappan, 1960; Johnson, 1964; Sutherland & Cressey, 1966). As far as criminological research is concerned, students of crime have investigated such correctional topics as social organization of the prison (Sykes, 1958; Cressey, 1961), probation and parole (Glaser, 1964), and rehabilitation (McCorkle, Elias, & Bixby, 1957). In addition, criminologists have studied and experimented with programs to combat gang delinquency (Miller, 1962; Short & Strodtbeck, 1965) and with community programs for prevention of crime and delinquency (Kobrin, 1959). Suggestions have also been proposed for the treatment of types of offenders (Gibbons, 1965).

An indication of the interdependence between research and practice is found in the recent governmental sponsorship of criminological research for the President's Commission on Law Enforcement and Administration of Justice (1967). The research was used in the Commission's recommendations on crime reporting, juvenile delinquency, law enforcement, administration of justice, correctional institutions, organized crime, narcotics abuse, drunkenness, control of firearms, and crime detection and control. However, even if the recommendations do become incorporated into concrete programs, their thrust will be basically conservative since they are aimed primarily at the enforcement of the law and the control and rehabilitation of the 'criminal' rather than at an alteration in the use of the criminal sanction.

There is no doubt that in terms of informal public reaction, crime is regarded as one of the most serious of all domestic problems. In fact, a chief reason for establishing the President's Commission on Law Enforcement and Administration of Justice was public concern about crime. In specific research sponsored by the Commission, it was found that there is a widespread anxiety about crime in the United States (President's Commission on Law Enforcement and Administration of Justice, 1967:49–53). Furthermore, the Commission reported that crime is linked in the public mind to other social problems, that people are more inclined to think of crime in moral rather than social terms, that public concern about crime is mounting, that public anxiety about crime is not necessarily related to the probability of being victimized. As far as action is concerned, most people believe that crime is the responsibility of the police and the courts. In other words, the public would fight crime by tightening controls rather than by changing the conditions and legal procedures that give rise to the behaviors that may be defined as criminal. Such public reaction does not give encouragement to those who would solve social problems by means of social engineering or to those who would change the social and legal structure.

What we need now is a radical perspective that will inform both our understanding of crime and our public reactions. Until there is an awareness that crime is a construct created by the ruling class, any solutions will be naive and inadequate. The task for the student of crime is to expose the meaning of crime as a phenomenon and a problem.

References

Abrahamsen, D.
1952   *Who Are the Guilty?* New York: Rinehart.

Adler, H. M., and M. R. Worthington.
1925   "The scope of the problem of delinquency and crime as related to mental deficiency." *Journal of Psycho-Asthenics* 30: 47–57.

Akers, R. L.
1964 "Socio-economic status and delinquent behavior: a retest." *Journal of Research in Crime and Delinquency* 1: 38–46.

Alexander, F., and H. Staub.
1956 *The Criminal, the Judge, and the Public.* Revised Edition. Glencoe, Ill.: Free Press.

Aschaffenburg, G.
1913 *Crime and Its Repression.* Translation by A. Albrecht. Boston: Little, Brown.

Banton, M.
1964 *The Policeman in the Community.* London: Tavestock.

Barnes, H. E.
1931 "Criminology." Pp. 584–592 in *Encyclopedia of the Social Sciences.* New York: Macmillan.

Beattie, R. H.
1955 "Problems of criminal statistics in the United States." *Journal of Criminal Law, Criminology, and Police Science* 46: 178–186.

Becker, H. S.
1953 "Becoming a marijuana user." *American Journal of Sociology* 59: 235–243.
1963 *The Outsiders: Studies in Social Deviance.* New York: Free Press of Glencoe.

Best, H.
1930 *Crime and Criminal Law in the United States.* New York: Macmillan.

Bianchi, H.
1956 *Position and Subject Matter of Criminology: Inquiry Concerning Theoretical Criminology.* Amsterdam: North-Holland Publishing Company.

Bierstedt, R.
1959 "Nominal and real definitions in sociological theory." Pp. 121–144 in L. Gross (ed.), *Symposium in Sociological Theory.* Evanston, Ill.: Row, Peterson.

Blumberg, A. S.
1967 *Criminal Justice.* Chicago: Quadrangle Books.

Bonger, W. A.
1916 *Criminality and Economic Conditions.* Translation by H. P. Horton. Boston: Little, Brown.
1936 *Introduction to Criminology.* Translation by E. Van Loo. London: Methuen.

Booth, C.
1892– *Life and Labour of the People of London.* 9 vols. Second Edition.
1897   London: Macmillan.

Bordua, D. J. (ed.).
1967   *The Police: Six Sociological Essays.* New York: Wiley.

Brace, C. L.
1872   *The Dangerous Classes of New York.* New York: Wynkoop & Hallenbeck.

Brasol, B.
1927   *The Elements of Crime.* New York: Oxford University Press.

Bridgman, P. W.
1961   "Determinism in modern science." Pp. 57–75 in S. Hook (ed.), *Determinism and Freedom in the Age of Modern Science.* New York: Collier.

Brown, R. R.
1963   *Explanation in Social Science.* Chicago: Aldine.

Bunge, M. A.
1963   *Causality: The Place of the Causal Principle in Modern Science.* New York: Meridian Books.

Burgess, E. W.
1923   "The study of the delinquent as a person." *American Journal of Sociology* 28: 657–680.

Burgess, E. W., and R. L. Akers.
1966   "A differential association-reinforcement theory of criminal behavior." *Social Problems* 14: 128–147.

Burt, C.
1925   *The Young Delinquent.* New York: D. Appleton.

Cantor, N. F.
1932a *Crime, Criminals and Criminal Justice.* New York: Holt.
1932b "The search for causes of crime." *Journal of Criminal Law, Criminology and Police Science* 22: 854–863.
1939   *Crime and Society.* New York: Holt.

Chambliss, W. J.
1964   "A sociological analysis of the law of vagrancy." *Social Problems* 12: 67–77.

Clark, A. L., and J. P. Gibbs.
1965   "Social control: a reformulation." *Social Problems* 12: 398–415.

Clinard, M. B. (ed.).
1964   *Anomie and Deviant Behavior.* New York: Free Press of Glencoe.

Clinard, M. B., and R. Quinney.
1967   *Criminal Behavior Systems: A Typology*. New York: Holt, Rinehart and Winston.

Cloward, R. A., and L. E. Ohlin.
1960   *Delinquency and Opportunity*. New York: Free Press of Glencoe.

Cohen, A. K.
1955   *Delinquent Boys: The Culture of the Gang*. Glencoe, Ill.: Free Press.

Cohen, A. K., A. R. Lindesmith, and K. F. Shuessler (eds.).
1956   *The Sutherland Papers*. Bloomington: Indiana University Press.

Colquhoun, P.
1806   *Treatise on the Police of the Metropolis*. Seventh Edition. London: J. Mawman.

Crapsey, E.
1872   *The Nether Side of New York*. New York: Sheldon.

Cressey, D. R.
1953   *Other People's Money*. Glencoe, Ill.: Free Press.
1957   "The state of criminal statistics." *National Probation and Parole Association Journal* 3: 230–241.
1966   "Crime." Pp. 136–192 in R. K. Merton and R. A. Nisbet (eds.), *Contemporary Social Problems*. Second Edition. New York: Harcourt, Brace and World.

Cressey, D. R. (ed.).
1961   *The Prison: Studies in Institutional Organization and Change*. New York: Holt, Rinehart and Winston.

DeFleur, M. L., and R. Quinney.
1966   "A reformation of Sutherland's differential association theory and a strategy for empirical verification." *Journal of Research in Crime and Delinquency* 3: 1–22.

Drähms, A.
1900   *The Criminal, His Personnel and Environment: A Scientific Study*. New York: Macmillan.

Dugdale, R. L.
1877   *The Jukes: A Study in Crime, Pauperism, Disease and Heredity*. New York: Putnam's.

Ellis, H.
1892   *The Criminal*. New York: Scribner's.

Erikson, K. T.
1962   "Notes on the sociology of deviance." *Social Problems* 9: 307–314.

Erickson, M. L., and L. T. Empey.
1963   "Court records, undetected delinquency and decision-making."
       Journal of Criminal Law, Criminology and Police Science 54:
       456–469.

Estabrook, A. H.
1916   *The Jukes in 1915*. Washington, D. C.: Carnegie Institute.

Ettinger, C. J.
1932   *The Problem of Crime*. New York: Long and Smith.

Ferri, E.
1881   *I nuovi orizzonti del diritto e della procedura penale*. 2 volumes.
       Turin: UTET. (Title changed to *La sociologia criminale* in 1884.)
1917   *Criminal Sociology*. Translation by J. I. Kelly and J. Lisle. Boston:
       Little, Brown.

Fink, A. E.
1938   *Causes of Crime: Biological Theories in the United States*. Philadel-
       phia: University of Pennsylvania Press.

Frank, L. K.
1925   "Social Problems." *American Journal of Social Problems* 30:
       462–473.

Friedlander, K.
1947   *The Psychoanalytic Approach to Juvenile Delinquence*. New York:
       International Universities Press.

Fuller, R. C.
1938   "The problem of teaching social problems." *American Journal of
       Sociology* 44: 415–425.

Fuller, R. C., and R. H. Meyers.
1941   "Some aspects of a theory of social problems." *American Sociologi-
       cal Review* 6: 24–32.

Garofolo, R.
1885   *Criminologia*. Naples.
1914   *Criminology*. Translation by R. Wyness Millar. Boston: Little,
       Brown.

Gault, R. H.
1932   *Criminology*. Boston: Heath.

Geis, G.
1959   "Sociology, criminology and criminal law." *Social Problems* 7: 40–47.

Gibbons, D. C.
1965   *Changing the Lawbreaker: The Treatment of Delinquents and Crim-
       inals*. Englewood Cliffs, N. J.: Prentice-Hall.

Gillin, J. L.
1926   *Criminology and Penology*. New York: Century.

Glaser, D.
1956   "Criminality theories and behavioral changes." *American Journal of Sociology* 61: 433–444.
1964   *The Effectiveness of a Prison and Parole System*. Indianapolis: Bobbs-Merrill.

Glueck, S., and E. Glueck.
1950   *Unraveling Juvenile Delinquency*. New York: Commonwealth Fund.
1956   *Physique and Delinquency*. New York: Harper.

Goddard, H. H.
1914   *Feeblemindedness: Its Causes and Consequences*. New York: Macmillan.
1920   *Human Efficiency and Levels of Intelligence*. Princeton, N. J.: Princeton University Press.

Goldman, E. F.
1952   *Rendezvous with Destiny*. New York: Random.

Goring, C.
1913   *The English Convict: A Statistical Study*. London: His Majesty's Stationary Office.

Guillot, E. E.
1943   "Social factors in crime: as explained by American writers of the Civil War and post-Civil War period." Ph.D. dissertation (published), University of Pennsylvania.

Hakeem, M.
1958   "A critique of the psychiatric approach to crime and correction." *Law and Contemporary Problems* 23: 650–682.

Hall, A. C.
1902   *Crime in its Relation to Social Progress*. New York: Columbia University Press.

Hall, J.
1952   *Theft, Law and Society*. Second Edition. Indianapolis: Bobbs-Merrill.

Hanson, N. R.
1965   *Patterns of Discovery*. London: Cambridge University Press.

Hathaway, S. R. and E. D. Monachesi.
1953   *Analyzing and Predicting Delinquency with the MMPI*. Minneapolis: University of Minnesota Press.

Haynes, F. E.
1930   *Criminology*. New York: McGraw-Hill.

Healy, W.
1915   *The Individual Delinquent*. Boston: Little, Brown.

Heisenberg, W.
1958   *Physics and Philosophy: The Revolution in Modern Science*. New York: Harper and Row.

Henderson, C. R.
1901   *An Introduction to the Study of Dependent, Defective, and Delinquent Classes*. Second Edition. Boston: Heath.

von Hentig, H.
1947   *Crime: Causes and Conditions*. New York: McGraw-Hill.

Hooton, E. A.
1939   *The American Criminal: An Anthropological Study*. Cambridge, Mass.: Harvard University Press.

House, F. N.
1936   *The Development of Sociology*. New York: McGraw-Hill.

Jeffery, C. R.
1956   "The structure of American criminological thinking." *Journal of Criminal Law, Criminology and Police Science* 46: 658–672.

Johnson, H. E.
1964   *Crime, Correction, and Society*. Homewood, Ill.: Dorsey Press.

Kaplan, Abraham.
1964   *The Conduct of Inquiry*. San Francisco: Chandler.

Karpman, B.
1935   *The Individual Criminal*. Washington, D. C.: Nervous and Mental Disease Publication.

Kellor, F. A.
1901   *Experimental Sociology*. New York: Macmillan.

Key, V. O., Jr.
1958   *Politics, Parties, and Pressure Groups*. New York: Thomas Y. Crowell.

Kinberg, O.
1935   *Basic Problems in Criminology*. Copenhagen: Levin and Munkgaard.

Kitsuse, J. I.
1962   "Societal reaction to deviance: problems of theory and method." *Social Problems* 9: 247–256.

Kitsuse, J. I., and A. V. Cicourel.
1963   "A note on the uses of official statistics." *Social Problems* 11: 131–139.

Kobrin, S.
1959   "The Chicago area project—a 25-year assessment." *Annals of the American Academy of Political and Social Science* 322: 19–29.

Korn, R. R., and L. W. McCorkle.
1959   *Criminology and Penology*. New York: Holt, Rinehart and Winston.

LaFave, W. R.
1965   *Arrest: The Decision to Take a Suspect into Custody*. Boston: Little, Brown.

Lange, J.
1930   *Crime and Destiny*. Translation by C. Haldane. New York: Boni.

Lejins, P. P.
1951   "Pragmatic etiology of delinquent behavior." *Social Forces* 29: 317–321.
1966   "Uniform crime reports." *Michigan Law Review* 64: 1011–1030.

Lemert, E. M.
1951   *Social Pathology*. New York: McGraw-Hill.

Levin, Y., and A. R. Lindesmith.
1937   "English ecology and criminology of the past century." *Journal of Criminal Law, Criminology and Police Science* 27: 801–816.

Lindesmith, A. R.
1947   *Opiate Addiction*. Bloomington, Ind.: Principia Press.

Lindesmith, A. R., and W. H. Dunham.
1941   "Some principles of criminal typology." *Social Forces* 19: 307–314.

Lindesmith, A. R., and Y. Levin.
1937   "The Lombrosian myth in criminology." *American Journal of Sociology* 42: 653–671.

Lindner, R.
1944   *Rebel Without a Cause*. New York: Greene and Stratton.

Lombroso, C.
1876   *L'Uomo delinquente*. 3 volumes. Milan: Hoepli.
1911a   *Criminal Man According to the Classification of Cesare Lombroso*. 1 volume (abridged). Translation by Gina Lombroso-Ferrero. New York: Putnam's.
1911b   *Crime, Its Causes and Remedies*. Translation by H. P. Horton. Boston: Little, Brown.

McCorkle, L. W., A. Elias, and F. L. Bixby.
1957   *The Highfields Story*. New York: Holt.

MacDonald, A.
1892   *Criminology*. New York: Funk and Wagnalls.

McKinney, J. C.
1966   *Constructive Typology and Social Theory*. New York: Appleton-Century-Crofts.

Martin, J. M., and J. P. Fitzpatrick.
1964   *Delinquent Behavior: A Redefinition of the Problem*. New York: Random.

Matza, D.
1964   *Delinquency and Drift*. New York: Wiley.

Merton, R. K.
1938   "Social structure and anomie." *American Sociological Review* 3: 672–682.

Michael, J., and M. J. Adler.
1933   *Crime, Law and Social Science*. New York: Harcourt, Brace.

Miller, W. B.
1962   "The impact of a 'total community' delinquency control project." *Social Problems* 10: 168–191.

Morris, T.
1958   *The Criminal Area: A Study in Social Ecology*. London: Routledge and Kegan Paul.

Murchison, C.
1926   *Criminal Intelligence*. Worchester, Mass.: Clark University Press.

Nagel, E.
1961   *The Structure of Science*. New York: Harcourt, Brace and World.

Newman, D. J.
1962   "The effect of accommodations in justice administration on criminal statistics." *Sociology and Social Research* 46: 144–155.
1966   *Conviction: The Determination of Guilt or Innocence Without Trial*. Boston: Little, Brown.

Nowak, S.
1960   "Some problems of causal interpretation of statistical relationships." *Philosophy of Science* 27: 23–38.

Ohlin, L. E.
1956   *Sociology of Corrections*. New York: Russell Sage.

Park, R. E. (ed.).
1925   *The City*. Chicago: University of Chicago Press.

Parmelee, M.
1908   *The Principles of Anthropology and Sociology in Their Relations to Criminal Procedure*. New York: Macmillan.
1918   *Criminology*. New York: Macmillan.

Parsons, P. A.
1926   *Crime and the Criminal*. New York: Knopf.

Pike, L. O.
1873– *A History of Crime in England*. 2 volumes. London: Smith, Elders.
1876

Piliavin, I., and S. Briar.
1964   "Police encounters with juveniles." *American Journal of Sociology*
       70: 206–214.

Pittman, D. J., and W. F. Handy.
1962   "Uniform crime reporting: suggested improvements." *Sociology and
       Social Research* 46: 135–143.

Ploscowe, M.
1931   "Some causative factors in criminology: a critical analysis of the
       literature," in *Report on the Causes of Crime*. Volume 1. Wash-
       ington, D. C.: National Commission on Law Observance and
       Enforcement.

Polsky, N.
1967   *Hustlers, Beats and Others*. Chicago: Aldine.

Porterfield, A. L.
1946   *Youth in Trouble*. Fort Worth: Leo Potishman Foundation.

Pound, R.
1943   "A survey of social interests." *Harvard Law Review* 62: 1–39.

Powers, E., and H. Witmer.
1951   *An Experiment in the Prevention of Delinquency: The Cambridge-
       Somerville Youth Study*. New York: Columbia University Press.

President's Commission on Law Enforcement and Administration of Jus-
       tice.
1967   *The Challenge of Crime in a Free Society*. Washington, D. C.: U. S.
       Government Printing Office.

Quinney, R.
1964   "Crime in political perspective." *American Behavioral Scientist* 8:
       19–22.
1966   "Structural characteristics, population areas, and crime rates in the
       United States." *Journal of Criminal Law, Criminology and Police
       Science* 57: 45–52.
1970   *The Social Reality of Crime*. Boston: Little, Brown.

de Quirós, C. B.
1911   *Modern Theories of Criminality*. Translation by A. de Salvio.
       Boston: Little, Brown.

Radzinowicz, L.
1962   *In Search of Criminology.* Cambridge, Mass.: Harvard University Press.

Reckless, W. C.
1940   *Criminal Behavior.* New York: McGraw-Hill.
1961   *The Crime Problem.* Third Edition. New York: Appleton-Century-Crofts.

Reckless, W. C., S. Dinitz, and B. Kay.
1957   "The self component in potential delinquency and potential non-delinquency." *American Sociological Review* 22: 566–570.

Reiss, A. J., Jr., and L. Rhodes.
1964   "An empirical test of differential association theory." *Journal of Research in Crime and Delinquency* 1: 5–18.

Riley, M. W.
1963   *Sociological Research.* New York: Harcourt, Brace and World.

Robison, S. M.
1936   *Can Delinquency Be Measured?* New York: Columbia University Press.
1966   "A critical view of the uniform crime reports." *Michigan Law Review* 64: 1031–1054.

Roebuck, J. B.
1967   *Criminal Typology: The Legalistic, Physical-Constitutional-Hereditary, Psychological-Psychiatric and Sociological Approaches.* Springfield, Ill.: Charles C. Thomas.

Rooney, E. A., and D. C. Gibbons.
1966   "Reactions to 'crimes without victims'." *Social Problems* 13: 400–410.

Rosenblum, V. G.
1955   *Law as a Political Instrument.* New York: Random.

Schlapp, M. G., and E. H. Smith.
1928   *The New Criminology.* New York: Boni and Liveright.

Schuessler, K. F., and D. R. Cressey.
1950   "Personality characteristics of criminals." *American Journal of Sociology* 55: 475–484.

Schulman, H. M.
1966   "The measurement of crime in the United States." *Journal of Criminal Law, Criminology and Police Science* 57: 483–492.

Schutz, A.
1963   "Common-sense and scientific interpretation of human action." Pp. 302–346 in M. Natanson (ed.), *Philosophy of the Social Sciences.* New York: Random.

Sellin, T.
1931 "The basis of a crime index." *Journal of Criminal Law, Criminology and Police Science* 22: 335–356.
1938 *Culture Conflict and Crime.* New York: Social Science Research Council.
1950 "The uniform criminal statistic act." *Journal of Criminal Law, Criminology and Police Science* 40: 679–700.

Sellin, T., and M. E. Wolfgang.
1964 *The Measurement of Delinquency.* New York: Wiley.

Selltiz, C., M. Jahoda, M. Deutsch, and S. W. Cook.
1959 *Research Methods in Social Relations.* New York: Holt, Rinehart and Winston.

Shaw, C. R.
1929 *Delinquency Areas.* With the collaboration of Frederick M. Zorbaugh, Henry D. McKay, and Leonard S. Cottrell. Chicago: University of Chicago Press.
1930 *The Jack-Roller.* Chicago: University of Chicago Press.
1931 *Natural History of a Delinquent Career.* Chicago: University of Chicago Press.
1938 *Brothers in Crime.* Chicago: University of Chicago Press.

Sheldon, W. H.
1949 *Varieties of Delinquent Youth.* New York: Harper.

Short, J. F., Jr.
1957 "Differential association and delinquency." *Social Problems* 4: 233–239.

Short, J. F., Jr., and I. Nye.
1958 "Extent of unrecorded juvenile delinquency: tentative conclusions." *Journal of Criminal Law, Criminology and Police Science* 49: 296–302.

Short, J. F., Jr., and F. L. Strodtbeck.
1965 *Group Process and Gang Delinquency.* Chicago: University of Chicago Press.

Simey, T. S., and M. B. Simey.
1960 *Charles Booth, Social Scientist.* London: Oxford University Press.

Skolnick, J. H.
1966 *Justice Without Trial: Law Enforcement in Democratic Society.* New York: Wiley.

Sorokin, P. A.
1928 *Contemporary Sociological Theories.* New York: Harper.

Sudnow, D.
1964 "Normal crimes: sociological features of the penal code in a public defender's office." *Social Problems* 12: 255–276.

Sutherland, E. H.
1929   "Crime and the conflict process." *Journal of Juvenile Research* 13: 38–48.
1937   *The Professional Thief.* Chicago: University of Chicago Press.
1939   *Principles of Criminology.* Third Edition. Philadelphia: Lippincott.
1947   *Principles of Criminology.* Fourth Edition. Philadelphia: Lippincott.
1950   "The diffusion of sexual psychopath laws." *American Journal of Sociology* 56: 142–148.

Sutherland, E. H., and D. R. Cressey.
1966   *Principles of Criminology.* Seventh Edition. Philadelphia: Lippincott.

Sykes, G. M.
1958   *The Society of Captives.* Princeton, N. J.: Princeton University Press.

Taft, D. R., and R. W. England, Jr.
1964   *Criminology.* Fourth Edition. New York: Macmillan.

Tannenbaum, F.
1938   *Crime and the Community.* Boston: Ginn.

Tappan, P. W.
1960   *Crime, Justice and Correction.* New York: McGraw-Hill.

Tarde, G.
1912   *Penal Philosophy.* Translation by R. Howell. Boston: Little, Brown.

Thomas, W. I.
1923   *The Unadjusted Girl.* Boston: Little, Brown.

Thomas, W. I., and F. Znaniecki.
1927   *The Polish Peasant in Europe and America.* 2 volumes. Second Edition. New York: Knopf.

Thrasher, F. M.
1927   *The Gang: A Study of 1,313 Gangs in Chicago.* Chicago: University of Chicago Press.

Truman, D.
1951   *The Governmental Process.* New York: Knopf.

Tulchin, S. H.
1939   *Intelligence and Crime.* Chicago: University of Chicago Press.

Turk, A. T.
1966   "Conflict and criminality." *American Sociological Review* 31: 338–352.
1969   *Criminality and Legal Order.* Chicago: Rand McNally.

Vold, G. B.
1958   *Theoretical Criminology.* New York: Oxford University Press.

Voss, H. L.
1966   "Socio-economic status and reported delinquent behavior." *Social Problems* 13: 314–324.

Waller, W.
1936   "Social problems and the mores." *American Sociological Review* 1: 922–933.

Wallerstein, J. S., and C. J. Wyle.
1947   "Our law-abiding law-breakers." *Probation* 25: 107–112.

Wheeler, S.
1962   "The social sources of criminology." *Sociological Inquiry* 32 (Spring): 139–159.

White, M.
1949   *Social Thought in America: The Revolt Against Formalism.* New York: Viking Press.

Wigmore, J. H.
1909   *A Preliminary Bibliography of Modern Criminal Law and Criminology.* Chicago: Northwestern University Law School Bulletin No. 1.

Wilkins, L. T.
1965   "New thinking in criminal statistics." *Journal of Criminal Law, Criminology and Police Science* 56: 277–284.

Wilks, J. A.
1967   "Ecological correlates of crime and delinquency." Pp. 138–156 in *President's Commission on Law Enforcement and Administration of Justice, Crime and Its Impact—An Assessment.* Washington, D. C.: U. S. Government Printing Office.

Wolfgang, M. E.
1963   "Uniform crime reports: A critical appraisal." *University of Pennsylvania Law Review* 111: 708–738.

Wood, A. E., and J. B. Waite.
1941   *Crime and Its Treatment.* New York: American Book Company.

Zeleny, L. D.
1933   "Feeblemindedness and criminal conduct." *American Journal of Sociology* 38: 564–576.

TWO

The Social Reality of Crime

The history of contemporary sociology is characterized by a progressive loss in faith—faith that anything exists beyond man's imagination. We are consequently being led to new assumptions about our craft and the substance of our labors. New ways of attacking old problems are making this a dynamic period for sociology.

Perhaps in no other sociological realm is intellectual revisionism more apparent than in the study of crime. In these pages I will indicate how current thoughts and trends in the sociological study of crime can culminate in a theory of crime. The theory that I will present—*the theory of the social reality of crime*—rests upon theoretical and methodological assumptions that reflect the happenings of our time; it is meant to provide an understanding of crime that is relevant to our contemporary experiences.[1]

Assumptions: Explanation in the Study of Crime

Until fairly recent times studies and writings in criminology were shaped almost entirely by the criminologist's interest in 'the criminal.' In the last few years, however, those who study crime have realized that crime is relative to different legal systems, that an absolute conception of crime—outside of legal definitions—had to be replaced by a relativistic (that is, legalistic) conception. Many criminologists have therefore turned to studying how criminal definitions are constructed and applied in a society.

Original source: Chapter 1 in Richard Quinney, *The Social Reality of Crime*. Boston: Little, Brown, 1970.

Two schools of thought have developed. Some argue that crime is properly studied by examining offenders and their behavior. Others are convinced that the criminal law is the correct object: how it is formulated, enforced, and administered. The two need not become deadlocked in polemics. The long overdue interest in criminal definitions happily corrects the absurdities brought about by studying the offender alone; the two approaches actually complement one another. A synthesis of the criminal behavior and criminal definition approaches can provide a new theoretical framework for the study of crime.

The theory I am proposing rests upon certain assumptions about theoretical explanation: these assumptions are in regard to (1) ontology, (2) epistemology, (3) causation, and (4) theory construction.

Ontology. What is the world really like? I mean, what is it we pretend to separate ourselves from when we go about our observations? I adopt a nominalistic position contrary to that of the positivists. Accordingly, I can accept no universal essences. The mind is unable to frame a concept that corresponds to an objective reality. We cannot be certain of an objective reality beyond our conception of it. Thus, we have no reason to believe in the objective existence of anything. We must, instead, formulate theories that give meaning to our experiences.[2]

Epistemology. Implied in the ontological assumption is the epistemological assumption that we as observers cannot 'copy' anything that may be regarded as an objective reality, since we are skeptical of the existence of such a reality. Our observations, instead, are based on our own mental constructions, not on essences beyond our experiences. Expressed in a more romantic way: "Beauty is in the eye of the beholder." Thus, our concern is not with any correspondence between 'objective reality' and observation, but between observation and the utility of such observations in understanding our own subjective, multiple social worlds.

Causation. Much of criminological theory, based on positivistic assumptions, has sought to explain the 'causes' of crime. That search continues, but the modern concept of causation employed in the philosophy of science is considerably different from that used by criminologists.[3] The strategy toward causation that I propose for a theory of crime is consistent with the above assumptions about the world and the way in which we understand it, as well as with current usage in the philosophy of science. This strategy has three parts.

First, causal explanation need not be the sole interest of criminologists.[4] The objective of any science is not to formulate and verify theories of causation, but to construct an order among observables. Explanations as generalized answers to the question 'why' may be presented in other than causal form. For example, explanations in terms of probability statements, functional relationships, and developmental stages can be formulated into propositions that do not depend upon causal explanation. A science of human social behavior is obviously possible without the notion of causation.

Second, a statement of causation does not necessarily state the nature of reality, but is a *methodological construction* of the observer: "Causes certainly are connected by effects; but this is because our theories connect them, not because the world is held together by cosmic glue."[5] Scientists who define causal relationships have to see that they are constructs imposed by themselves in order to give meaning to a significant theoretical problem. Confused, we often inadvertently turn the causational construct into a description of reality.[6] Initially a heuristic device, a methodological tool, causation does not necessarily describe the substance of our observations.

Third, we must not use the causational construct as it has often been applied in physical science. Causative explanations of crime have tended in particular to be based on the mechanistic conception of causation. What is required in the explanation of crime, if a causative explanation is formulated, is a conception of causation that is attuned to the nature of social phenomena.

The world of social phenomena studied by the social scientist has meaning for the human beings living within it. The world of nature, on the other hand, which the physical scientist studies, means nothing to the physical objects. Therefore, the social scientist's constructs have to be founded upon the *social reality* created by human beings: "The constructs of the social sciences are, so to speak, constructs of the second degree, that is, constructs of the constructs made by the actors on the social scene, whose behavior the social scientist has to observe and to explain in accordance with the procedural rules of his science."[7] As social scientists we may well conceive of a *substantive causal process*, as part of a social reality that is constructed by human beings, and distinct from the causal constructs formulated as methodological devices by the physical scientist. Thus, causation could be used substantively to explain crime in the special sense of *social causation*. To the extent that human beings define situations, that is, construct their own worlds in relation to others, the student of social life may conceive of a social causation as part of a social reality.

Theory Construction. The appropriate structure of a theory is far from certain in sociology. Many have worked toward establishing a research methodology, but little has been done about developing theoretical methods. Since we lack criteria for building theories, Homans has suggested that a theory must consist of propositions that state relationships and form a deductive system.[8] But we cannot ignore explanations that may be formulated in forms other than the deductive. These may contain propositions which are not deductive, but which are probabilistic, functional, or generic.[9] Such propositions need not necessarily be deductive, in the sense that another set of propositions must be deduced from them in order for the original set of propositions to be regarded as a theory.

More important, propositions must be consistent with one another and must be integrated into a system.[10] The conclusions drawn from one proposition must not contradict those derived from another, and any conclusions obtained from the theory must be derivable within the system. Other standards to be adhered to in constructing theories are: the propositions must be testable; their validity must be determined by subsequent research; and they must be useful, enabling us to understand the problem that inspired us to formulate the theory.

Within the theory that I am constructing are several propositions that are consistent and integrated into a theoretical system. One or more specific statements express in probability form the relationships within the proposition. Further, the propositions are arranged according to a *system of proposition units*. The propositions express relationships that are both coexistent and sequential. The theory thus assumes that patterns of phenomena develop over a period of time.[11] Each proposition unit within the theoretical model requires explanation, and each unit relates to the others. Ultimately, the theoretical system provides the basis for an integrated theory of crime.

Assumptions in a Theory of Crime

In studying any social phenomenon we must hold to some general perspective. Two of those used by sociologists, and by most social analysts for that matter, are the *static* and the *dynamic* interpretations of society. Either is equally plausible, though most sociologists take the static viewpoint.[12] This emphasis has relegated forces and events, such as deviance and crime, which do not appear to be conducive to stability and consensus, to the pathologies of society.

My theory of crime, however, is based on the dynamic perspective. The theory is based on assumptions about (1) process, (2) conflict, (3) power, and (4) social action.

Process. The dynamic aspect of social relations may be referred to as 'social process.' Though in analyzing society we use static descriptions—that is, we define the structure and function of social relations—we must be aware that social phenomena fluctuate continually.[13]

We apply this assumption to all social phenomena that have duration and undergo change, that is, all those which interest the sociologist. A social process is a continuous series of actions, taking place in time, and leading to a special kind of result: "a system of social change taking place within a defined situation and exhibiting a particular order of change through the operation of forces present from the first within the situation."[14] Any particular phenomenon, in turn, is viewed as contributing to the dynamics of the total process. As in the "modern systems approach," social phenomena are seen as generating out of an interrelated whole.[15] The methodological implication of the process assumption is that any social phenomenon may be viewed as part of a complex network of events, structures, and underlying processes.

Conflict. In any society conflicts between persons, social units, or cultural elements are inevitable, the normal consequences of social life. Conflict is especially prevalent in societies with diverse value systems and normative groups. Experience teaches that we cannot expect to find consensus on all or even most values and norms in such societies.

Two models of society contrast sharply: one is regarded as 'conflict' and the other, 'consensus.' With the consensus model we describe social structure as a functionally integrated system held together in equilibrium. In the conflict model, on the other hand, we find that societies and social organizations are shaped by diversity, coercion, and change. The differences between these contending but complementary conceptions of society have been best characterized by Dahrendorf.[16] According to his study, we assume in postulating the consensus (or integrative) model of society that (1) society is a relatively persistent, stable structure, (2) it is well integrated, (3) every element has a function—it helps maintain the system, and (4) a functioning social structure is based on a consensus on values. For the conflict (or coercion) model of society, on the other hand, we assume that (1) at every point society is subject to change, (2) it displays at every point dissensus and conflict, (3) every element contributes to change, and (4) it is based on the coercion of some of its members by others. In other words, society is held together by force and constraint and is characterized by ubiquitous conflicts that result in continuous change: "values are ruling rather than common, enforced rather than accepted, at any given point of time."[17]

Although in society as a whole conflict may be general, according to the conflict model, it is still likely that we will find stability and consensus on values among subunits in the society. Groups with their own cultural elements are found in most societies, leading to social differentiation with conflict between the social units; nonetheless integration and stability may appear within specific social groups: "Although the total larger society may be diverse internally and may form only a loosely integrated system, within each subculture there may be high integration of institutions and close conformity of individuals to the patterns sanctioned by their own group."[18]

Conflict need not necessarily disrupt society. Some sociologists have been interested in the *functions* of social conflict, "that is to say, with those consequences of social conflict which make for an increase rather than a decrease in the adaptation or adjustment of particular social relationships or groups."[19] It seems that conflict can promote cooperation, establish group boundaries, and unite social factions. Furthermore, it may lead to new patterns that may in the long run be beneficial to the whole society or to parts of it.[20] Any doubts about its functional possibilities have been dispelled by Dahrendorf: "I would suggest . . . that all that is creativity, innovation, and development in the life of the individual, his group, and his society is due, to no small extent, to the operation of conflicts between group and group, individual and individual, emotion and emotion within one individual. This fundamental fact alone seems to me to justify the value judgment that conflict is essentially 'good' and 'desirable.'"[21] Conflict is not always the disruptive agent in a society; at certain times it may be meaningful to see it as a cohesive force.

Power. The conflict conception of society leads us to assume that coherence is assured in any social unit by coercion and constraint. In other words, *power* is the basic characteristic of social organization. "This means that in every social organization some positions are entrusted with a right to exercise control over other positions in order to ensure effective coercion; it means, in other words, that there is a differential distribution of power and authority."[22] Thus, conflict and power are inextricably linked in the conception of society presented here. The differential distribution of power produces conflict between competing groups, and conflict, in turn, is rooted in the competition for power. Wherever human beings live together, conflict and a struggle for power will be found.

Power, then, is the ability of persons and groups to determine the conduct of other persons and groups.[23] It is utilized not for its own sake, but is the vehicle for the enforcement of scarce values in society, whether the values are material, moral, or otherwise. The use of power affects the distribution of values and values affect the distribution of power. The 'authoritative allocation of values' is essential to any society.[24] In any society, institutional means are used to officially establish and enforce sets of values for the entire population.

Power and the allocation of values are basic in forming public policy. Groups with special interests become so well organized that they are able to influence the policies that are to affect all persons. These interest groups exert their influence at every level and branch of government, in order to have their own values and interests represented in the policy decisions.[25] Any interest group's ability to influence public policy depends on the group's position in the political power structure. Furthermore, access to the formation of public policy is unequally distributed because of the structural arrangements of the political state. "Access is one of the advantages unequally distributed by such arrangements; that is, in consequence of the structural peculiarities of our government some groups have better and more varied opportunities to influence key points of decision than do others."[26] Groups that have the power to gain access to the decision-making process also inevitably control the lives of others.

A major assumption in my conception of society, therefore, is the importance of interest groups in shaping public policy. Public policy is formed so as to represent the interests and values of groups that are in positions of power. Rather than accept the pluralistic conception of the political process, which assumes that all groups make themselves heard in policy decision-making, I am relying upon a conception that assumes an unequal distribution of power in formulating and administering public policy.[27]

Social Action. An assumption of human behavior that is consistent with the conflict-power conception of society asserts that the actions of human beings are purposive and meaningful, that they engage in voluntary behavior. This *humanistic* conception contrasts with the oversocialized conception of human behavior. Human beings are, after all, capable of considering alternative actions, of breaking from the established social order.[28] Once they gain an awareness of self, by being members of society, they are able to choose their actions. The extent to which they do conform depends in large measure upon their own self-control.[29] Nonconformity may also be part of the process of finding self-identity. It is thus *against* something that the self can emerge.[30]

By conceiving of human beings as able to reason and choose courses of action, we may see them as changing and becoming, rather than merely being.[31] The kind of culture that humans develop shapes their ability to be creative. Through their culture they may develop the capacity to have greater freedom of action.[32] Not only are they shaped by their physical, social, and cultural experiences, they are able to select what they are to experience and develop. The belief in realizing unutilized human potential is growing and should be incorporated in a contemporary conception of human behavior.[33]

The *social action* frame of reference that serves as the basis of the humanistic conception of human behavior is drawn from the work of such writers as Weber, Znaniecki, MacIver, Nadel, Parsons, and Becker.[34] It was originally suggested by Max Weber: "Action is social in so far as, by virtue of the subjective meaning attached to it by the acting individual (or individuals), it takes account of the behavior of others and is thereby oriented in its own course."[35] Hence, human behavior is intentional, has meaning for the actors, is goal-oriented, and takes place with an awareness of the consequences of behavior.

Because humans engage in social action, a *social reality* is created. That is, individuals in interaction with others construct a meaningful world of everyday life.

> It is the world of cultural objects and social institutions into which we are all born, within which we have to find our bearings, and with which we have to come to terms. From the outset, we, the actors on the social scene, experience the world we live in as a world both of nature and of culture, not as a private but as an intersubjective one, that is, as a world common to all of us, either actually given or potentially accessible to everyone; and this involves intercommunication and language.[36]

Social reality consists of both the social meanings and the products of the subjective world of persons. Accordingly, human beings construct activities and patterns of actions as they attach meaning to their everyday existence.[37] Social reality is thus both a *conceptual reality* and a *phenomenal reality*. Having constructed social reality, humans find a world of meanings and events that is real to them as conscious social beings.

Theory: The Social Reality of Crime

The theory contains six propositions and a number of statements within the propositions. With the first proposition I define crime. The next four are the explanatory units. In the final proposition the other five are collected to form a composite describing the social reality of crime. The propositions and their integration into a theory of crime reflect the assumptions about explanation and about humankind and society outlined above.[38]

PROPOSITION 1 (DEFINITION OF CRIME): *Crime is a definition of human conduct that is created by authorized agents in a politically organized society.*

This is the essential starting point in the theory—a definition of crime—which itself is based on the concept of definition. Crime is a *definition* of behavior that is conferred on some persons by others. Agents of the law (legislators, police, prosecutors, and judges), representing segments of a politically organized society, are responsible for formulating and administering criminal law. Persons and behaviors, therefore, become criminal because of the *formulation* and *application* of criminal definitions. Thus, crime is created.

By viewing crime as a definition, we are able to avoid the commonly used 'clinical perspective,' which leads one to concentrate on the quality of the act and to assume that criminal behavior is an individual pathology.[39] Crime is not inherent in behavior, but is a judgment made by some about the actions and characteristics of others.[40] This proposition allows us to focus on the formulation and administration of the criminal law as it touches upon the behaviors that become defined as criminal. Crime is seen as a result of a process which culminates in the defining of persons and behaviors as criminal. It follows, then, that the greater the number of criminal definitions formulated and applied, the greater the amount of crime.

PROPOSITION 2 (FORMULATION OF CRIMINAL
   DEFINITIONS): *Criminal definitions describe behaviors that
   conflict with the interests of the segments of society that have
   the power to shape public policy.*

Criminal definitions are formulated according to the interests
of those *segments* (types of social groupings) of society which have
the *power* to translate their interests into *public policy*. The interests—based on desires, values, and norms—which are ultimately
incorporated into the criminal law are those which are treasured by
the dominant interest groups in the society.[41] In other words, those
who have the ability to have their interests represented in public
policy regulate the formulation of criminal definitions.

That criminal definitions are formulated is one of the most
obvious manifestations of *conflict* in society. By formulating criminal law (including legislative statutes, administrative rulings, and
judicial decisions), some segments of society protect and perpetuate
their own interests. Criminal definitions exist, therefore, because
some segments of society are in conflict with others.[42] By formulating criminal definitions these segments are able to control the
behavior of persons in other segments. It follows that the greater
the conflict in interests between the segments of a society, the
greater the probability that the power segments will formulate
criminal definitions.

The interests of the power segments of society are reflected not
only in the content of criminal definitions and the kinds of penal
sanctions attached to them, but also in the *legal policies* stipulating
how those who come to be defined as 'criminal' are to be handled.
Hence, procedural rules are created for enforcing and administering
the criminal law. Policies are also established on programs for treating and punishing the criminally defined and for controlling and
preventing crime. In the initial criminal definitions or the subsequent procedures, and in correctional and penal programs or policies
of crime control and prevention, the segments of society that have
power and interests to protect are instrumental in regulating the
behavior of those who have conflicting interests and less power.[43]
Finally, law changes with modifications in the interest structure.
When the interests that underlie a criminal law are no longer relevant to groups in power, the law will be reinterpreted or altered to
incorporate the dominant interests. Hence, the probability that
criminal definitions will be formulated is increased by such factors
as (1) changing social conditions, (2) emerging interests, (3) increas-

ing demands that political, economic, and religious interests be protected, and (4) changing conceptions of the public interest. The social history of law reflects changes in the interest structure of society.

PROPOSITION 3 (APPLICATION OF CRIMINAL
    DEFINITIONS): *Criminal definitions are applied by the
    segments of society that have the power to shape the
    enforcement and administration of criminal low.*

The powerful interests intervene in all stages in which criminal definitions are created. Since interests cannot be effectively protected by merely formulating criminal law, enforcement and administration of the law are required. The interests of the powerful, therefore, operate in *applying* criminal definitions. Consequently, crime is "political behavior and the criminal becomes in fact a member of a 'minority group' without sufficient public support to dominate the control of the police power of the state."[44] Those whose interests conflict with the interests represented in the law must either change their behavior or possibly find it defined as 'criminal.'

The probability that criminal definitions will be applied varies according to the extent to which the behaviors of the powerless conflict with the interests of the power segments. Law enforcement efforts and judicial activity are likely to be increased when the interests of the powerful are threatened by the opposition's behavior. Fluctuations and variations in the application of criminal definitions reflect shifts in the relations of the various segments in the power structure of society.

Obviously, the criminal law is not applied directly by the powerful segments. They delegate enforcement and administration of the law to authorized *legal agents*, who, nevertheless, represent their interests. In fact, the security in office of legal agents depends on their ability to represent the society's dominant interests.

Because the interest groups responsible for creating criminal definitions are physically separated from the groups to which the authority to enforce and administer law is delegated, local conditions affect the manner in which criminal definitions are applied.[45] In particular, communities vary in the law enforcement and administration of justice they expect. Application is also affected by the visibility of acts in a community and by its norms about reporting possible offenses. Especially important are the occupational organization and ideology of the legal agents.[46] Thus, the probability that criminal definitions will be applied is influenced by such community and organizational factors as (1) community expectations of law enforcement and administration, (2) the visibility and public reporting of offenses, and (3) the occupational organization, ideology, and actions of the legal agents to whom the authority to enforce and administer criminal law is delegated. Such factors determine how the dominant interests of society are implemented in the application of criminal definitions.

The probability that criminal definitions will be applied in specific situations depends on the actions of the legal agents. In the final analysis, a criminal definition is applied according to an *evaluation* by someone charged with the authority to enforce and administer the law. In the course of "criminalization," a criminal label may be affixed to a person because of real or fancied attributes: "Indeed, a person is evaluated, either favorably or unfavorably, not because he *does* something, or even because he *is* something, but because others react to their perceptions of him as offensive or inoffensive."[47] Evaluation by the definers is affected by the way in which the suspect handles the situation, but ultimately their evaluations and subsequent decisions determine the criminality of human acts. Hence, the more legal agents evaluate behaviors and persons as worthy of criminal definition, the greater the probability that criminal definitions will be applied.

PROPOSITION 4 (DEVELOPMENT OF BEHAVIOR PATTERNS
   IN RELATION TO CRIMINAL DEFINITIONS): *Behavior
   patterns are structured in segmentally organized society in
   relation to criminal definitions, and within this context persons
   engage in actions that have relative probabilities of being
   defined as criminal.*

Although behavior varies, all behaviors are similar in that they represent the *behavior patterns* of segments of society. Therefore, all persons—whether they create criminal definitions or are the objects of criminal definitions—act according to *normative systems* learned in relative social and cultural settings.[48] Since it is not the quality of the behavior but the action taken against the behavior that makes it criminal, that which is defined as criminal in any society is relative to the behavior patterns of the segments of society that formulate and apply criminal definitions. Consequently, persons in the segments of society whose behavior patterns are not represented in formulating and applying criminal definitions are more likely to act in ways that will be defined as criminal than those in the segments that formulate and apply criminal definitions.

Once behavior patterns are established with some regularity within the respective segments of society, individuals are provided with a framework for developing *personal action patterns*. These patterns continually develop for individuals as they move from one experience to another. It is the development of these patterns that gives individual human behavior its own substance in relation to criminal definitions.

Humans construct their own patterns of action in participating with others. It follows, then, that the probability that a person will develop action patterns that have a high potential of being defined as criminal depends on the relative substance of (1) structured opportunities, (2) learning experiences, (3) interpersonal associations and identifications, and (4) self-conceptions. Throughout their experiences, individuals create conceptions of themselves as social beings. Thus prepared, they behave according to the anticipated consequences of their actions.[49]

During experiences shared by the criminal definers and the criminally defined, personal action patterns develop among the criminally defined because they are so defined. After such persons have had continued experience in being criminally defined, they learn to manipulate the application of criminal definitions.[50]

Furthermore, those who have been defined as criminal begin to conceive of themselves as criminal; as they adjust to the definitions imposed upon them, they learn to play the role of the criminal.[51] Because of others' reactions, therefore, persons may develop personal action patterns that increase the likelihood of their being defined as criminal in the future. That is, increased experience with criminal definitions increases the probability of developing actions that may be subsequently defined as criminal.

Thus, both the criminal definers and the criminally defined are involved in reciprocal action patterns. The patterns of both the definers and the defined are shaped by their common, continued, and related experiences. The fate of each is bound to that of the other.

PROPOSITION 5 (CONSTRUCTION OF CRIMINAL
 CONCEPTIONS): *Conceptions of crime are constructed
 and diffused in the segments of society by various means
 of communication.*

The "real world" is a social construction: human individuals, with the help of others, create the world in which they live. Social reality is thus the world a group of people create and believe in as their own. This reality is constructed according to the kind of 'knowledge' they develop, the ideas they are exposed to, the manner in which they select information to fit the world they are shaping, and the manner in which they interpret these conceptions.[52] Humans behave in reference to the *social meanings* they attach to their experiences.

Among the constructions that develop in a society are those which determine what members of the society regard as crime. Wherever we find the concept of crime, there we will find conceptions about the relevance of crime, the offender's characteristics, and the relation of crime to the social order.[53] These conceptions are constructed by communication. In fact, the construction of criminal conceptions depends on the portrayal of crime in all personal and mass communications. By such means, criminal conceptions are constructed and diffused in the segments of a society. The most critical conceptions are those held by the power segments of society. These are the conceptions that are certain of becoming incorporated into the social reality of crime. In general, then, the more the power segments are concerned about crime, the greater the probability that criminal definitions will be created and that behavior patterns will develop in opposition to criminal definitions. The formulation and application of criminal definitions and the development of behavior patterns related to criminal definitions are thus joined in full circle by the construction of criminal conceptions.

PROPOSITION 6 (THE SOCIAL REALITY OF CRIME):
The social reality of crime is constructed by the formulation and application of criminal definitions, the development of behavior patterns related to criminal definitions, and the construction of criminal conceptions.

The first five propositions can be collected into a composite. The theory, accordingly, describes and explains phenomena that increase the probability of crime in society, resulting in the social reality of crime.

Since the first proposition is a definition and the sixth is a composite, the body of the theory consists of the four middle propositions. These form a model which relates the propositions into a theoretical system. Each proposition is related to the others, forming a theoretical system of developmental propositions interacting with one another. The phenomena denoted in the propositions and their relationships culminate in what is regarded as the amount and character of crime in a society at any given time, that is, in the social reality of crime.

A Theoretical Perspective for Studying Crime

The theory as I have formulated it is inspired by a change currently altering our view of the world. This change, found at all levels of society, has to do with the world that we all construct and, at the same time, pretend to separate ourselves from in assessing our experiences. Sociologists, sensing the problematic nature of existence, have begun to revise their theoretical orientation, as well as their methods and subjects of investigation.

For the study of crime, a revision in thought is directing attention to the process by which criminal definitions are formulated and applied. In the theory of the social reality of crime I have attempted to show how a theory of crime can be consistent with some revi-

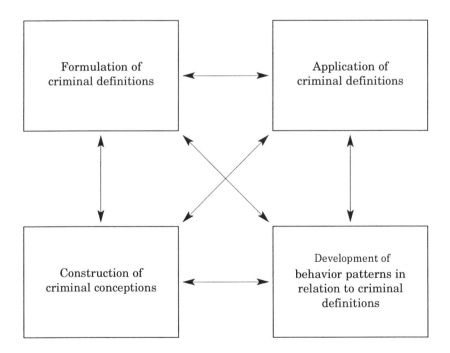

Model of the Social Reality of Crime

sionist assumptions about theoretical explanation and about human beings and society. The theory is cumulative in that the framework incorporates the diverse findings from criminology.

The synthesis has been brought about by conceiving of crime as a constructive process and by formulating a theory according to a system of propositions. The theory is integrative in that all relevant phenomena contribute to the process of creating criminal definitions, the development of the behaviors of those who are involved in criminal defining situations, and the construction of criminal conceptions. The result is the social reality of crime that is constantly being constructed in society.

The theory of the social reality of crime is used as a *theoretical perspective* throughout this book. It has allowed me to organize a considerable amount of material into a coherent framework, giving a perspective for a sociological study of crime. The theory can be useful to the extent that it helps us to understand crime as we experience it today.

THREE

There's a Lot of Folks
Grateful to the Lone Ranger:
With Some Notes on the Rise and Fall
of American Criminology

No matter how terrible things seemed
I knew you were always there.
Every Monday, Wednesday, and Friday night at 6:30 p.m.
    radio time, as the sun was setting in the west over
    my Aunt Lizzie's hay field,
You came galloping up on Silver
With silver bullets blazing into the sky.
I knew once again that my world
    was much more than a dairy farm in the Midwest.

THIS IS THE LEGEND OF A MAN WHO BURIED HIS IDENTITY TO DEDICATE
HIS LIFE TO THE SERVICE OF HUMANITY AND COUNTRY. IT IS THE STORY OF
THE ORIGIN OF THE LONE RANGER.

And then after you informed me in your adventure of what one
man could do against the forces of evil, my brother Ralph and I
would jump on our bicycles and head into the sunset of a Wisconsin
summer night. On my Silver King—its real name—bought outgrown on a farm near Darien—that one bicycle with an enormous
shock absorber on the front column just above the wheel to make
riding easy on even the roughest terrain.

      HI YO, SILVER. BANG . . . BANG . . .
      A FIERY HORSE WITH THE SPEED OF LIGHT . . .

Original Source: *The Insurgent Sociologist* 4 (Fall 1973): 56–64.

A CLOUD OF DUST . . . AND A HEARTY, "HI YO, SILVER."
THE LONE RANGER.

Lone Ranger, it has been twenty years now down the road. You have had a hold on me all this time. Yes, I heard that the real-life man who played your part (I always, intentionally I'm sure, forget his name) died in Detroit. There was some news about Silver being sent to a zoo. But these were things of another world made by others to make you less real to me.

But I must confess, Lone Ranger, that lately I have been having some uneasy feelings about you and about what you did to me. It all started when I saw that old photograph of myself, with my Lone Ranger cap pistol, taking deadly aim at an imaginary enemy.

You see, since my adventures with you I have been through some other worlds. There was the high school in town where I came up against those small town sophisticated kids who made me feel like I was from the backwoods—"farmer," they called me. (Yet I knew you were with me.) There was a small denominational college where I over-excelled (rising to student body president to show them I was really all right after all), two graduate schools where I learned liberal ideas and the virtues of value-free science, and marriage and babies—where for the first time I saw that life was more than sunsets and Saturday afternoon matinees, looking up at you, Hoppy, Gene, and Roy. And there was a time when neither you nor those things that I learned in spite of you gave me much contact with my real-life experiences. It is only now that I can talk to you.

Lone Ranger, there is an alternative to you and your world, one that could mark the end to the myth you made me hold so dearly. I have some ideas that might make you vanish without my firing a single shot. I know now that you were a part of a larger myth that prevailed in those years—and that still prevails today. I finally realize that you were part of the hegemony established by those who would benefit from our ignorance. You were the creation of a commercialized image, an image that made both of us believe that reality was something other than what we experienced. They made a world, those who ruled, and they manipulated our minds just as they determined our conditions. They led us to believe that America was something other than it really was. Lone Ranger, we were both deceived.

What was it you told little Dan, your nephew, about his grandmother and father, ambushed by the Apaches and the Butch Cavendish Gang?

SHE AND YOUR FATHER LEFT YOU A GREAT HERITAGE. THEY AND OTHERS LIKE THEM HAVE HANDED DOWN TO YOU THE RIGHT TO WORSHIP AS YOU CHOOSE. AND THE RIGHT TO WORK AND PROFIT FROM YOUR ENTERPRISE. THEY HAVE GIVEN YOU A LAND WHERE THERE IS TRUE FREEDOM, TRUE EQUALITY OF OPPORTUNITY. A NATION THAT IS GOVERNED BY THE PEOPLE. BY LAWS THAT ARE BEST FOR THE GREATEST NUMBER. YOUR DUTY, DAN, IS TOO PRESERVE THAT HERITAGE AND STRENGTHEN IT. THAT IS THE HERITAGE AND DUTY OF EVERY AMERICAN.

Intellectually I shared the frontier theory of Frederick Jackson Turner. This was fitting since we both came from rural, small town, southern Wisconsin: frontier country—or so we thought. Ironically I had never heard of Turner; his ideas were simply the way of the Midwest. But that didn't matter. (Even the seventy-three years that separated our birth dates—his in 1861 and mine in 1934—did not pose any great division. The mentality of the place was fixed.)

It was in the Spring of 1972, flying to the University of Montana where I was to talk on "The Law and Order Theories of Criminologists," that I read Frederick Jackson Turner for the first time. I knew that I was going to Montana to find something. Cowboys standing at bars in Great Falls and Missoula? I had seen this—in greater detail—a thousand times on the screen. Was I coming home? Or was this a trip to find an unknown country beyond the myth?

Even then Turner struck a responsive note in his assertion that "the true point of view in the history of this nation is not the Atlantic coast, it is the Great West." To me the East had always represented the place of cities (much larger than Delavan), congestion, and Eastern manners. Wisconsin, on the contrary, was on the western frontier. In mind if not in reality.

Then I began to get uncomfortable. Turner was informing me that "The American had continually before him the vision of a continent to be subdued, challenging his courage and ambition, calling out his endeavor in the presence of unparalleled opportunities, raising the competitive spirit to its highest point, stimulating nervous energy, inventiveness, optimism, practical capacity and largeness of design." And at the end of his essay on "Contributions of the West to American Democracy," Turner wrote:

Best of all, the West gave, not only to the American, but to the
unhappy and oppressed of all lands, a vision of hope, and assurance
that the world held a place where were to be found high faith in
man and the will and power to furnish him the opportunity to grow
to the full measure of his own capacity. Great and powerful as are
the new sons of her loins, the Republic is greater than they. The
paths of the pioneer have widened into broad highways. Let us see
to it that the ideals of the pioneer in his log cabin shall enlarge into
the spiritual life of a democracy where civic power shall dominate
and utilize individual achievement for the common good.

Was I being told that frontier individualism from the beginning promoted democracy in America? This is a questionable thesis to say
the least. Given my experiences between Wisconsin and Montana,
I knew there had to be an alternative reality to the myth of the
frontier. Clearly for me, and for generations of Americans, the West
had been mystified.

"Oh, give me land, lots of land under starry skies above. Don't
fence me in." Cole Porter, no less, from Warner Brothers' "Holly-
wood Canteen"—1944. Sung by country-western singers, and we
called it "cowboy music." This was our world at the end of World
War II. The individual reigned supreme. Or so we thought.

And we daydreamed a lot. You were all we had, Lone Ranger, as
we worked all day on a grain binder or the back of a hay wagon, trying to make enough to survive on the family farm. The neighbors were
more competitors than friends. Friday night we went to town, once
with a leghorn hen on the front bumper of the truck, not expecting her
roost to be removed from the shed after dark. Winters snowed us in
for days. Cows had to be milked at 5:30 a.m. Music during the morning milking hours from Chicago's WLS (long before going Rock)—
Arkie the Arkansas Woodchopper, and Lulu Belle and Scottie.

Perhaps at one time in America the frontier mentality
worked. But to live after World War II as if frontier individualism
applied shows only the poverty of our imaginations. America long
ago ceased to be a land of unlimited possibilities for everyone, if
indeed it ever was. Belief in limitless abundance—without material substantiation—serves a ruling economic class that benefits
from this ideology. The frontier myth was an ideology that worked
against those who believed in it. Few people would venture an
understanding of their country as a capitalist, class-divided,
expansionist-imperialistic nation. Thus, the frontier mentality

prevented the emergence of a socialist, revolutionary tradition.

Where is the real America? In a way Turner was right: America has always needed a frontier. That need, coupled with a supporting ideology, has become self-fulfilling in the policies and practices of the American state and its ruling class. This is the message of radical historian William Appleman Williams in his book *The Roots of the Modern American Empire*. In a reinterpretation of the frontier thesis, Williams argues that the frontier-expansionist ideology has guided American policies from the nineteenth century to this day. Writing about the administrations of Adams, Roosevelt, and Wilson in particular, Williams observes:

> They thought about American relations with the rest of the world in terms of the continuing need to expand in order to sustain the dynamic relationship between expansion, prosperity, democracy, and domestic well-being (and order), and they acted on that conception of the world. In their view, the new frontiers would be supplied by the continued overseas expansion of the American marketplace, and they formulated their foreign policies in order to create and maintain the momentum required to achieve that broad objective. They dealt with the more narrow and specific political and strategic (meaning military) aspects of foreign policy within the framework (and limits) created by that underlying evaluation of the American political economy.

American capitalism has to be continuously sustained through an expanding marketplace. The American political economy is still based on a frontier mentality.

In modern terms this means that the United States pursues its manifest destiny in an attempt to control the world. After the American Indian was subdued and conquered, after the frontier reached the shores of the Pacific, the American economy had to seek new frontiers in the rest of the world. This naturally led to war—wars of American intervention, where we defended the freedom of the American empire (and its capitalist ruling class) to prosper at the expense of the lives and welfare of people abroad as well as at home.

On your great white horse you have pursued the enemy to the end of the earth. Lone Ranger-America, you won the West. Then you crossed the Pacific, where you tried to wipe out the dread Yellow Kid. Watch out, Lone Ranger! The hour of the dragon is near. Your silver bullets cannot pierce time.

∞

You may have begun to ask, "What does this have to do with criminology?" What I am suggesting is that our understanding of crime in America is tied to a myth. Rather than basing our thought on social theory, whether of Emile Durkheim or of Max Weber, we have allowed our thinking to be shaped by the prevailing American frontier ideology. We have been party to a myth. *Law and order. Support your local sheriff. My country. To rule the world.*

And beware of evil. What would a world look like that was not divided into the good and the bad? I can't say, can you? The reel spinning before me always shows men in white hats chasing men in black hats; cowboys and Indians; cops and robbers; Americans and Communists; believers and non-believers. To this day I cannot conceive of a world that does not pit the forces of good against those of evil.

But the bad guys in my criminology have changed of late. Earlier I was in pursuit of The Criminal. As a life's work, like the Lone Ranger, I chose to fight the bad guys, TURNING THE BLINDING LIGHT OF JUSTICE ON CRIMINALS. . . . The criminal consisted of anyone who violated the law—that is, anyone who violated laws that preserved the American Way of Life. Someplace along the way, however, it occurred to me that there were others who were violating criminal laws, such as businessmen and politicians. But this was only a transition period, for soon I realized that the really bad guys were those who make laws to protect their own selfish interests, those who oppress others.

This ultimately led me to a critique of the orthodox assumptions about the American Experience, including our conventional wisdom about crime in America. The United States itself, as the perpetrator of an immoral war and the attempted ruler of the world, has become the enemy.

No, Lone Ranger, we can have it no other way. You taught us to stamp out evil. And now that we have come to recognize the real enemy, we are still riding hard in pursuit of the Cavendish Gang.

Your failing, Lone Ranger, was in not having the good fortune of a critical mind. I know, it is hard to have one when you are so busy chasing and being chased. The frontier is no place for self-reflection. How could you know that you were actually protecting the economic interests of Eastern capitalists? You thought the problem was uniquely Western, that 'outlaws' were violating the 'laws of the people.' Lone Ranger, the outlaws were rebels (without a revolutionary consciousness) who were threatening the territory of the financiers, railroad men, and large landowners. The cavalry was your real enemy. You, unknowingly I think, were duped into believing that the lawmen were the good guys, when they were in reality murderers protecting the interests of the capitalists. This unorthodox view of your West is closer to the truth than that perpetuated by conventional wisdom.

What makes one turn from the conventional ideas of the time? Is there a dialectic built into human thought that prompts us to contradict what we hold? This seems clearly to be the case: the dialectic is the natural form of thought. Perhaps there is in every situation a subterranean tradition that stands ready to counter the prevailing culture. That such a tradition exists in middle America accounts for the ideas and actions that rise above the dominant American ideology.

Even the frontier contained its own dialectic. For all the myths about individualism, male dominance, manifest destiny, expansionism, and the like, there did exist a radical critique of the American experience. Even the Lone Ranger, in his fervor to promote justice, attempted to rise above the mean elements (as he saw them) of frontier life. While frontier society never produced a Karl Marx or a socialist tradition, there was always a radicalism that challenged oppressive authority. This radicalism emerged in the course of everyday practice.

Even in the heart of Republican country there was a populism which challenged that system which promoted the monopoly of the few, the disassociation of people from each other through competition, the oppression of the working man. True, this populism never developed into a coherent theory that dealt with the means of production, the division of labor, and alienation; there was no sophisticated analysis of surplus-value. Nevertheless, the West and the Midwest have always had their own radical tradition that provided an alternative 'other side' to the frontier.

This is the alternative that has finally come to inform my notions about crime in America. The sensibility was there all the time. Only years of liberal education and academic sociology could dull its edge. Now, as I free myself from this 'training,' I find the underside of America. Only when we allow ourselves to break out of the conventional wisdom are we able to develop a critical understanding of crime and the legal order. This marks the end of a liberal criminology, a deceptive and oppressive criminology, and the beginning of a critical criminology. The task now is to create a socialist tradition in America—in thought and in action.

∞

The purpose of a critical understanding of crime in America is to expose the meaning of law and order in capitalist society. The false reality by which we live, the one that supports the established system, must be understood and thereby demystified. It is through a critical criminology that we can understand how American law preserves the existing social and economic order. Criminal law is used in the capitalist state to secure the survival of the capitalist system and its ruling class.

And as capitalist society is further threatened by its own contradictions, criminal law is increasingly used in the attempt to maintain domestic order. The underclass, the class that must remain oppressed for the triumph of the dominant economic class, will continue to be the object of criminal law as long as the dominant class seeks to perpetuate itself. To remove the oppression, to eliminate the need for further revolt, would necessarily mean the end of the ruling class and the capitalist economy.

Criminal law continues to assure the colonial status of the oppressed in the social and economic order of the United States. The events of the last few years relating to crime, including both so-called disruption and its repression, can be understood only in terms of the crisis of the American system. Moreover, the oppression within the United States cannot be separated from American imperialism abroad. The crisis of the American empire is complete. The war waged against people abroad is part of the same war waged against the oppressed at home. The ruling class, through its control of the state, has had to resort to a worldwide counterrevolution. A counterinsurgency program is being carried out—through the CIA abroad and the FBI, LEAA, and local police at home. A military war is being fought in Asia, while a war on crime with its own weaponry is being fought within the United States. And all of this is to avoid changing the capitalist order, indeed to protect it and to promote its continuation.

The consequences are revolutionary. Crime and the criminal law can be understood only within the context of this crisis. As David Horowitz has written in *Empire and Revolution*:

> By posing on the national level the central issues of the international conflict, by linking the international struggle for self-determination with the internal quest for social equality and social control, the crisis of democracy increasingly presents itself as the revolutionary crisis of the epoch. The movement for the sovereignty of the people within the imperial nation coincides with the struggle for self-determination in the international sphere. Just as

domestically the demand for domestic power is a demand to overthrow the corporate ruling class and to make the productive apparatus responsive to social needs, so internationally the precondi-
tion of democratic sovereignty and inter-state coexistence is the
dissolution of the government of the international corporations
and financial institutions which have expropriated the sovereignty of nations in order to appropriate the wealth of the world.

Never before has our understanding of legal order been so crucial. Never before has our understanding been so related to the way
we must live our lives. Today, to think critically and radically is to
be revolutionary. To do otherwise is to side with oppression. Our
understanding of the legal order is essential; and our actions in
relation to it must be to remove that oppression, to be a force in a
socialist revolution.

In the meantime, American criminologists continue to serve
the capitalist state. The modern era of repression is being realized
in the rationalization of crime control. The legal order itself, as the
most rationalized form of regulation, demands the latest theoretical and technical knowledge of control. It is only logical, then, that
bourgeois science should serve the capitalist state in the control of
crime.

The move to apply the latest in science and technology to
crime control began in the mid-1960's, particularly through the
efforts of the President's Commission on Law Enforcement and
Administration of Justice. The capitalist state's application of science and technology to crime control was probably inevitable, however, given its tendency to rationalize all systems of management
and control. Yet it was with the President's Crime Commission,
staffed by social scientists and criminologists, that scientific crime
control was justified and, as such, presented to the public. The
Commission's recommendations (published as *The Challenge of
Crime in a Free Society*) were soon made concrete and instituted by
the newly created crime control agencies. Science and technology
give today's crime control systems their most advanced and insidi-
ous form; they provide the modern state with the most advanced
system of control for the maintenance of domestic order, that is, for
the perpetuation of capitalist society.

Thus, the capitalist state is now engaged in the militarization
of crime control. The similarities between military operations
abroad and domestic crime control are clear. As advisors to the

President's Crime Commission observed (in the *Science and Technology* report), the talents of all scientists can contribute to the modern, militarized, control of crime.

> Crime control, being largely a social problem, may appear to be outside the realm of the scientists' skills. Indeed, many aspects of the problem do fall outside their scope. The experience of science in the military, however, suggests that a fruitful collaboration can be established between criminal justice officials on one hand and engineers, physicists, economists, and social and behavioral scientists on the other. In military research organizations these different professions, working with military officers in interdisciplinary teams, have attacked defense problems in new ways and have provided insights that were new even to those with long military experience. Similar developments appear possible in criminal justice.

American criminologists are contributing to the capitalist state's new methods of crime control. They are a part of the process by which the maintenance of frontiers abroad is combined with the establishment of domestic order at home. Criminologists are making their contribution to the hegemony of the capitalist system. American criminology is an integral part of capitalism.

Only with a critical criminology can we break out of the ideology and practice of American capitalism. It will allow us to demystify our own American experience, exposing capitalist ideology and practice. This is a criminology that is part of the movement to bring about a socialist society.

WOULD YOU DO JUST ONE THING BEFORE I SLEEP?
WOULD YOU TAKE OFF THAT MASK AND SHOW ME YOUR FACE?
WHY, OF COURSE.
OH, IT'S A GOOD FACE.
YES, A GOOD FACE.

Always the mask. To expose the underside of reality, to open the gate to the self, means facing something much more real than the illusion of the mask. Such analysis, however, was not usually appropriate to the needs of frontier life. Only with the alienation of post-frontier America does such scrutiny emerge as a conscious activity.

Each age in America has produced its own myth, its own form of estrangement. In the rural Midwest of the forties and fifties we were still living the alienation of the frontier. The mask we wore was the mask of a former time. We avoided the reality of the present. We coped with our modern problems in terms of an outdated reality. The frontier had passed; yet we lived the present according to the image of our past.

Work hard, no matter what the nature of the work. Do 'good,' according to the authoritative conception of the good. Never question the prevailing code. Avoid that not tried by others. The compliment to the parents of the two year son: "He's a little old man."

The alternative to this world, buried however deeply, was known to many of us behind the mask of the Lone Ranger. This was our secret. There *is* a reality beyond what we live daily! There is something to our being that no myth can take from us. There is a way of life that is apart from the official reality. We had, if not in practice at least in form, the potential for critical imagination.

We were perhaps the last to obscure life through Heroes and Innocence. ("Take it easy, greasy, you've got a long ways to slide." We refused to believe that Roy Rogers was Leonard Slye from Duck Run, Ohio.) But innocence also had its two sides.

The contradictions of innocence. Innocence that served to mask experience on occasion allowed us to break from the conventions of time and place. We entered 'unreal' worlds. Innocence cut both ways; we moved back and forth between two kinds of experience, one in life and one in the mind. In such flight we began to entertain the possibilities of actually living an alternative reality. Years later the process might serve us well.

Could there have been another way? Was the Lone Ranger really necessary? Given America's history, the life and consciousness of the Lone Ranger was probably inescapable. And yet we survived. There is another way. We can begin.

A socialist consciousness negates the frontier mentality. We are now into an age where the frontier mind is not only obsolete but dangerous to our survival. We are in an age that requires the understanding and practice that only a socialist consciousness can provide. The frontier way of life can only further our alienation, perpetuate the capitalist system, and prevent our liberation. The dialectic of the frontier may allow us to cope sporadically with our condition; but a new consciousness—a new life—beyond the frontier is now necessary.

Intellectually we must work together within a socialist tradition. As I have been suggesting, our understanding of crime has been shaped by the conditions of the American frontier experience. As such, our current understanding of crime—our criminology—is archaic and dangerous. Criminology today serves an existing system that is as obsolete as it is oppressive. Even a dialectic that would allow us to transcend established thought is usually lacking in our theories and our research. We must begin to think and act in terms of a socialist tradition. We must build a body of ideas that will allow us to critically understand crime and the legal order in America. In this way will we not only understand our contemporary experiences but we will be able to change our social world. This is the thought and practice that is appropriate to our age.

The rise and fall of American criminology is at the same time the rise and fall of the frontier. The cowboy, the outlaw, the lawman—all gave rise to a way of thought and ultimately to a myth. Criminology is part of that myth. As the frontier is removed from our mind so is most of our current criminology. Our new dialectic is in the removal of the old myth and the creation of a critical form of theory and practice.

Goodbye, Lone Ranger.

THERE'S A LOT OF FOLKS GRATEFUL TO THE LONE RANGER.
COME ON, SILVER
(GET 'EM UP, SCOUT.)
HI YO, SILVER . . . AWAY!

You helped us once. Now we are on our own—working together in the real world, struggling to build a world that is authentic to our being.

FOUR

A Critical Philosophy of Legal Order

We do not adequately understand our contemporary existence. Our comprehension of the present, as well as of the past, is
obscured by our current consciousness—a consciousness developed
within the existing order and serving only to maintain that order.
If we are ever to remove the oppression of the age, we must critically understand the world about us. Only with the development of
a new consciousness—a critical philosophy—can we begin to realize the world of which we are capable. My position is thus a critical one: critical not only in an assessment of our current condition,
but critical in working toward a new existence—toward a negation
of what *is* through thinking about and practicing what *could be*.
Any possibility for a different life will come about only through
new ideas formed in the course of altering the way we think and
the way we live. What is required is no less than a whole new way
of life. What is necessary is a new beginning—intellectual, spiritual, and political.

Nowhere is the inadequacy of our understanding more apparent than in our thoughts and actions in relation to legal order. Our
thinking about law and crime only confirms an official ideology that
supports the existing social and economic order. As long as we fail
to understand the nature of law in contemporary society, we will be
bound by an oppressive reality. What is urgently needed is a critical philosophy of legal order.

The development of a critical philosophy of legal order should
allow us to contemplate and act toward the fulfillment of a new
reality. To accomplish this, it is necessary to understand where we

Original source: Chapter 1 in Richard Quinney, *Critique of Legal Order.*
Boston: Little Brown, 1975.

have been in regard to our thinking about the legal order and also to understand the relation of our thoughts and actions to the official reality. In order to determine where we have been and where we are going, several modes of thought must be distinguished. Each mode embodies its own epistemology and ontology—its own way of thinking and its own assumptions about reality. Each takes a particular stance toward the philosophical issues of objectivity, reflexivity, and transcendence. Furthermore, each mode carries with it a specific relation to the dominant order. Each has its own potential for either oppressing us or liberating us. The four modes of thought are (1) the positivistic, (2) the social constructionist, (3) the phenomenological, and (4) the critical. My objective in analyzing them is to develop a critical philosophy of legal order. The result will be a Marxian theory of crime control in capitalist society. This theory will be expanded in subsequent chapters into a critique of legal order.

The Positivistic Mode

The positivistic mode of thought begins with the realist assumptions about existence. These assumptions are shared by anyone who has not reflected about the problems of perception and experience. At best, the positivist has only a naive acquaintance with epistemological and ontological concerns. Rather, methodology is the positivist's chief concern—how to develop a method to grasp or discover the laws of the physical world.

Positivism follows the simple epistemology that absolutely separates the knower from the known. Objectivity is assumed to be possible because order is believed to exist independent of the observer. The observer's cognitive apparatus supposedly does not affect the nature of what is known. Given enough knowledge, accumulated systematically, the scientist presumably could predict future events and control their occurrence. An orderly universe could be established through humanity's knowledge and manipulation of the external world.

The overriding emphasis of positivistic thought is on the *explanation* of events. And in following a mechanistic conception of the relation of social facts, positivists usually couch their explanations in terms of causality. What is ignored in this approach to explanation is an *examination* (or even an awareness) of the philosophical assumptions by which the observer operates.[1] There is neither a recognition that the nature of explanation depends upon the kinds of things investigated nor that explanation requires a description of the unique context in which events occur. Likewise, the positivist refuses to recognize that to assess and make statements about human actions is to engage in a moral endeavor. Instead, positivists regard their activity as being 'value free.'

The intellectual failure of positivism is that of not being reflexive. It makes little or no attempt to examine or even question the metaphysics of inquiry, to turn the activity of explanation back upon itself. Positivists refuse to be introspective. Their concern is to get on with the task of explaining, without considering what they are doing. Positivistic thought is of a particular kind; it is calculative thinking as described by Heidegger: "Its peculiarity consists in the fact that whenever we plan, research, or organize, we always reckon with conditions that are given."[2] In other words, there is little time to ask the crucial philosophical questions that ultimately affect the operations of investigation. "Calculative thinking races from one prospect to the next. Calculative thinking never stops, never collects itself. Calculative thinking is not meditative thinking, not thinking which contemplates the meaning which reigns in everything that is."[3]

The political failure of positivist thought, as related to its intellectual failure, is its acceptance of the status quo. There is no questioning of the established order, just as there is no examination of scientific assumptions. The official reality is the one within which positivists operate—and the one that they accept and support. The positivist takes for granted the dominant ideology that emphasizes bureaucratic rationality, modern technology, centralized authority, and scientific control.[4] Positivistic thought, in fact, naturally lends itself to the official ideology and the interests of the ruling class. Little wonder that the talents of positivistic social scientists are in such demand by those who rule. Social scientists have failed to break out of the interpretations and practices of the official reality, that reality within which they comfortably operate, never asking what could be and never seeking to transcend the established order.

Most of the research and theoretical developments in the sociology of law have been dominated by the positivistic mode of thought.[5] The legal order is taken for granted, and research is directed toward an understanding of how the system operates. Little attention is devoted to questions about why law exists, whether law is indeed necessary, or what a just system would look like. If the value of justice is considered at all, the concern is with the equitability of the system rather than with whether the system should exist in the first place. Suggestions may be made for changing particular laws, but the outlines of the legal system are to remain intact.[6] Inadequacies in the administration of justice may be noted, but prescriptions for change merely call for more technical and efficient procedures.

The efforts of criminologists have been devoted almost solely to the most conservative interests. Attention traditionally has been on the violator of criminal law rather than on the legal system itself.[7] Solutions to the crime problem have proposed changing the lawbreaker rather than the legal system. Only recently have some criminologists, realizing that law is problematic, turned their attention to a study of criminal law. But for the most part these studies have been based on the positivistic mode of thought.[8]

The conservative nature of most research and theory on law and crime is logically related to the social scientist's emphasis on social order. In the search for the natural laws of society, social scientists have favored any existing arrangements that would assure an orderly society. Anything that would threaten the existing order has been regarded as a violation of natural law, a social pathology to be eradicated, ameliorated, or punished in some way. Social scientists have formed an easy alliance with the ruling class that profits from the preservation of the status quo. Research and theory in criminology and the sociology of law have done little more than provide a rationale for the established order. A social theory that would allow for human liberation has been excluded. It now seems evident that positivistic thought cannot provide a liberating conception of human existence. Instead, we must turn to alternative modes of thought.

The Social Constructionist Mode

Social constructionist thought begins with a recognition of philosophical idealism. Social constructionists work with an ontology that questions the existence of an objective reality apart from the individual's imagination. Whether there are universal essences is indeed problematic. What can be assumed is that objects cannot exist independently of our minds, or at least that any such existence is important only as long as it can be perceived.

The epistemological assumption of social constructionist thought is that observations are based on our mental constructions, rather than on the raw apprehension of the physical world. The concern of the social constructionist is not primarily with the correspondence between 'objective reality' and observation, but between observation and the utility of such observation in understanding our own subjective, multiple worlds. Therefore, the social scientist's constructs have to be founded upon the world created by social actors. As Schutz conceptualized the problem: "The constructs of the social sciences are, so to speak, constructs of the second degree, that is, constructs of the constructs made by the actors on the social scene, whose behavior the social scientist has to observe and to explain in accordance with the procedural rules of his science."[9] The world that is important to the social constructionist, then, is the one created by the social actions of human beings, through interaction and intercommunication with others. This *social reality* involves the social meanings and the products of the subjective world of actors.[10] People construct activities and patterns of action as they attach meanings to their everyday life.

The social constructionist mode of thought makes a major advance over positivistic thought in respect to the crucial matter of reflexivity. Social constructionists question the process by which they know, instead of taking it for granted. In the course of this consideration, they reflect on their activity as observers, using to advantage the social and personal nature of their observations. That this reflexivity does not extend to a political stance, and possibly to political action, is a shortcoming inherent in the social constructionist mode.

Since social constructionist thought generally concentrates on the world of meanings created by social actors, its emphasis, especially in ethnomethodological studies, is on the construction of social order. Such concentration tends to ignore a world of events and structures that exists independent of the consciousness of social actors. This conservative side of social constructionist thought makes it inadequate for a critical perspective. As Richard Lichtman has written about this inadequacy: "It is overly subjective and voluntaristic, lacks an awareness of historical concreteness, is naive in its account of mutual typification and ultimately abandons the sense of human beings in struggle with an alien reality which they both master and to which they are subordinate. It is a view that tends to dissolve the concept of 'ideology' or 'false consciousness' and leaves us, often against the will of its advocates, without a critical posture toward the present inhuman reality."[11]

Therefore, it is often necessary to revise or reject the world as some social actors conceive it. To accept the world that social actors portray is often to accept the view of reality that the ruling class perpetuates to assure its own dominance. Social constructionist thought fails to provide a stance that would allow us to transcend the official reality and, ultimately, our current existence. Although social constructionists furnish us with the beginnings for an examination of multiple realities, they fail to provide a yardstick for judging the goodness of one reality over another. Social relativism prevails at the expense of a critical understanding of the social world.

The social constructionist perspective, however, has given new vitality to the study of crime and the law. Departing significantly from positivistic studies, social constructionists have tuned attention to the problematic nature of the legal order. They view crime and other forms of stigmatized behavior first as categories created and imposed upon some persons by others.[12] Crime exists because of the social construction and the application of the label.

Similarly, criminal law is not autonomous within society, but is itself a construction, created by those in positions of power. The administration of justice is a human social activity that is constructed as various legal agents interpret behavior and impose their order on those they select for processing.[13] The social reality of crime is thus a process whereby conceptions of crime are constructed, criminal laws are established and administered, and behaviors are developed in relation to these criminal definitions.[14]

The legal order, accordingly, is a human activity. It is an order created for political purposes, to ensure the hegemony of the ruling class. However, social constructionist thought stops at this point. To be sure, there are critical implications. There is the libertarian ideal that individuals should not be controlled by others, that people must be free to pursue their human potential. But there is, nevertheless, a failure to provide an image of what a new world should look like. Without such an image of what could be, an understanding of the current reality lacks a critical perspective. The ideal of liberation may be present, but unless that ideal is accompanied by a critique of the present and an image of an authentic existence, transcendence of the existing order is unlikely. Critical thought and action must be informed by a critical philosophy.

The Phenomenological Mode

Phenomenological thought departs markedly from positivistic and social constructionist thought in its basic intention. Whereas the other modes of thought are concerned with the explanation of social life, phenomenological thought begins by examining the process by which we understand the world. Explanation as a form of thought is itself examined. Hence, the philosophical problems of epistemology and ontology are a major concern of the phenomenologist.

Phenomenologists, though differing considerably among themselves, generally agree that our knowledge of the physical world comes from our experiences. But, they continue, when we talk about the physical world we are not limited by our experiences. That is, we are not limited by our actual experiences; we are able to talk about *possible* experiences, thus altering our perception of things in the world. As long as a physical object exists in the world, it is possible to experience it. What is important is that an object is perceivable.

The phenomenologists may proceed by 'bracketing,' or setting aside, the question of objective reality in order to turn attention to the reality in *consciousness*. The phenomenon in question, then, is that which manifests itself immediately in consciousness. Following Kant's distinctions, the phenomenologist is primarily concerned with the *phenomenon*, or the appearance of reality in itself.[15] Yet it is possible to think about what is not known, the 'thing-in-itself,' or *noumenon*, of which the phenomenon is the known aspect. Our knowledge of phenomena, therefore, is always subject to revision.

Consciousness itself is the source of our understanding of the world. Any knowledge of an objective thing can come about only through our consciousness of the thing. Reality is not to be found existing independently of our consciousness.[16] Any objectivity is to be achieved by means of our own subjectivity—that is, through our consciousness. Essence, or the essential, is what the human mind understands through its consciousness, in the course of its experiences in the world. We are thus capable of perceiving the essence of things.

Phenomenological thought is thought in its purest form. Following Kant's further distinction between thinking and knowing, phenomenologists are engaged in thinking beyond the limitations of knowledge. There is the urge to think and understand in contrast to the urge solely to construct verifiable knowledge.[17] Though knowledge is not denied, room is made for thinking, for thinking about the possibilities. This allows the phenomenologist to think about such otherwise unthinkable topics as the meaning of our existence.

The urge to think forces us to transcend our conventional knowledge about the world and our place in it. It allows us momentarily to remove ourselves from our concrete experiences. This is, as Heidegger has termed it, meditative thinking: "Meditative thinking demands of us not to cling one-sidedly to a single idea, nor to run down a one-track course of ideas. Meditative thinking demands of us that we engage ourselves with what at first sight does not go together at all."[18] A comportment that enables us to keep open the meaning hidden in the world, in the arrangements of modern society, is what Heidegger further describes as the "openness to the mystery." Related to this is a "releasement toward things." Through the two, in the course of meditative thinking, we seek our true nature. And, as Heidegger writes, "They grant us the possibility of dwelling in the world in a totally different way. They promise us a new ground and foundation upon which we can stand and endure in the world of technology without being imperiled by it."[19]

The idea of some form of transcendence has been basic to most phenomenological thought. For Kant the phenomenological method was transcendental in that we attend to our experiencing of an object, rather than to the object directly. Therefore, to be transcendental is to be reflexive. Phenomenology, as Richard Zaner has recently written, "is 'transcendental' because it is *foundational*, seeking to uncover and explicatively analyze the necessary presuppositions of every actual and possible object and process of consciousness, leading ultimately to the grounds for philosophical reflection itself (reflexivity)."[20] The essence of a thing can be attained only through a transcendental philosophy—by being reflexive.

It is in the transcendental thinking of some of the phenomenologists that we find the inspiration for moving beyond the conventional wisdom of the age, including our contemporary knowledge of the legal order. Instead of reifying the social order in the manner of the positivists, or giving an account of ordered existence in the manner of the social constructionists, the phenomenologists move toward a transcendence of our experience. This is a necessary step as we begin to act in a way that will truly reveal the social world. Our primary interest is not in the development of a new social science (which would still be a reified science) but in the creation of a new existence, an existence free of all reifications.

Phenomenological thought by itself, however, is incomplete for attaining our objectives. Although it provides a drastic and necessary move beyond the other modes of thought, it lacks the critical edge that would allow us to truly transcend the present, in life as in mind. Phenomenology does make us question the assumptions by which we know and by which we live. This is its major achievement. But what is needed is a philosophy that would allow us to actively transcend the existing order, one that would allow us to be committed. We must turn to the development of a critical philosophy.

Critical Philosophy

A critical philosophy is one that is *radically* critical. It is a philosophy that goes to the roots of our lives, to the foundations and the fundamentals, to the essentials of consciousness.[21] In the rooting out of presuppositions, we are able to assess every actual and possible experience. The operation is one of demystification, the removal of the myths—the false consciousness—created by the official reality. Conventional experience is revealed for what it is—a reification of an oppressive social order. The underside of official reality is thereby exposed. The liberating force of radical criticism is the movement from revelation to the development of a new consciousness and an active life in which we transcend the established existence. A critical philosophy is a form of life.

Thinking in itself is the beginning of a critical philosophy. For in the act of thought we engage in a particular kind of life, a reflective life that liberates us from preconceptions. Such theorizing, Alan Blum contends, expresses self, is a display of mind. Furthermore: "This 'calling to mind,' following an interpretation of Wittgenstein, is a way of recovering what one has all along, it is a way of seeing and as such it is inextricably tied to a way of living. More than this, it is to reconstitute or re-create out of one's life and the history of a society another possibility for seeing. To theorize is to re-formulate one's self."[22] The theorist is thus showing another possibility for seeing and living. Such theorizing has the potential of allowing us to comprehend a version of a possible society. Our selves are transformed in the course of theorizing.

The concept of thought in relation to a form of life is firmly based in the classic philosophical tradition. This is the theoretical attitude that ideas are to inform actions, that life is to be enlightened by thought. A critical philosophy, as Jurgen Habermas has suggested, is one that destroys the illusion of objectivism (of a reality apart from consciousness).[23] Conceived in this way, thought itself is necessarily critical. In demystifying our lives of all presuppostions, our attention is directed to a critique of our current existence. In a critical philosophy, truth is linked to the intention of finding the good and true life.

The chief characteristic of thinking, as Hannah Arendt notes in an essay on thinking and moral considerations, is that it interrupts all doing, all ordinary activity.[24] We are momentarily removed from our worldly associations; it is as though we entered into a different existence. Arendt adds that "thinking, the quest for meaning—rather than the scientist's thirst for knowledge for its own sake—can be felt to be 'unnatural,' as though men, when they begin to think, engage in some activity contrary to the human condition."[25] Arendt then concludes that only with thought that is aimed toward certain ideals (with the desiring of love, wisdom, beauty, and justice) are we prepared with a kind of thought that promotes a moral existence. Only when we are filled with what Socrates called "eros," a love that desires what is not, can we find what is good.

Without critical thought we are bound to the only form of social life we know—that which currently exists. We are not then free to choose a better life; our only activity is in further support of the system in which we are enslaved. Our current cultural and social arrangements, supported as they are by a bureaucratic-technological system of production and distribution, are a threat to individual freedom—including the freedom to know that this system is oppressive and may be altered. Such a system tends to preclude the possibility of an opposition emerging within it. In aspiring to the rewards that the system holds out to us, we are unable to consider an alternative existence. Such is the message of Herbert Marcuse in his discussion of the "one-dimensional" character of our present reality.[26] Only in a negation of the present can we experience something else.

It is apparent, then, that what prevents us from seeing clearly is the ideology of the age. The modern institutional order finds its legitimation in an ideology that stresses the rationality of science and technology.[27] A generalized belief in the importance of controlled scientific-technical progress gives legitimacy to a particular class—the one that utilizes science and technology. The extent to which this ideology pervades the whole culture limits the possibility of emancipation, limits even the perception of the need for liberation. Moreover, the technocratic consciousness prevents a critical philosophy. Our understanding about the legal order, in particular, is limited by the ideology on which the legal order itself rests. That is, the legal order is founded on the rationality of science and technology, and the dominant mode of thought in understanding that order is based on this same ideology. Little wonder that we have been unable to break out of our conventional wisdom.

It is in a critical philosophy that we are able to break with the ideology of the age. For built into the process of critical thinking is the ability to think negatively. This dialectical form of thought allows us to question current experience.[28] By being able to entertain an alternative, we can better understand what exists. Rather than merely looking for an objective reality, we are concerned with the negation of the established order. Through this negation we are better able to understand what we experience. Possibly only by means of this dialectic can the present be comprehended. Certainly the present cannot be surpassed until the dialectic is applied to our thought.

But more than negative thinking is required in a philosophy that will move us to a radical reconstruction of our lives—indeed, to revolution itself. In order to reject something, we must have some idea of what things could be like. It is at this point that a critical philosophy must ultimately develop a Marxist perspective. In the Marxian notion of the authentic human being, we are provided with a concrete image of the possible. Current realities are judged according to how they alienate human beings. Only in the conscious grasp of the world can we change the world. The process is a collective one—consciousness and action developed in association with others. The imagery is transcendental—to attain what is natural to us by removing that which obstructs our lives. It is in the contradiction of an oppressive existence, between what exists and what is authentically human, that we understand our reality and act to bring about a liberating existence.

To think in a Marxian fashion is to be genuinely critical, to the fullest extent of our critical resources. For most of us, however, Marxian thought has been presented in two forms: either in the liberal reactionary version, as a response to the Cold War mentality of the last twenty years, or in the orthodox realpolitik version. That we accepted these versions and resorted to positivistic thought, is the stark measure of our lack of critical faculties.

In contrast, what we are experiencing today is the creation of an underground Marxism.[29] In the course of developing our critical capacities, we are rediscovering and recreating a form and body of thought that finds its grounding in Marxian analysis. Marxism is the one philosophy of our time that takes as its focus the oppression produced by a capitalist society. It is the one form of analysis that is historically specific and locates the problems of the age in the economic-class relations.[30] A Marxian critique provides, most importantly, a form of thought that allows us to transcend in thought and action that kind of existence. Contrary to both liberal and orthodox interpretations, Marxism is highly creative thought, open to the interpretations of each generation. And with the changes in capitalism itself, from industrial capitalism to advanced monopoly capitalism, new and critical readings of Marx are necessary.[31] Critical thought makes possible a new understanding of Marx in each age. Which is also to say, a new understanding of Marx makes critical thought possible.

All thinking, all life, is subject to critical philosophy. A critical philosophy of legal order, in particular, allows us to understand what has been otherwise unexamined. In an understanding of the true meaning of the legal order, in a Marxian critique, we are able to transcend the present and create an alternative existence. Liberation is the ultimate objective of a critical philosophy of legal order.

Developing a Critical Philosophy of Legal Order

To summarize thus far, I have argued that current modes of thought have prevented us from understanding the legal order. The dominant modes of thought, including the positivistic, social constructionist, and much of the phenomenological, have been tied to an age that can do little more than oppress, manipulate, and control human beings as objects. The legal order has been viewed in the social sciences as a necessary force to assure order in capitalist society. Positivists have regarded law as a natural mechanism; social constructionists have regarded it relativistically, as one of the individual's conveniences; and even the phenomenologists, though examining underlying assumptions, have done little to provide or promote an alternative existence. We must conclude that our thoughts and our ways of thinking are wanting, are inappropriate and inadequate.

With a sense of the more authentic life that may be possible for us, I am suggesting that a critical philosophy for understanding the legal order should be based on a development of Marxist thought for our age. Marx had little to say about criminal law and crime control. Our purpose, then, will be to develop a critical-Marxian analysis of crime control in capitalist society.

Although the legal order consists of more than criminal law, criminal law is the foundation of that order. It is the coercive instrument of the state, used by the state and its ruling class to maintain the existing social and economic order. A critical theory of crime control in American society can be outlined systematically as follows:

1. American society is based on an advanced capitalist economy.

2. The state is organized to serve the interests of the dominant economic class, the capitalist ruling class.

3. Criminal law is an instrument of the state and ruling class to maintain and perpetuate the existing social and economic order.

4. Crime control in capitalist society is accomplished through a variety of institutions and agencies established and administered by a governmental elite, representing ruling class interests, for the purpose of establishing domestic order.

5. The contradictions of advanced capitalism—the disjunction between existence and essence—require that the subordinate classes remain oppressed by whatever means necessary, especially through the coercion and violence of the legal system.

6. Only with the collapse of capitalist society and the creation of a new society, based on socialist principles, will there be a solution to the crime problem.

Criminal law is used by the state and the ruling class to secure the survival of the capitalist system, and, as capitalist society is further threatened by its own contradictions, criminal law will be increasingly used in the attempt to maintain domestic order. The underclass, the class that must remain oppressed for the triumph of the dominant economic class, will continue to be the object of crime control as long as the dominant class seeks to perpetuate itself, that is, as long as capitalism exists. Only with the building of a socialist society will there be a world without the need for crime control. Never before has our understanding of legal order been so crucial. Never before has our understanding been so related to the way we must live our lives. To think critically and radically today is to be revolutionary. To do otherwise is to side with the oppression of the capitalist state. Our understanding of the legal order and our actions in relation to it must work to remove that oppression, must be a force in liberation.

FIVE

The Production of a Marxist Criminology

We are at the same time products of our culture and creators of it. People make their own history, Marx noted, "but they do not make it just as they please; they do not make it under circumstances chosen by themselves, but under circumstances directly encountered, given and transmitted from the past."[1] The objective material conditions of the time provide the setting for the possibilities of creation, change, and revolution. While our daily struggle is one of transforming the existing order, of removing conditions of oppression and making an authentic existence, the old social order will not perish until all the productive forces and contradictions of that order have become obstacles to its further development. Thus history is made both subjectively and objectively, as the result of class struggle *and* as the development of the economic modes of production: two sides of the same process, two codes for understanding our human history.

The problem with which we begin and end is one of reconciling spirit and matter—subject and object, internal and external, self and the world. We are beyond the moment when the separation took place, where we the subjects in the historical process (the 'movers' of history) became the objects of forces beyond our immediate control. Self-consciousness as well as historical conditions divided us into spirit and matter. Dialectical thought—thinking about the way we think about our condition—has become our nature.[2]

Human consciousness and action are now separated from an external material world of things, events, institutions, and productive forces. We attempt a reconciliation by creating the forms that

---

Original source: *Contemporary Crises* 2 (July 1978): 227–292.

will allow us to bring our consciousness and our material world together. What, we ask, is the society—what is the culture—that will permit us to be whole again? What mode of production (and its further refinement) allows us truly to be in the world, to be alive? To be ourselves one with another. This is undoubtedly the never-ending struggle and search.

In the meantime, as always, we must produce our material means of subsistence. Production is the necessary requirement of existence. Social production is the primary process of all social life. And in the social production of our existence we enter into relations that are appropriate to the existing forces of production. It is this 'economic' structure that provides the material foundation for our social and political institutions, for everyday life, and for social consciousness. Thus, all social life, including everything associated with crime, must be understood in terms of the objective economic conditions of production and the subjective struggle between classes that is related to these conditions. In other words, in capitalist society the social and cultural life of any person or group of people is understood according to the class relations produced by the capitalist system of production.

So it is also that our cultural productions are connected to the capitalist mode of production and the class struggle associated with capitalist production. The study of crime—*criminology*—is associated with the capitalist mode of production. The practice of criminology—especially *criminal justice work*—is likewise part of the capitalist structure. Criminological theory and practice are materially based. Moreover, criminology is a *cultural production* under the late stages of capitalism. It is a form of production: the production of knowledge and consciousness. In a Marxist critique of capitalist society, we also critically examine our own place as criminologists in the production system. Are we only the objects of the prevailing order, or are we also subjects who are able to move beyond it? To what extent are we engaged in the class struggle? Our product is criminology. What, we must ask, is the nature of our production?

Class Position of Criminologists

On a concrete, daily basis, the forms of work within the field we call 'criminology' are remarkably diverse and distinct. Criminology is, in fact, a cluster of fields and employments that all bear some relation to crime and its control. Criminology is far from being (will never be) a unitary and autonomous discipline and occupation. Instead, criminology continues to bring together in a very amorphous manner people who do the following (not necessarily mutually exclusive) kinds of work: 1) academicians (often sociologists) who teach students a subject called criminology, including those criminologists who also do research and write on the subject; 2) teachers who train other people for professional roles in crime control and criminal justice work; 3) those who are involved in policy research within the criminal justice system; and 4) those who 'apply' criminology, that is, all the people who are employed in criminal justice agencies, ranging from policemen, to lawyers, to prison wardens, to correctional workers. Even this list of broad groupings does not exhaust the possibilities as criminology and criminal justice increasingly play prominent roles in the further development of capitalist society.

Yet, in spite of this diversity within criminology, there are factors and forces that bring us all together in important ways. The development of criminology has been the formation of an ideology, a theoretical framework, a practice, and a complex of employment forms that all have as their primary purpose the protection of the existing social and economic order. Criminology has been, and continues in large measure to be, a body of thought and practice that seeks to control anything that threatens the capitalist system of production and its social relations. We have been among the agents of the capitalist state.

Our role has become increasingly more dynamic—and dialectical—in recent years. In the middle of the 1960s, what had been a traditional criminology was transformed by two opposing movements. On the one hand the 'war on crime,' itself a reaction to changes, challenges, and crises in the United States, gave birth to the criminal justice movement. A new criminology has emerged that has even closer, more explicit ties to the state and its control of threatening social behavior. On the other hand, partly in response to the same forces, there has emerged a 'radical' criminology that questions both traditional criminology and the new developments in criminal justice. The two emerging groups within criminology differ from each other in their objectives, values, and actions. The differences, to say the least, are significant.

However, it is in a class analysis that the various roles within criminology are best understood. While our daily work and actions as criminologists remain diverse, it is important to see ourselves in the larger class structure of the United States.[3] With this under-standing, our choice of alternatives within the objective material world becomes evident. Our possibility as subjects—rather than mere objects—in the historical process is thereby enhanced. We do make decisions and commitments that place us in the struggle of modern times.

A class analysis begins with the recognition that, first, classes are an expression of the underlying forces of the capitalist mode of production and that, second, classes are not fixed entities but rather ongoing processes in the development of capitalism. On the abstract level, the class structure of developing capitalism is an expression of the antagonistic relation between two opposing classes, those who own and control the means of production and those who do not. One class, the capitalist class, exploits the labor power of the working class. The capitalist class survives by appro-priating the surplus labor of the working class, and the working class as the exploited class exists as long as surplus labor is required in the productive process: each class depends on the other for its character and existence. Empirically, however, in the con-crete analysis of specific capitalist societies at particular points in history, the class structure is much more complex.[4] The primary focus, nevertheless, is on the nature of class structure in relation to the present level of capitalist development.

Since capitalism is constantly transforming itself, it follows that class analysis must be attuned to the changes in the class rela-tions that occur in the development of capitalism. Although all stages of capitalist development involve a dialectic between owner-ship and non-ownership, control and non-control, domination and resistance, the fundamental opposition between the capitalist class and the working class continues. Yet it is becoming apparent that a class analysis of advanced capitalism requires a more elaborate description of this relationship. The class structure of advanced capitalism is in transition; new forms are emerging within the dynamic of the capitalist mode of production.

While the class composition changes under advanced capital-ism, around new forms of economic activity and occupations, capi-talist development does not necessarily give rise to major new classes within capitalism. Rather, it gives rise to what Marx described as "fractions" within classes.[5] The basic dialectic between the capitalist class and the working class still predominates, but added to this is a dialectic between divisions within these classes.

The expansion of capitalism, in fact, necessitates divisions within classes. These new fractions are of such importance that several class theorists have posited the formation of a new class of 'petty bourgeoisie' (including civil servants, intellectuals, and professional workers).[6] However, while the subjective consciousness of the petty bourgeoisie may be different from that of the industrial working class, this does not mean that the fundamental objective antagonism of the capitalist mode of production has been altered in any important way. As Francesca Freedman has written,

> The subjective and objective must be united in a dialectical manner for a dynamic analysis of classes, since classes are in their essence the expression of the antagonistic contradictions upon which a mode of production is based. Thus, class struggle is the highest form in which these contradictions are expressed.[7]

The class struggle between the working class and the capitalist class continues, and continues at an even faster and higher level under advanced capitalism.

The fractioning of the working class is taking place in response to the development of different sectors of the economy. This century has seen a tremendous shift in relative and absolute numbers from industrial to non-industrial labor. The more capitalist industry has grown, the greater has been the need for a mass of labor to provide the unproductive activities for the diversion and distribution of capital goods. Following the classical Marxian labor theory of value, this *unproductive* labor is in contrast to *productive* labor.[8] That is, productive labor under capitalism consists of labor that produces commodity value for capital; money is exchanged for labor with the purpose of appropriating that value which it creates over and above what is paid (the *surplus* value). Unproductive labor, on the other hand, is labor that is not exchanged for capital and that does not produce surplus value, hence, profit, for capitalists. Clerical, sales, and service workers (primarily employed by corporations and the state) make up the largest segment of the classical category of unproductive labor. Unproductive labor, that used by the capitalist for 'unproductive' purposes, is increasing significantly under advanced capitalism.

The mass of workers now included in unproductive labor has been transformed into a modern commercial proletariat. This wage-working segment, as Harry Braverman has shown, has become a major element in the capitalist mode of production.[9] In the process, these workers have lost many of the characteristics that formerly separated them from the traditional productive workers. Their growth in the labor force has brought them into the modern proletariat.

A large portion of these workers (including professional and technical workers, clerical and sales workers, and various other service workers) are employed by the state. In order to assure continuing accumulation under advanced capitalism, the capitalist state has expanded, employing new forms of labor to carry out the work of the state apparatus.[10] Workers are now involved in the functions of servicing (and controlling) the population and maintaining the legitimacy of the capitalist system. Work under late capitalism has become both productive and unproductive in the Marxist sense. That is, while profit still continues to be appropriated through the surplus value of labor, much labor is unproductive—or, better, *indirectly productive*—in that the capitalist mode of production is being supported by other necessary forms of labor.

This has led some neo-Marxists to turn from a strictly labor theory of value, suggesting that in the present context such activities as science and technology are among the leading productive forces.[11] It is true that late capitalist development has transformed liberal capitalism into a system of welfare capitalism. The construction of a wide range of social policies is a vital characteristic of late capitalism. The social order is stabilized by the capitalist state with its pervasive intervention into the economy and the population. Nevertheless, while legitimization and stabilization are secured by a large unproductive labor force, including (and in particular) criminal justice workers, appropriation of surplus value from the traditional productive labor force continues. The condition in late capitalism is that all labor is *production* in either the direct, surplus value sense or in the indirect, unproductive sense.[12] The present system needs both kinds of production in order to survive.

Moreover, with the further development of capitalism, fractions within the working class are occurring along hierarchical lines, ranging from the industrial reserve army at the bottom to the various levels of the labor force.[13] Included in the labor force hierarchy are 1) the unskilled workers in industrial, service, and office occupations—composed largely of minorities and women; 2) the skilled workers, industrial and non-industrial; 3) the low-level and middle-level technical workers, including teachers and nurses; and 4) the middle-level management personnel, salaried professionals, university professors, and middle-level government bureaucrats. The hierarchical fracturing of the working class enforces class discipline and division, thus further reproducing class relations under capitalism.

One of the largest segments of the working class, cutting across all levels of the working class hierarchy, are the workers whose primary purpose is to maintain *social peace*. In the course of performing a wide range of activities, largely financed by the state, these workers control by various means large portions of the population, establish the legitimacy of the capitalist mode of production (often by providing services), and generally assist in reproducing the capitalist system.[14] It is within this increasing segment of the working class that criminologists and criminal justice workers are located. Their labor has the use value (rather than the exchange value) of reproducing the formal structures of capitalism and maintaining capitalist production relations. The commodity of their labor is not a physical product or surplus value, but the reproduction of the capitalist system, without which further capitalist accumulation would be impossible.

Workers in the criminal justice system, numbering well over a million employees, provide in their labor one of the most important links in the reproduction of capitalism. Many, such as those who are employed as police, are the 'repressive workers' in that they engage in the actual or threatened use of physical force and legal punishment. The concrete use value of their work is maintaining domestic order, making capitalist society safe for capitalist accumulation and promoting class relations. Inasmuch as these workers occupy a position within the working class, and are not therefore members of the 'ruling class,' they act against their own working-class interests. This contradiction obscures their class struggle and at the same time provokes a tension that undermines the possibility of continued domination by the capitalist state.

Those of us, as criminologists, who are not employed daily in repressive criminal justice work are likely also to be engaged (however dialectically) in some aspects of maintaining the social peace of late capitalism. At least our objective location and role in the class structure place us in a position to readily assist in securing the domestic order. Our work is in the sphere of the *ideological reproduction* of capitalism. We are the workers in the colleges and universities, in the criminal-justice research agencies, and in the schools of criminal justice. The objective task of the criminologist is to transmit bourgeois ideology to the working class as a whole, to ensure harmonious relations between the working class and the capitalist class according to the interests of the latter. The use value of our work is to promote identification with bourgeois ideology. The assumed objectivity and value-free stance of our science is the illusion that masks an identification with the interests of capitalism. Even a critical stance—as long as it does not overstep its bounds, moving into practice—serves to rationalize capitalism. The role of bourgeois ideological work is to legitimize the capitalist system.

However, the dialectic of ideological work makes problematic the ultimate direction and consequence of this work. Our membership in a fraction of the working class whose real interests contradict those of capital makes it far from certain what political role will be played by worker-intellectuals in the course of increased class struggle. Some of the recent criminological developments mark an ideological struggle within criminology, a struggle between those members who openly defend or tacitly accept the interests of the capitalist class and those who defend the interests of the working class. On the ideological level, and sometimes on the daily practical level, a struggle is being waged in criminology that is part of the larger class struggle. In a recognition of our class position as criminologists, we can move to the kind of daily work that assists in removing the oppressions of the capitalist system by building a socialist society.

Our class position as criminologists is a contradictory one.[15] We are not firmly located within a developing petty bourgeois class, in that we do not have full economic ownership and control over the physical means of production. Yet, like the bourgeoisie and the petty bourgeoisie (and unlike the proletariat), we do have some immediate control over our conditions of work. We occupy, instead, if not a definite class position, a contradictory position that is torn between the basic contradictory class relations of late capitalism. We are 'semi-autonomous employees' who retain relative control over our immediate labor process and thus occupy a contradictory location between the working class and the petty bourgeoisie.[16] We are not, however, without class. We take our characteristics from both class locations; we have one foot in each class; we are of both the petty bourgeoisie and the working class.

What is it, then, that concretely makes us at one moment members of the working class and at another members of the petty bourgeoisie? Our location is not so much economic as it is political and ideological. Occupying a contradictory location in the class structure makes increasingly important our ideology and politics. Our class position as criminologists under late capitalism is determined by our subjective life in the class struggle. It becomes a matter of class consciousness. And we have a choice: whether to aid in further legitimizing the capitalist system (operating as the petty bourgeoisie) or to engage in the class struggle for socialism with the working class. We are *cultural workers*, and the politics we choose and the class consciousness that we develop make all the difference.

Class Consciousness and Marxist Criminology

Our understanding of the world, our knowledge and our theory, is materially connected to our location in the class structure of advanced capitalism. Ideas—like people—are not detached from object reality. Nevertheless they are dialectically related to social and economic foundations, having consequences that may be as contradictory as the locations from which they spring. This makes our subjective world and our daily class struggle even more important. In the doing of criminology—especially the writing and teaching of criminology—our subjective reality is crucial. Correct criminology can be pursued only in the course of developing the appropriate (socialist), class consciousness.

Our thought and our practice in criminology are so materially bound by the capitalist structures within which we operate, and by the bourgeois roles we are assigned to perform, that breaking out of the mold is itself a constant struggle. The normal knowledge we create and impart is supposed to fit into the conventional wisdom of a liberal education, providing the ideology for capitalist relations. The educational and agency structures within which we work have as their purpose the preservation of a capitalist society. Without dialectical thought, and without working class consciousness and struggle, our efforts easily fulfill capitalist interests.

When not engaged in the socialist struggle, when we do not identify with the working class, when we perform as petty-bourgeois intellectuals, our thoughts and actions are principally bourgeois. The condition is self-fulfilling: bourgeois intellectual life sets a priori limits to speculative-critical-dialectical thought, and without this kind of thought we tend not to become aware of other possibilities—of our true class interest in building a working-class, socialist society. Bourgeois thought is dependent on the inner logic of bourgeois (and petty-bourgeois) life.

Bourgeois thought and life both are tied to an Anglo-American empirical realism whose mission is essentially to serve as a check on social and class consciousness. Doubts about capitalism are kept from arising by concentrating on narrowly-defined questions of law, freedom, and equality. Frederic Jameson observes in his book *Marxism and Form*,

> The method of such thinking, in its various forms and guises, consists in separating reality into airtight compartments, carefully distinguishing the political from the economic, the legal from the political, the sociological from the historical, so that the full implications of any given problem can never come into view, and in limiting all statements to the discrete and the immediately verifiable, in order to rule out any speculative and totalizing thought which might lead to a vision of social life as a whole.[17]

Dialectical thinking and living represent a threat to this form of class ideology.

Bourgeois ideology is a mystification of objective reality. When pursued as a basis for science, as well as for living, it is not only a misrepresentation and distortion of the real world but a source of our continued alienation in the world. Bourgeois ideology is a corrupt form of consciousness that emerges from an identification with the capitalist class. It is a class consciousness, nevertheless, which has all the *a priori* limits conferred by identification with the bourgeoisie.[18] What is needed, instead, by all who will produce a Marxist criminology, is a class consciousness that has the advantages provided by affiliation with the working class. For it is in a working class, socialist society that the needs of all of us who labor can be satisfied. It is only in a working-class consciousness, coming from an affiliation with the working class, that a socialist-Marxist criminology can be pursued. Through such consciousness we become the subjects (rather than the objects) in the transformation of human society.

The problem for us is how to confirm and live daily our working-class affiliation and identification. And then, how to practice a Marxist criminology. Possibly we can get there by thinking, by allowing ourselves to think, dialectically. But dialectical-critical thinking has to be done with a commitment to proletarian, socialist revolution. Only by uniting with the working class and by developing a working-class consciousness can intellectuals (those who already have a foot in the working class) be on the side of human liberation. We are then ready to develop a socialist criminology, creating ourselves in history, producing the conditions for our own development.

The Marxist Dialectic in Criminology

The criminologist—as with all other intellectuals—is not unattached, but is grounded in the class structure. Although our position contains its own contradictions, it is still an integral part of the class relations of advanced capitalist society. Our productions—whether theoretical or practical—are initially founded on our material existence.

Such is the source of the external and internal restrictions on our production of criminology. To move beyond these limits takes the form of (to use existential language) a leap, a leap that finds oneself transported from one's own conditions of existence and one's own mind. However, as I will argue, to move beyond the limits of bourgeois thought and actions involves harder work and more conscious thought than the romantic imagery of the 'leap' implies. The process is one that requires 1) a shift in our alliances, including a recognition of the alliances that we already have, and 2) a kind of thought (dialectical thinking) that makes personal and social change possible. Finally, by being involved in the class struggle, on the side of the working class, we can live the Marxist dialectic. In practice we move from speculation and doubt to the relative certainty of our cause.

Our criminology is a cultural production. It is a part of the structure that shares the functions of such other productions as philosophy, religion, and art. Criminology, in fact, is all of these. It is a product of human labor, and the same processes that produce other cultural productions also produce criminology. I am suggesting, in particular, that criminology resembles the art form. In an analogous fashion, its productions are subject to the same forces that Marxist aesthetics has found to operate in the world of art and literature. How, then, to read and view the production of criminology as an art form?

As in art, the criminologist is engaged in a social practice. The role is one of making something that has some cultural meaning in the existing society.[19] The commodities we produce, whether in the physical form of a book, the transmission of ideas and an ideology or consciousness in the classroom, or the administration of criminal justice, are all shaped by the underlying capitalist mode of production. There is a connection (however dialectical) between the dominant mode of production and the content of our art—as well as its form.

The characteristic of all human beings, as Adolfo Sánchez Vázquez has noted, is "the creation or production of human objects through which essential human powers can be externalized."[20] The human need to produce is a real need for material subsistence, but it is also in production that human creativity is necessarily exercised. Work is the basic human activity; it is (in a Marxian sense) an attempt to alter the subject-object relationship, to have control over our labors, to make us the movers of our history. "Labor is thus not only the creation of useful objects that satisfy specific human needs, but also the art of objectifying or molding human goals, ideas, or feelings in and through material, concrete-sensuous objects."[21] It is at the same time the transcendence of our existence, to which we return with new light.

In capitalist society, however, there is the innate tendency to turn creative work (that is, art) into alien labor. Work no longer fulfills the human need for expression and communication; we no longer realize ourselves through creation. The alienation experienced in our work becomes the condition of the worker in all areas of life. Ownership and control of life in general have been surrendered to alien hands.[22] The production of life itself under capitalism is alienated. Our lives as well as our production of art and criminology tend to become subverted and alienated when lived and practiced in the context of capitalism. The creative essence of art and criminology is negatively affected when the artist and criminologist are restrained by the inner need to produce according to the conditions of the capitalist mode of production.

The substance and form of all our productions, then, are expressions of the underlying structure of capitalism to the extent that production has become alienated under capitalism. Our productions in art and criminology are thus mediated by capitalism.[23] The final products of our labor (of our cultural work) are filtered through a multiplicity of mediations between the economic mode of production, the social structure, and the consciousness through which the artist-criminologist perceives reality. Through our productions we express the underlying structure of capitalism. Whether our expressions are critical and reflexive or merely reflections of capitalism is shaped by our ability to think dialectically and by our conscious involvement in the class struggle.[24]

Art differs from the positivistic-scientific mode of understanding in that it consciously seeks to transcend the objective, material world—in both theory and practice. Art as a way of seeing, feeling, and perceiving is prophetic in its forms and content.[25] Not only does it penetrate beneath the surfaces of social reality to the underlying structures, but it aspires to go beyond that reality in actual life. Art suggests how the world could be. It is a form of knowledge that has as its objective a transcendence of the everyday life of the existing order.

Reality thus may become transformed in the course of artistic production. Even momentarily, we are made to see the possibilities of another existence. The task of revolutionary theater according to Bertolt Brecht is not to reflect a fixed reality, but to demonstrate how character and action are historically produced, and so how they could have been different, and still can be transformed. "The play itself, therefore, becomes a model of that process of production; it is less a reflection *of*, than a reflection *on*, social reality."[26] The play is an experiment, testing its own presuppositions, just as it tests the reality within which it is produced. It becomes a public demonstration of its own form. It makes possible a transformation of reality as perceived and constructed by the audience in the course of the production. All art—I contend all dialectical criminology—aims to evoke. It aims to awaken in the observer, listener, or reader thoughts and emotions to opposition and to action. Art and criminology when thus practiced are part of the class struggle, are part of socialist revolution.

How are we to do criminology, in our wild moments to construct criminological theory? There must be an interrelation between 1) awareness of our class location, 2) development of proletarian-socialist consciousness, 3) engagement in the class struggle, and 4) the correct form of artistic-dialectical thinking. Which factor or process comes first is not the answerable question, but rather how they come together to produce a Marxist-socialist criminology. At the moment, in my argument, I am interested in our form of thinking.

Dialectical thought, as I have been indicating throughout, is, in its very structure, self-conscious and may be described as "the attempt to think about a given object on one level, and at the same time to observe our own thought processes as we do so: or to use a more scientific figure, to reckon the position of the observer into the experiment itself."[27] This is the Marxist dialectic in which the thinker (the criminologist as theorist) is aware of his or her position in society and in history, and is conscious of the limits and possibilities of one's class position. Our thought, at the beginning, is situational, objectively determined. But with self-consciousness and class consciousness we transcend that restriction. "Thus our thought no longer takes official problems at face value, but walks behind the screen to assess the very origin of the subject-object relationship in the first place."[28] Dialectical thinking (in the Marxist form), thought about preexisting thought and its conditions, plays a necessary part in the process of transforming the dominant social and economic conditions of capitalist society.

In such a way we break the tie that has made the producer the product of the external world of capitalist production. Severing the bonds of the present, our thinking is now historical thinking—that is to say, thinking about the future. We see ourselves and our class (as well as our thought) as a part of the basic historical situation in which all of this takes place. We are now free with a relative degree of freedom to transcend existing conditions. We are in the class struggle for a new society. We are in the position intellectually and socially—to think about and act upon the production of a socialist future.

Now that our internal world is one that is located in the class struggle, our production becomes socialist. Our criminology comes out of the conditions of the class struggle. Dialectical thinking, nevertheless, continues to operate in our theorizing. But dialectical thinking now takes place within a socialist tradition. Rather than all the effort being expended on transcending capitalist restrictions (which are nevertheless real and must continually be combated), our work is directed to a critical understanding of and involvement in the socialist struggle itself. The Marxist dialectic continues to serve us in the production of a socialist criminology.

Socialist Theory and Practice

A Marxist criminology is a form of *cultural politics*. We are creating (producing) a way of understanding and a way of living in the world. Our cultural production is specialized in speaking to other criminologists, but it is also popular as it becomes part of everyday consciousness and action. Although many of us will continue to work within that ideological apparatus known as the university, it is nevertheless one of the forums available to us for the dialectical expression of criminological production. Criminology as cultural politics has to be developed and practiced in this institution, as in other (and possibly alternative) institutions in capitalist society. The production of knowledge is a political act.

What we need to produce in the transition to socialism is a social theory (a criminological theory) that supports socialist rather than capitalist development. This is a *socialist theory* that provides the knowledge and politics for the working class, rather than knowledge for the survival of the capitalist class. In other words, the social theory appropriate for capitalism is quite different from the social theory needed for socialism. Moreover, as socialism develops, social theory will be modified from that necessary for the transition to socialism to that necessary for the further development of socialist society. For the moment, however, we need a social theory in criminology that allows us to move from late capitalism to the first stages of socialism.

As I have been arguing throughout, Marxist theory and practice provide the necessary basis for a socialist criminology. Increasingly, social scientists are recognizing that Marxism is the one tradition that takes as its focus the conditions of capitalist society; it is the one form of analysis that is historically specific and locates the problems of the age in the material conditions of our time. Thus the most dynamic and significant movement in the social sciences today is the development of a Marxist (or 'neo-Marxist') social science. Marxism is the most suitable and all-embracing philosophy in which to produce our criminology. We will produce a criminology that takes us beyond capitalist ideology and practice to the everyday reality of the class struggle. As this takes place we are creating the theory and practice for the transition to socialism and for the eventual transition to communism.

In a Marxist criminology there is no such thing as a theory that is produced in detached, contemplative observation. A theory without a practice not only makes bad theory but also shuts off the possibility of actual political struggle. On the other hand, practice without theory leads to incorrect action for socialist revolution. The only way to confront the problem is to combine social theory and social practice. The process is a never-ending one, being subject to reformulations of both theory and practice.[29]

As social science has developed within the capitalist hegemony, its theory has tended to furnish a practice that supports the political economy of capitalism. A social theory by and for the working class, however, is aimed at liberation and emancipation rather than at the capitalist domination of nature and human beings. Bourgeois social science attempts to dominate and control other people, mainly those who labor. The theory of bourgeois liberal criminology (including 'criminal justice') assists in the manipulation and control of the working class. Marxist criminology, in contrast, is allied to the popular struggles against capitalist oppression and is for the creation of a socialist society.

The purpose of criminology (and criminological theory) in the transition to socialism is to subvert the capitalist hegemony that maintains its hold over the working class. Socialist criminology provides people with an understanding of their alienation and oppressed condition, and provides a means of expression that is the beginning of socialist revolution.[30] To engage in social theory under these conditions is to engage in educational, political, and cultural work. The production of socialist social theory assists in the development of class consciousness. "The intellectual," Theotonio Dos Santos observes, "considered not as an individual isolated in an ivory tower but as a militant intellectual of a class, is thus a key factor in working out and developing class consciousness."[31] A conscious working-class culture of emancipation is being created.

Criminology, to conclude, is to serve the working class in the struggle for a socialist society. As bourgeois criminology has served the capitalist class under capitalism, Marxist criminology will serve the working class under socialism and assist in the transition to socialism. In the struggle, criminological theory (social theory) will be revised and practice will be altered to better achieve the goal of a socialist society. The only purpose in knowing the world, as Mao has noted, is to change it.[32] Our criminology does not stop with reflecting on the world, but rather is a part of the process through which the world is transformed.

In understanding crime and criminal justice we produce a theory and a practice that have as their objective changing the world. The importance of criminology is that it moves us dialectically to reject the capitalist order and to struggle for a socialist society. We are thus engaged in the working class struggle—producing the conditions for our own development in history. The struggle is shared in common and goes to the core of our being. As the theologian and socialist Paul Tillich reminded us: "The most intimate motions within the depths of our souls are not completely our own. For they belong also to our friends, to mankind, to the universe, and to the Ground of all being, the aim of our life."[33] We are in the struggle together, always.

SIX

The Prophetic Meaning of Social Justice

The conditions of our existence provide the setting for the possibilities of creation and fulfillment. Our future, Karl Marx (1963:15) noted, is to be made "under circumstances directly encountered, given and transmitted from the past." We are thus the products of our culture and the creators of it. While our daily struggle is one of transforming the existing order, of removing conditions of oppression and making an authentic existence, a new social order will emerge only out of the productive forces and contradictions of the old order. History is made both subjectively and objectively, as the result of conscious struggle and as the development of the economic mode of production.

Our destiny, moreover, is directed by the powers of our origin. In the prophetic tradition of Jewish and Christian thinking, as the theologian Paul Tillich (1977:108) has reminded us, the symbol of providence expresses to us "the confidence that what is is not utterly removed from what should be; that in spite of the present lack of fulfillment, being is moving in the direction of fulfillment." The unity of the "is" and the "ought" is expressed in our prophetic understanding. Both Marx and Tillich reaffirm for us the prophetic tradition. Being moves in the direction of that which is demanded.

The basic question asked in both Marxism and prophetic theology is the relation between existence and essence—between our existential situation and our essential nature. In the theology of Tillich, consistent with the existential Marx, three fundamental concepts characterize the problem of existence and essence:

Original source: Chapter 1 in Richard Quinney, *Class, State, and Crime.* Second Edition. New York: Longman, 1980.

First: *Esse qua esse bonum est.* This Latin phrase is a basic dogma of Christianity. It means "Being as being is good," or in the biblical mythological form: God saw everything that he had created, and behold, it was good. The second statement is the universal fall—fall meaning the transition from this essential goodness into existential estrangement from oneself, which happens in every living being and in every time. The third concept refers to the possibility of salvation. We should remember that salvation is derived from *salvus* or *salus* in Latin, which means "healed" or "whole," as opposed to disruptiveness (Tillich 1959:118–119).

These three considerations—essential goodness, existential estrangement, and the possibility of something else through which the cleavage is overcome—necessarily point to the fundamental nature of our contemporary condition.

In the contemporary historical situation, under capitalism, our essential being is deprived. The separation of existence and essence is the tragic condition of human life in capitalist society. The contemporary capitalist world is caught in what Tillich (1948:60), going beyond Marx's materialist analysis of capitalism, calls a *sacred void*, the human predicament on both a spiritual and a sociopolitical level. Among the vacuous characteristics of present civilization are a mode of production that enslaves workers, an analytic rationalism that saps the vital forces of life and transforms all things (including human beings) into objects of calculation and control, a loss of feeling for the translucence of nature and the sense of history, a demotion of our world to a mere environment, and a hopelessness about the future.

From the existential condition of capitalist society emerges the possibility of a transformation that will allow us to achieve the full potential of our being. Because the conditions under which we live in capitalist society divorce us from our essential nature, a transformation of the world becomes necessary (see Avineri 1969:202–249). The socialist demand is confirmed by our being. "The promise of socialism grows out of the analysis of being itself" (Tillich 1959:109).

In closing the separation between existence and essence, we create a reality in which our wholeness is more fully realized. Through human *praxis* the unity of production and product, subject and object, and spirit and matter becomes known. We become the subjects (the 'movers of history') in the world we create. Thus, Karel Kosik (1976:7) observes, "The world of reality is not a secularized image of paradise, of a readymade and timeless state, but is a process in which mankind and the individual *realize* their truth, i.e., humanize man." The specifics of truth are not given and preordained; they are constructed in the process of searching for the unity of being in the world. Being essentially human is realized in the course of consciously transforming our human history, always with an image of what it is to be truly human and spiritually whole.

Being human in the world is thus a social and moral endeavor. In the human praxis of transformation—in bridging the gap between existence and essence—we create a world of shared meanings and actions. As human beings we construct a language of communication charged with the moral meaning of our being. The categories of human language contain and presuppose definite forms of life (see Gadamer, 1975). Thus it is that justice—one of the most significant terms in any language—is a fundamental key to the form of life in a society. The substance of the term certainly differs from one society to another, and from one class to another within a society, but in the varying conceptions of justice, the character of social and moral life is registered and conducted.

The way we talk about justice—that is, the concept of justice we consciously hold—is a guide to the state of our being. And our commonsensical notion of justice is a most important part of the process of transforming our social and moral world, of resolving the separation between our existence and the essence that may be realized. That notions of justice may actually increase the separation is the contradiction and the moral failure built into some societies, especially that sense of justice found in contemporary society.

Justice in Capitalist Society

Justice is an absolute statement of an ideal. Nevertheless, justice as an ideal rests on a concrete historical foundation. In practice, justice is inevitably shaped by social reality: it is an integral part of the social, economic, and political structure of society. Rather than being removed from the material world, justice plays a crucial role in establishing and reproducing social order.

Nowhere is justice more important—in theory and practice— than in capitalist society. The concept of justice has evolved with the development of capitalism. At each stage of economic development, the particular notion of justice has been tied to the material basis of production, playing a part in securing the existing order. The struggle between classes, central to developing capitalism, is regulated by capitalist justice. Justice in capitalist society, today as always, is an ideological and practical instrument in the class struggle.

The notion of justice we conventionally know is an accumulation of ideas formed in the course of the development of capitalism. However mystified, justice is a social norm that is a directive for guiding human action (Bird, 1967). Actions are judged in terms of the directive; and justice is dispensed according to some notion of equality for people in similar situations. But as social norm, following our Greek heritage, justice complies with the interests of the stronger, mainly with the needs of the ruling class as expressed in law.

Although justice is to be applied to individual cases, the general objective is the promotion of social order. Thus conceived, individualistic needs and social order are combined to form the "healthy" whole:

> The problem of justice is closely related to the problem of a healthy order of society. It is concerned with the healthfulness of the parts as well as with sound condition of the whole. These two aspects of justice are, of course, inseparable. If the needs and aspirations of the individuals composing society are reasonably taken care of by the system of justice, and if reciprocal concern for the health of the social body exists among the members of society, there is a good chance that a harmonious and flourishing society will be the result (Bodenheimer 1967:8).

In capitalist society the healthy order is the one that primarily benefits the capitalist class, the class that owns and controls the productive process.

To our contemporary mind, questions of justice are generally restricted to a consideration of 'equal justice'—and severely limited even within that realm. Again following the Greek path, justice originates in the belief that equals should be treated equally and unequals unequally (Ginsberg 1965:7). In practice this has come to mean that discrimination in dispensing justice for infractions should not occur beyond what is justified by relevant differences. This leaves wide open such questions as the concrete meaning of equality, the social reality of equality and inequality, the existence of class conflict and state power, and the struggle for a better society beyond a narrow sense of justice.

Justice in contemporary capitalist society equates the limited idea of equal justice with the formulation and administration of positive law. Capitalist justice, in other words, is made concrete in the establishment of legal order. All notions of goodness, evil, and the earthly kingdom become embodied in capitalist law. And in everyday life questions of justice are confined to whether or not the law is arbitrarily administered. Justice is grounded, not in some alternative idea of social good or natural order, but in the survival needs of the capitalist system. Judgment is now in the hands of legal agencies of the capitalist state. Legality and the 'rational' administration of the law have become the capitalist symbols of justice.

In recent years, in response to a crisis in the legitimation of capitalist institutions as well as the more general crisis in the capitalist system, there has been renewed interest in the concept of justice. Such diverse presentations as John Rawls's *A Theory of Justice* (1971) and Robert Nozick's *Anarchy, State, and Utopia* (1974) attest to the chaos in our thinking about justice. Both philosophical treatises are in defense of some version of capitalism. Serious academic attention is being directed to the philosophical underpinnings for modern capitalist society. Marxist critiques, theories, and practices are beginning to emerge, however.

The current theories of justice are rooted in the moral and political problems generated by advanced capitalism. The solutions presented by Rawls and Nozick are within the liberal bourgeois tradition. Nevertheless, while Nozick espouses a pure form of laissez-faire capitalism, today called 'libertarianism,' Rawls bases his discussion on a philosophy of the liberal welfare state. Justice for Nozick is a world of separate individuals, with individual rights, who exist and act irrespective of being in society. From this "state of nature" follows the right to property, a free market of competition, and very little interference from a "minimal state." Rawls's theory of justice, while similarly attentive to the freedom of individuals to achieve their own good, considers the principles necessary to govern the distribution of the means to achieve individual goods. It is the modern welfare state that assures and regulates this distribution.

Rawls bases his theory of justice on a hypothetical condition where rational people live in an "original position." There is consensus on the principles of living together, a liberal agreement of what is important for the fulfillment of individual goals. Omitted from this individualistic view are the realities of class conflict, exploitation, and ruling-class power (see Nagel, 1973; Miller, 1974). Moreover, the original position is neutral toward values that emphasize cooperative relations between people and collective or communal activity. Opposed is any conception of society that sees human life as the collective achievement of a social good.

The liberal version of justice in capitalist society selectively and necessarily excludes a socialist vision of social order. The essence of liberalism is a society made up of autonomous units that associate only to further individual ends. Capitalist market relations are the paradigm for justice in the liberal philosophy of justice (Barry, 1972). An alternative theory of justice in society, one based on cooperative and collective action, must be founded in socialist philosophy. This is a philosophy worked out in the course of socialist practice.

The Rise of Criminal Justice

The capitalist notion of justice is most explicitly represented in its application to the problem of crime. Since the mid-1960s, with the increasing crisis of capitalism, official and public attention has focused on rising crime and its control. A solution to the crisis has become simply that of fighting the domestic enemy—crime. In a presidential message to Congress in 1965, the "war on crime" was launched. The President (March 8, 1965) declared that "we must arrest and reverse the trend toward lawlessness," suggesting that "crime has become a malignant enemy in America's midst." Congress responded by enacting the Omnibus Crime Control and Safe Streets Act, noting in its opening statement (1969) the scale of the project: "Congress finds that the high incidence of crime in the United States threatens the peace, security and general welfare of the Nation and its citizens. To prevent crime and to insure the greater safety of the people, law enforcement efforts must be better coordinated, intensified, and made more effective at all levels of government."

A new form of crime control was being established in capitalist society. Not only was the war on crime intensified by legislation, presidential commissions, and policy research by liberal academicians, but the capitalist state was now instituting a new system of domestic control. Especially with the newly created federal agency, the Law Enforcement Assistance Administration (LEAA), with appropriations amounting to millions of dollars, all levels of government were involved in planning and implementing an apparatus to secure the existing capitalist order (see Quinney 1974:95–135).

In the process, a new terminology was being created: that of criminal justice. Theoretically the terminology updates the ideology of 'law and order.' But adding to the conventional image, the terminology of criminal justice recognizes the new emphasis being placed on maintaining the existing order through the tools and agencies of the capitalist state. In practice criminal justice represents an innovation in control, indeed, the establishment of a new system of control, a criminal justice system. With the euphemism of criminal justice, a new system of control has been established and (at the same time) justified. Today we are all attuned in one way or another to criminal justice.

With the war on crime and the development of a new criminal justice system there has emerged the new field of criminal justice research and education. The need for criminal justice research was expressed by the President's Commission on Law Enforcement and Administration of Justice in 1967. Congress responded by establishing the National Institute of Law Enforcement and Criminal Justice through a provision in the Omnibus Crime Control and Safe Streets Act of 1968. The National Institute provides a mechanism for initiating and coordinating criminal justice research on a national level, providing resources beyond those already furnished by other federal agencies, such as the Center for Studies of Crime and Delinquency at the National Institute of Mental Health.

Since its creation in 1968, the activities of the National Institute of Law Enforcement and Criminal Justice have grown considerably in scope. The Crime Control Act of 1973 further expanded the role of the National Institute by giving it authority to develop training programs for criminal justice personnel, to create an international clearinghouse for the collection and dissemination of criminal justice information, including data on acts of crime, and to evaluate programs and projects. The criminal justice system in the United States was increasingly being rationalized through the introduction and application of a new scientific technology of criminal justice.

Recognizing that the new technology requires an educated and indoctrinated personnel, academic programs in criminal justice have developed rapidly in the last two decades. These programs have had the effect of changing the social sciences. Courses that consider the phenomenon of crime, such as criminology courses taught in sociology departments, now give more attention to criminal justice, and in many cases have adopted the criminal justice and administrative perspective. Furthermore, some criminal justice programs have grown out of former social science courses. At some colleges and universities, courses in the sociology of crime have been shifted to the criminal justice curriculum. The modern move to criminal justice, in other words, is shaping the nature of our lives and minds in many ways. We are in an age of criminal justice.

The criminal justice movement is a state-initiated and state-supported effort to rationalize mechanisms of social control. The larger purpose is to secure a capitalist order that is in grave crisis, likely in its final stages of development. The criminal justice system will surely be modified in response to further problems generated by late capitalism. Technological as well as ideological solutions will be attempted. There will be greater efforts at criminal justice planning, to develop a comprehensive system of criminal justice. Not only will the traditional agencies of the law be systematized, involving the police and the courts, but more emphasis will be placed on the prevention of crime.

In addition, alternatives to the existing criminal justice agencies are being proposed and implemented. Cases are to be diverted from the courts, and new agencies ('non-criminal justice institutions') process cases formerly handled by the police and the courts. This leaves the criminal justice system free to deal with serious offenses against the state and the economy and at the same time makes a wide range of social behavior subject to surveillance and control by the state. Criminal justice is expanding, and in the process will make further changes to provide greater control within the capitalist order.

Finally, the state is initiating the participation of the citizenry in crime control. Public concern about crime is being channeled into approved kinds of responses. The public is thus being enlisted into the criminal justice system. In cities large and small, citizens have been organized to fight crime, doing such specific things as (1) encouraging victims to report all crimes and testifying against the accused, (2) helping the police by patrolling their own neighborhoods, (3) serving as auxiliary police or sheriff's reserves, (4) keeping watch on neighbors' homes, (5) reporting suspicious activities in their neighborhoods, (6) securing their own homes from crime, (7) educating children to obey the laws and respect the police, (8) keeping watch on courts to spot judges who are soft on crime, and (9) demanding stronger anticrime laws.

We are all to be a part of the criminal justice system. However, the official programs for citizen participation are being contradicted by initiatives that are being taken by people outside state-sponsored programs. Built into the state efforts at citizen participation is a dialectic that supports autonomous community action removed from state control. Developing alongside the criminal justice system is a grass-roots approach that is beyond the design of the state. The dialectic undoubtedly will advance in coming years. Community actions themselves will be subject to criminal justice.

Crime and Punishment

The social, political, and economic events of recent years in the United States—and in the whole of the capitalist world—have forced social theorists to new formulations about the nature of the crisis in social order. A Marxist theory provides a critique of the crisis in capitalist societies. Meanwhile, conventional social theory seeks intellectual and policy solutions that attempt to preserve the existing order.

One of the crucial points at which conventional social theory is being revised is in reference to crime and criminal justice. Crime has come to symbolize the ultimate crack in the armor of the existing social order. And given the modern pessimism that social problems cannot really be solved—without drastically altering the established order—controls must be instituted to protect 'our society.' Recent thoughts about crime, combined with proposed policies, therefore have to be taken seriously as containing notions for the revision of social theory.

Several books about crime and criminal justice, and considerable empirical research, are providing important ideas for the formulations that would secure the capitalist order. These works bridge the interests of a range of social scientists including sociologists, economists, criminologists, legal behaviorists, and policy scientists. That most of these books are grounded in a moral philosophy, attending particularly to a notion of justice, makes their appearance even more important. What is emerging for the conventional social theorists, then, the theorists who would preserve the established system, is a new philosophy and likely a revised social theory for advanced capitalist society.

Most social theorists postulate some notion about the nature of human nature. For James Q. Wilson, in his book *Thinking About Crime*, a "clear and sober understanding of the nature of man" is required not only for purposes of theory but for "the proper design of public policies" (1975:xi). Human nature and subsequent policy are simply conceived: "Wicked people exist—Nothing avails except to set them apart from innocent people" (209). Crime, in all its reification, thus provides the metaphor for our human nature; crime represents human nature in its "less attractive" form. To think about crime as Wilson does is to advance one possible notion of being human and one possible way of controlling that nature.

Moreover, being wicked (and criminal) is a rational choice. In all our affairs, following this image, we are self-interested people rationally pursuing what is best for ourselves and, perhaps, our families. We are rational in the capitalistic, individual and economic, sense. And our criminality, according to the recent economic statement on crime, explicitly stated in an influential article by Gary S. Becker, is utilitarian: "A person commits an offense if the expected utility to him exceeds the utility he could get by using his time and resources at other activities" (1968:176). The obvious solution coming from the rational-utilitarian model is to deter crime by raising the risks of crime.

The notion of the capitalist (rational and utilitarian) individual gives support to the renewed interest in deterrence as social policy. Research by sociologists seeks to establish the importance of "certainty" and "swiftness" of punishment in deterring crime (see Tittle and Logan, 1973). In addition there are legal and philosophical works, such as *Deterrence* by Franklin E. Zimring and Gordon J. Hawkins (1973). In this book, legal scholars lend their weight to the new utilitarianism, arguing that the purpose of the criminal sanction is to deter criminal acts and that this is accomplished by declaring and administering pain in cases of noncompliance to the legal code of the existing order. While the book contains an elaborate framework for empirically determining the "deterrent effect" of punishment, the overall thrust is to make deterrence (i.e., punishment) "morally tolerable."

Although the traditional dichotomy between liberal and conservative may yet distinguish responses to some issues, when it comes to crime and criminal policy, the distinction is of diminishing importance. The practical possibilities of punishment characterize the modern debate. What binds Wilson's thinking to the scheme of Zimring and Hawkins, and these works with Ernest van Den Haag's conservative argument in his 1975 book explicitly called *Punishing Criminals*, is the contemporary justification for further instituting punishment in the capitalist state. As the 'rehabilitation' ideal proves itself bankrupt in practice, liberals and conservatives alike (all within the capitalist hegemony) resort to the utilitarianism of pain.

New emphasis is given to the prison as a place of punishment. Norval Morris, dean of the University of Chicago Law School, in *The Future of Imprisonment* furnishes "general principles under which imprisonment may be part of a rational criminal justice system" (1974:2). While some forms of rehabilitation may be attempted within the prison of the future, mainly in a "facilitative" capacity, the principal objective of the prison is to punish the criminal. Morris thus writes: "In my view, penal purposes are properly retributive and deterrent. To add reformative purposes to that mix—as a purpose of the sanction as distinct from a collateral aspiration—produces neither clemency nor justice" (58). Morris then tries to justify imprisonment as a rational form of control, providing a moral as well as rational framework for incarceration. Justice and rationality are thus linked.

With works and ideas such as these, combined with the sociological research that seemingly gives support, we have the reconstruction of a reality that takes as given the existing social order. Rather than suggest an alternative order, one based on a different conception of human nature, political economy, and social justice, the authors present us with schemes that merely justify further repression within the established order. The solutions being offered can only exacerbate the conditions of our existence.

It is with such convoluted rationality that Wilson turns his thinking to an epistemology of causal and policy analysis. In this discussion Wilson lays bare the elements of the new utilitarianism that increasingly characterizes both government policy and social theory. After reviewing traditional theorizing about crime, Wilson (48–54) argues that such theorizing about the "root causes" of crime fails because it cannot "supply a plausible basis for the advocacy of public policy." Policy based on causal analysis commits the "causal fallacy," which assumes "that no problem is adequately addressed unless its causes are eliminated." Public policy, therefore, should be directed to conditions that can more easily and deliberately be altered. A "policy analysis," as opposed to causal analysis, is accordingly addressed to those conditions that can be manipulated to produce the desired change. That is, for the reduction of crime, the policy analyst focuses on those instruments of control (primarily relating to deterrence) that will "at what cost (monetary and nonmonetary), produce how much of a change in the rate of a given crime."

Hence, policy analysis for the new criminal justice is grounded, in theory and practice, in individual utilitarianism. Wilson writes: "The policy analyst is led to assume that the criminal acts *as if* crime were the product of a free choice among competing opportunities and constraints. The radical individualism of Bentham and Beccaria may be scientifically questionable but prudently necessary" (56). The infrastructure of early capitalism is being revitalized to confront the problems of late capitalism.

The policies that follow from this version of reality emphasize deterrence and incapacitation. For Wilson there is little the police can do in reducing crime, since the police are not the crucial agency in the system. Moreover, rehabilitation does not deter crime. The best that rehabilitation can do is to isolate and incapacitate. "Of far greater importance are those agencies that handle persons once arrested and that determine whether, how soon, and under what conditions they will be returned to the communities from which they came. These agencies are the criminal courts and the correctional institutions" (163). And the function of the courts is not so much to determine guilt or innocence but, in fact, to decide what to do with criminals. Thus, what is needed is "good" sentencing, that is, dispositions that "minimize the chance of a given offender's repeating his crime," considering also the "effect any given sentence will have on actual or potential offenders" and the extent to which the sentence gives "appropriate expression to our moral concern over the offense" and conforms "to our standards of humane conduct" (164).

Such sentencing, Wilson continues, should increase the probability of imprisonment, since this seems to deter crime. While severity of penalties "cannot be the norm," certainty of punishment must be. The court system, therefore, is where legal control is best concentrated and dispensed. Nevertheless, Wilson warns, giving some attention to the problem of civil liberties, we in the United States must be willing to "accept both a higher level of crime and disorder and a larger investment in the resources and facilities needed to cope with those who violate the law and, despite our procedural guarantees, are caught by its agents" (182).

The resurgence of interest in crime and punishment is characterized by an even larger problem. In spite of the elaborate legal, philosophical, and behavioralist arguments presented in recent books and articles on crime and punishment, the works lack critical understanding. The thoughts are grounded within the sensibility of the existing conventional order. What we are given, whether

in Wilson's thinking about crime, Morris's proposal for imprisonment, Zimring and Hawkins's scheme for considering deterrence, or
in a book such as Jack Gibbs's *Crime, Punishment, and Deterrence*
(1975), which in spite of all its theoretical and empirical specifica-
tion revises the possibility of deterrence as social policy, is a defense
of punishment. But, more to the point, we are given a defense of
punishment that is to be applied within our unique historical context, in the protection of a social order based on late capitalist
development. Punishment becomes the solution when our vision is
confined within the problem itself. Being proposed, and adopted in
policy, is the "new justice model" based on punishment, which is
expressed in mandatory sentencing, "flat time," and the like (for a
critique, see Platt and Takagi, 1977). Social theory, if not public policy, should be capable of more than this.

The new justice model is represented in the influential report
of the Committee for the Study of Incarceration (1976). The report,
titled *Doing Justice*, combines the work of lawyers, philosophers,
historians, and social scientists over a period of several years.
Couched in the language of punitive reform, the purpose of the
report is to create a "fairer and less brutal penal system." The criminal sanction of punishment (mainly the length of the prison sentence) is to be limited, but the aim of the report is nevertheless to
provide a rationale for punishment. Rather than question the
nature of the society in the first place, a scheme of punishment is
designed to serve the ends of the existing society. In proposing a justice for the present and the future, there is a return to the justice
of the past:

> Some of our conclusions may seem oldfashioned. To our surprise,
> we found ourselves returning to the ideas of such Enlightenment
> thinkers as Kant and Beccaria—ideas that antedated notions of
> rehabilitation that emerged in the nineteenth century. We take
> seriously Kant's view that a person should be punished because he
> deserves it. We argue, as both Kant and Beccaria did, that sever-
> ity of punishment should depend chiefly on the seriousness of the
> crime. We share Beccaria's interest in placing limits on sentencing
> discretion (6).

Moreover, punishment is defended on grounds of its deterrent
effect and according to the value that those who are defined as
criminal deserve to be punished. The penalty is a penalty deserved
based on the seriousness of the past conduct of the "criminal" and
the seriousness of the act in question. Rehabilitation (or any

attempt to change behavior) is rejected in favor of a penalty for the behavior. The sentencing system of criminal justice becomes technically rational: "Graded levels of seriousness would be established, and the guidelines would specify which offense categories belong to which seriousness level" (99). Such is the nature of reform at the present stage of capitalist development.

When it comes specifically to justice, the revitalization of conventional social theory is restricted to a limited historical version of justice. For Wilson, in his thoughts about the death penalty, justice is reduced to whether the death penalty subscribes to considerations of "fitness and fairness" (184). Similarly, for Morris, in his defense of imprisonment, justice is a matter of "desert," as "the maximum of punishment that the community extracts from the criminal to express the severity of the injury his crime inflicted on the community as a condition of readmitting him to society" (74). Morris, in drawing from John Rawls's rationalistic treatise on justice (a variant within the utilitarian tradition), determines the extent of criminal punishment and imprisonment according to what is "deserved" by the crime of the offender.

All of these writings subscribe to a combination of two unique notions of justice. They conceive of justice as protecting acknowledged "rights" within the current order and as distributing punishment according to desert. The new justice model dispenses justice (i.e., punishment) for the purpose of preserving the capitalist social order and according to what the offender deserves in the pursuit of rational action. This notion of justice is appropriate for the capitalist order; it assumes a hierarchy of rights and competitive social relations.

There is an alternative to capitalist notions of justice. In sharp contrast to the new justice model (which is actually a mixture of old justice) is the idea of justice as distribution according to need. David Miller (1974), in "The Ideological Backgrounds to Conceptions of Social Justice," suggests that this latter form of justice is appropriate for a society based on cooperative social relations, a communal society, and a developing socialist society. It assumes that human beings behave (or are capable of behaving) cooperatively and altruistically without the use of financial rewards or penal sanctions. Although not likely to be found in capitalist societies, this notion of justice nevertheless has its own tradition. It is found in early and latter-day communal and religious movements, with basic elements present in socialist countries today.

As capitalist society continues to develop its own contradictions and crises, the contrasts between divergent conceptions of justice become evident. What we are witnessing in recent theories and practices of criminal justice is an attempt to reestablish a justice appropriate to a former age, a justice that ignores historical development but which would seemingly preserve the contemporary capitalist order.

However, our human development is also a struggle for a social justice. Beyond the conventional notions of crime and punishment is the creation of a new social order. In question is not merely the extent of justice but what kind and under what conditions. Now we are beginning to attend to a socialist sense of justice.

A Critique of Capitalist Justice

The classic dichotomy about the meaning of justice dominates contemporary social science and ethical discourse. That dichotomy is found in the debate between Socrates and Thrasymachus that Plato chronicles in the first book of the *Republic* (see Pitkin, 1972:169–192). When the question "What is justice?" is posed, Thrasymachus responds that "justice is the interest of the stronger," elaborating that what is regarded as just in a society is determined by the ruling elite acting on its own interest. Later Socrates gives his formulation of justice as "everyone having and doing what is appropriate to him," that is, people trying to do the right thing.

Obviously, Thrasymachus and Socrates are talking about two different problems. Whereas Thrasymachus is giving us a factual description of how justice actually operates, Socrates is telling us about what people think they are doing when they attend to that which is called "justice." There is justice as an ideal of goodness and justice in practice in everyday life. And justice as officially practiced in contemporary society is the idealized and practical justice of the capitalist state. The question for us, then, given a Marxist understanding of the class and state character of capitalist justice, is how do we attend to correct action and the creation of a better life?

The general concept of justice serves the larger purpose of providing a standard by which we judge concrete actions. We critically understand the actions of the capitalist state, including the administration of criminal justice, because we have an idea of how things could be. Critical thought and related actions are made possible because we transcend the conventional ideology of capitalism. Because we have a notion of something else, a socialist life, we refuse to accept capitalist justice either in theory or in practice. Critical thought, as Hannah Arendt has noted, allows us to interrupt all ordinary activity, entering into a different existence: "Thinking, the quest for meaning—rather than the scientist's thirst for knowledge for its own sake—can be felt to be 'unnatural,' as though men, when they begin to think, engage in some activity contrary to the human condition" (1971:424). In talking and thinking about how things *could* be, we engage in thoughts and actions directed to the realization of a different life. Arendt adds that only with the desiring love of wisdom, beauty, and the like are we prepared with a kind of life that promotes a moral existence. Only when we are filled with what Socrates called "eros," a love that desires what is not, do we attempt to find what is good. In critical and collective effort, we change our form of life and alter the mode of social existence.

If any body of thought has a notion of truth and beauty, of how things could be, it is that of Marxism. In fact, Marxism is the philosophy of our time that takes as its primary focus the oppression of capitalist society. It is an analysis that is historically specific and locates contemporary problems in the existing political economy. Marxist theory provides, most importantly, a form of thought that allows us to transcend in theory and practice the oppression of the capitalist order.

Marx avoided the use of a justice terminology (see McBride, 1975; Wood, 1972). He steered away from justice-talk because he regarded it as "ideological twaddle," detracting from a critical analysis of the capitalist system as a whole. Both Marx and Engels were in fact highly critical of the use of the justice notion, employed as a means of mystifying the actual operation of capitalism. At the same time, they found a way critically to understand capitalism that carried with it a condemnation that goes beyond any legal notion of justice. Thus, Marxist analysis provides us with an understanding of the capitalist system, a vision of a different world, and a political life in struggling for that society.

According to Marx and Engels, the problem with the concept of justice, as it is used in capitalist society, is that it is fundamentally a juridical or legal concept. As such, the concept is restricted to rational standards by which laws, social institutions, and human actions are judged (see Wood, 1972:246). Moreover, this restricted analysis fails to grasp the material conditions of society. Human life, instead, is to be understood in terms of the productive forces and relations of society, with the state as an expression of the prevailing mode of production (Marx, 1970:19–23). To focus on the juridical nature of social reality is to misunderstand the material basis of reality. An analysis limited to legalistic questions of justice systematically excludes the important questions about capitalist society.

The critique of capitalism for Marx is provided in the very form of the capitalist system. Capitalism rests on the appropriation of labor power from the working class. Capital is accumulated by the capitalist class in the course of underpaying the workers for products made by their labor. The capitalist mode of production depends on "surplus value," on unpaid labor. Capitalism itself is a system of exploitation. The servitude of the wage laborer to capital is essential to the capitalist mode of production. Marx's condemnation of capitalism and the need for revolutionary action is based on the innate character of capitalism, on an understanding of capitalism as a whole and on its position in human history.

We have thus moved out of the classical dichotomy between value and fact. In developing a Marxist analysis, value and fact are integrated into a comprehensive scheme. Values are always attached to what we take to be facts, and facts cannot exist apart from values. As Bertell Ollman observes in his discussion of Marx's method:

> It is not simply that the "facts" affect our "values," and our "values" affect what we take to be the "facts"—both respectable common sense positions—but that, in any given case, each includes the other and is part of what is meant by the other's concept. In these circumstances, to try to split their union into logically distinct halves is to distort their real character (1971:48).

In a Marxist analysis, the description of social reality is at the same time an evaluation. Nothing is 'morally neutral' in such an understanding. The description contains within itself its own condemnation and, moreover, a call to do something about the condition. The critique is at once a description of the condition and the possibility for transforming it. All things are in relation to one another—are one in the other.

Nevertheless, the more critical and general sense of justice will not disappear from philosophical and everyday discourse. That the terms 'justice' and 'social justice' continue to move us is an expression of their innate ability to join our present condition with an ultimate future. In our human struggle for existence, and for beauty, we will create the essential meaning of justice.

Prophetic Justice

The roots of our contemporary world, in spite of capitalist relations and extreme religious secularity, are firmly placed in the Judeo-Christian apprehension of human existence and fulfillment. We have an image of our essential nature and the possibilities for our human existence. But this essence has become separated from the conditions of this world; it is contradicted by human existence. The cleavage between reality and essence can be overcome only by human action. The modern historical consciousness, in other words, is derived from the historical thinking of the Judeo-Christian prophetic tradition. Through the dynamics of history we experience the meaning that guides and transcends our history. History and the transhistorical—time and the eternal—support our human existence.

Rooted deeply in the prophetic tradition is the urge toward justice in human affairs. This urge becomes the will of divine origin operating in history, providing the source of inspiration to all prophets and revolutionaries (see Dombrowski, 1936:25–26). The identification of religion with political economy can be seen in the Hebrew prophets, who looked on all history as the divine law in human life. The highly ethical religion of the Old Testament prophets and the New Testament Jesus sees human society from the perspective of a holy and just God who forgives human beings but also judges them. The prophetic soul is hopeful and optimistic in the "confidence that God will form a better society out of the ashes of the present world" (Dombrowski:26). The future in this world is built on the prophetic impulse that necessarily transcends this world.

Our prophetic heritage perceives the driving force of history as being the struggle between justice and injustice. We the people—in a covenant with God—are responsible for the character of our lives and our society, for the pursuit of righteousness, justice, and mercy. The social and moral order is consequently rooted in the divine commandments; morality rests on divine command and concern rather than on the relativity of reasonableness. We seek to realize a divine concern and command, the essence of perfect justice and love. The prophetic presence is real: "God is a living entity, closer than one's hands and feet, not a philosophic or theological abstraction" (Magnin, 1969:108).

Prophecy thus proclaims the divine concern for justice. The idea and belief that "God is justice" means the divine support and guidance for such human matters as the demystification of conventional thought, the humanization of work, the democratization and socialization of the economy, and the elimination of all forms of oppression (see Soelle, 1976). Apparent material issues are thus conceived in terms of the transcendent, adding the necessary element that is missing in a strictly materialist analysis. Prophetic justice is both sociological and theological. In fact, the dialectic of the theological and the sociological gives the prophetic its power as a critique and an understanding of human society.

To the prophets of the Old Testament, injustice (whether in the form of crime and corruption or in the wretched condition of the poor) is not merely an injury to the welfare of the people but a threat to existence. Moral comprehension, in other words, is rooted in the depth of the divine. This is a sense of justice that goes far beyond our modern liberal and legalistic notions of justice. For the prophets, the worldly virtue of justice is founded on the understanding that oppression on earth is a humiliation of God. Righteousness is not simply a value for the prophet; it is, as Abraham J. Heschel (1962, vol. 1:198) observes, "God's part of human life, God's stake in human history." The relation between human life and the divine is at stake when injustice occurs. Justice is more than a normative idea; it is charged with the transcendent power of the infinite and the eternal, with the essence of divine revelation.

For the prophets, justice is like a mighty stream, not merely a category or mechanical process. In contrast: "The moralists discuss, suggest, counsel; the prophets proclaim, demand, insist" (Heschel, vol. 1:215). Prophetic justice is charged with the urgency of the divine presence in the world. "Let judgment roll down like waters, And righteousness like a mighty stream" (Amos 5:24). In Heschel's (vol. 1:213) phrase, "What ought to be, shall be!" Prophetic justice has a sense of urgency and depth.

Justice—or the lack of it—is a condition of the whole people. An individual's act expresses the moral state of the many.

> Above all, the prophets remind us of the moral state of a people: Few are guilty, but all are responsible. If we admit that the individual is in some measure conditioned or affected by the spirit of

society, an individual's crime discloses society's corruption. In a community not indifferent to suffering, uncompromisingly impatient with cruelty and falsehood, continually concerned for God and every man, crime would be infrequent rather than common (Heschel, vol. 1:16).

Prophecy is directed to the whole world as well as to the inner spirit of the individual.

The purpose of prophecy—and of prophetic justice—is to revolutionize history. Divine compassion is expressed in our time. The call is personal: "And what does the Lord require of you but to do justice, and to love mercy, and to walk humbly with your God?" (Micah 6:8). And we are all judged collectively in the presence of corruption and oppression:

> From the heavens Thou didst utter judgment;
> The earth feared and was still,
> When God arose to establish judgment
> To save all the oppressed of the earth. (Psalm 76:8–9)

The possibilities of life are neither wholly economic nor wholly political; they are also religious. While the socialist struggle is necessarily temporal and in this world, the expectant goal is transhistorical and eternal.

We live in an era that tends to reject the claims of a religion-based prophetic theology. In his study of the Hebrew prophets, Heschel (1962, vol. 2:192) notes that "owing to a bias against any experience that eludes scientific inquiry, the claim of the prophets to divine inspiration was, as we have seen, *a priori* rejected." A scientific rationality based entirely on empirical observation of this world excludes the prophetic critique of our existential estrangement from essence. History and its concrete conditions, accordingly, are bounded solely by time; there is little that would guide us beyond the mortality of our earthly selves. Which also means that an evaluation of our current situation is limited by the particular historical consciousness that comprehends nothing beyond itself. Not only have we silenced God, we have silenced ourselves before our own history. But, remembering our heritage, we begin to recover the prophetic in our lives and in our understanding of history.

The prophetic meaning of justice is in sharp contrast to the capitalist notion of justice. Distinct from capitalist justice, with its emphasis on human manipulation and control, prophetic justice is a form of address that calls human beings to an awareness of their historical responsibility and challenges them to act in ways that will change the existing human condition. Human fulfillment is found in the exercise of moral will in the struggle for a historical future. The pessimistic character of a deterministic and predictive materialism is overcome in the prophetic hope for a humane and spiritually filled existence.

Through the prophetic tradition, a tradition that is present also in the prophetic voice of Marxism, a meaning of justice that can transform the world and open the future is once again emerging. Marxism and theology are confronting each other in ways that allow us to understand our existence and consider our essential nature. The human situation, no longer completely bounded by time, is "elevated into the eternal and the eternal becomes effective in the realm of time" (Tillich, 1971:91). Reconciliation and redemption are realized through an apprehension of the eternal.

References

Hannah Arendt, "Thinking and Moral Considerations," *Social Research* 38 (Autumn 1971):417–446.

Shlomo Avineri, *The Social and Political Thought of Karl Marx* (London: Cambridge University Press, 1969).

Brian Barry, *The Liberal Theory of Justice: A Critical Examination of the Principal Doctrines in a Theory of Justice by John Rawls* (New York: Oxford University Press, 1972).

Gary S. Becker, "Crime and Punishment: An Economic Approach," *Journal of Political Economy* 76 (March–April 1968):169–217.

Otto A. Bird, *The Idea of Justice* (New York: Praeger, 1967).

Edgar Bodenheimer, *Treatise on Justice* (New York: Philosophical Library, 1967).

James Dombrowski, *The Early Days of Christian Socialism in America* (New York: Columbia University Press, 1936).

Hans-Georg Gadamer, *Truth and Method* (New York: Seabury, 1975).

Jack R. Gibbs, *Crime, Punishment, and Deterrence* (New York: Elsevier, 1975).

Morris Ginsberg, *On Justice in Society* (Baltimore: Penguin, 1965).

Ernest van Den Haag, *Punishing Criminals: Concerning a Very Old and Painful Question* (New York: Basic, 1975).

Abraham J. Heschel, *The Prophets*, vol. 1 (New York: Harper & Row, 1962).

———, *The Prophets*, vol. 2 (New York: Harper & Row, 1962).

Andrew Von Hirsch, *Doing Justice: The Choice of Punishments*, Report of the Committee for the Study of Incarceration (New York: Hill & Wang, 1976).

Karel Kosik, *Dialectics of the Concrete* (Dordrecht, Holland, 1976).

William Leon McBride, "The Concept of Justice in Marx, Engels, and Others," *Ethics* 85 (April 1975):204–218.

Edgar R. Magnin, "The Voice of Prophecy in This Satellite Age," in *Interpreting the Prophetic Tradition*, ed. Harry M. Orlinsky (Cincinnati: Hebrew Union College Press, 1969).

Karl Marx, *The Eighteenth Brumaire Of Louis Bonaparte* (New York: International Publishers. 1963).

———, *A Contribution to the Critique of Political Economy*. ed. M. Dobb (New York: International Publishers, 1970).

David Miller, "The Ideological Backgrounds to Conceptions of Social Justice," *Political Studies* 22 (December 1974):387–399.

Richard Miller, "Rawls and Marxism," *Philosophy and Public Affairs* 3 (Winter 1974):167–191.

Norval Morris, *The Future of Imprisonment* (Chicago: University of Chicago Press, 1974).

Thomas Nagel, "Rawls and Justice," *Philosophical Review* 82 (April 1973):220–234.

Robert Nozick, *Anarchy, State, and Utopia* (New York: Basic, 1974).

Bertell Ollman, *Alienation: Marx's Conception of Man in Capitalist Society* (New York: Cambridge University Press, 1971).

Hanna Fenichel Pitkin, *Wittgenstein and Justice* (Berkeley: University of California Press, 1972).

Tony Platt and Paul Takagi, "Intellectuals for Law and Order: A Critique of the New Realists," *Crime and Social Justice* 8 (Fall–Winter 1977):1–16.

Richard Quinney, *Critique of Legal Order: Crime Control in Capitalist Society* (Boston: Little, Brown, 1974).

John Rawls, *A Theory of Justice* (Cambridge, Mass.: Harvard University Press, 1971).

Dorothee Soelle's review of *Marx and the Bible* by Jose Miranda in the *Union Seminary Quarterly Review* 32 (Fall 1976):49–53.

Paul Tillich, *The Protestant Era* (Chicago: University of Chicago Press. 1948).

——, *Theology of Culture*. ed. Robert C. Kimball (New York: Oxford University Press. 1959).

——, *Political Expectation* (New York: Harper and Row, 1971).

——, *The Socialist Decision*. trans. Franklin Sherman (New York: Harper & Row, 1977).

Charles R. Tittle and Charles .H. Logan, "Sanctions and Deviance: Evidence and Remaining Questions," *Law and Society Review* 7 (Spring 1973):371–392.

United States House of Representatives, "Crime, Its Prevalence, and Measures of Prevention," Message from the 89th Cong., 8 March 1965, Document No. 103.

United States Statutes at Large, "Omnibus Crime Control and Safe Streets Act," PublicLaw 90–351, 1968 (Washington, D.C.: U.S. Government Printing Office, 1969):197.

James Q. Wilson, *Thinking About Crime* (New York: Basic, 1975).

Allen W. Wood, "The Marxian Critique of Justice," *Philosophy and Public Affairs* 1 (Spring 1972):244–282.

Franklin E. Zimring and Gordon J. Hawkins, *Deterrence: The Legal Threat in Crime Control* (Chicago: University of Chicago Press, 1973).

SEVEN

Crime and the Development of Capitalism

Our desire is to understand the conditions of our contemporary historical existence. We are located in the material world, but a comprehension of that world and our place in it requires an imagination that exceeds the details of daily finite existence. It is in both social analysis and prophetic theology that our imagination is enhanced. The myths and images of human nature and social life by which we understand our contemporary condition transcend the concrete historical situation.

Under capitalism our actual condition has become mistakenly regarded as the essential condition. We have increasingly become the objects of our own history, left to drift without an ultimate end. Moreover, the methodology for understanding our world suffers from the same condition, limiting reality to the technical and scientific conquest of time and space. This truly is the contemporary human predicament.

The Understanding of Crime

An understanding of crime in our society begins with the recognition that the crucial phenomenon to be considered is not crime per se, but the historical development and operation of capitalist society.[1] The study of crime involves an investigation of such natural products and contradictions of capitalism as alienation, inequality, poverty, unemployment, spiritual malaise, and the economic crisis of the capitalist state. To understand crime we have to

---

Original source: Chapter 2 in Richard Quinney, *Class, State, and Crime.* 2nd edition. New York: Longman, 1980.

149

understand the development of the political economy of capitalist society.

The necessary condition for any society is that its members produce their material means of subsistence. Social production is therefore the primary process of all social life. Furthermore, in the social production of our existence we enter into relations that are appropriate to the existing forces of production.[2] According to Marx, it is this economic structure that provides a grounding for social and political institutions, for everyday life, and for social consciousness. Our analysis thus begins with the conditions of social life.

The *dialectical method* allows us to comprehend the world as a complex of processes, in which all things go through a continuous process of coming into being and passing away. All things are studied in the context of their historical development. Dialectical analysis allows us to learn about things as they are in their actual interconnection, contradiction, and movement. We critically understand our past, informing our analysis with possibilities for our future.

A Marxist analysis shares in the larger *socialist struggle*. There is the commitment to eliminating exploitation and oppression. Being on the side of the oppressed, only those ideas are advanced that will aid in transforming the capitalist system. The objective of understanding is change—revolutionary change. The purpose of our intellectual labors is to assist in providing knowledge and consciousness for building a socialist society. Theories and strategies are developed to increase conscious class struggle; ideas for an alternative to capitalist society are formulated; and strategies for achieving the socialist alternative are proposed. In the course of intellectual-political work we engage in activities and actions that will advance the socialist struggle.

Finally, the questionable character of spiritual as well as material life under capitalism is understood in an analysis of crime. Marxism is a necessary method for unmasking the hidden levels of the material world. The far-reaching implications, however, are found in the *prophetic understanding* of reality. Recovered is the urgency of the human nature revealed in the contemporary condition and in its transformation. Socialism, Tillich observes, "acts in the direction of the messianic fulfillment; it is a messianic activity to which everybody is called."[3]

With these characteristics of understanding—encompassing a dialectical and historical analysis of the conditions of capitalist society in relation to socialist revolution—we begin to formulate significant substantive questions about crime. In recent years, as socialists have turned their attention to the study of crime, the outline for these questions has become evident. At this stage in our intellectual development the important questions revolve around the meaning of crime in capitalist society. Furthermore, there is the realization that the meaning of crime changes in the course of the development of capitalism.

The basic question in the analysis of crime is thus formulated: what is the meaning of crime in the development of capitalism? In approaching this question, we give attention to several interrelated processes: (1) the development of capitalist political economy, including the nature of the forces and relations of production, the formulation of the capitalist state, and the class struggle between those who do and those who do not own and control the means of production; (2) the systems of domination and repression established in the development of capitalism, operating for the benefit of the capitalist class and secured by the capitalist state; (3) the forms of accommodation and resistance to the conditions of capitalism by all people oppressed by capitalism, especially the working class; and (4) the relation of the dialectics of domination and accommodation to patterns of crime in capitalist society, producing the crimes of domination and the crimes of accommodation. These processes are dialectically related to the developing political economy. Crime is to be understood in terms of the development of capitalism.

The Development of a Capitalist Economy

As noted, crime is a manifestation of the conditions—material and spiritual—of society. The failure of conventional criminology is to ignore, by design, the conditions of capitalism. Since the phenomena of crime are products of material and spiritual conditions, any explanation of crime in terms of other elements is no explanation at all. Our need is to develop a general framework for understanding crime, beginning with the underlying historical processes of social and moral existence.

Production, as the necessary requirement of existence, produces its own forces and relations of social and economic life. The material factors (such as resources and technology) and personal factors (most importantly the workers) present at any given time form the productive *forces* of society. In the process of production, people form definite relations with one another. These relations of

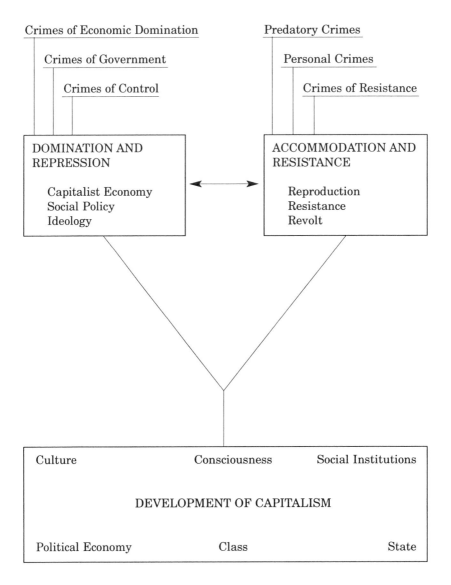

Crime and the Development of Capitalism

production, in reference to the forces of production, constitute the particular *mode* of production of any society at any given time.

Once the outlines of political economy (the productive forces, the relations of production, and the superstructure) have been indicated, the class structure and its dynamics can be recognized. A class society arises when the system of production is owned by one segment of the society to the exclusion of another. All production requires ownership of some kind; but in some systems of production ownership is private rather than social or collective. In these economies social relations are dependent on relations of domination and subjection. Marxist economists thus observe: "Relations of domination and subjection are based on private ownership of the means of production and express the exploitation of man by man under the slave-owning, feudal and capitalist systems. Relations of friendly cooperation and mutual assistance between working people free of exploitation are typical of socialist society. They are based on the public ownership of the means of production, which cut out exploitation."[4]

Social life in capitalist society, which includes crime, therefore, is related to the economic conditions of production and the struggle between classes produced by these conditions. In other words, in capitalist society the behavior of any group or any individual is part of the conflict that characterizes class relations, a conflict produced by the capitalist system of production. The life of one class is seen in relation to that of the other. As E. P. Thompson observes, an analysis of class entails the notion of the historical relationship of classes:

> Like any other relationship, it is a fluency which evades analysis if we attempt to stop it dead at any given moment and anatomise its structure. The finest-meshed sociological net cannot give us a pure specimen of class, any more than it can give us one of deference or of love. The relationship must always be embodied in real people in a real context. Moreover, we cannot have two distinct classes, each with an independent being, and then bring them *into* relationship with each other. We cannot have love without lovers, nor deference without squires and laborers. And class happens when some men, as a result of common experiences (inherited or shared), feel and articulate the identity of their interests as between themselves, and as against other men whose interests are different from (and usually opposed to) theirs. The class experience is largely determined by the productive relations into which men are born—or enter involuntarily.[5]

Hence, class in capitalist society is analyzed in reference to the relationship to the process of production and according to the relationship to other classes in the society.

Moreover, the problematics of *labor* characterize the nature and specific relationship of the classes. For the capitalist system to operate and survive, the capitalist class must exploit the labor (appropriate the *surplus labor*) of the working class. Maurice Dobbs notes:

> The relationship from which in one case a common interest in preserving and extending a particular economic system and in the other case an antagonism of interest on this issue can alone derive must be a relationship with a particular mode of extracting and distributing the fruits of surplus labour, over and above the labour which goes to supply the consumption of the actual producer. Since this surplus labour constitutes its life-blood, any ruling class will of necessity treat its particular relationship to the labour process as crucial to its own survival; and any rising class that aspires to live without labour is bound to regard its own future career, prosperity and influence as dependent on the acquisition of some claim upon the surplus labour of others.[6]

The capitalist class survives by appropriating the labor of the working class, and the working class as an exploited class exists as long as labor is required in the productive process: each class depends on the other for its character and existence.

The amount of labor appropriated, the techniques of labor exploitation, the conditions of working-class life, and the level of working-class consciousness have all been an integral part of the historical development of capitalism.[7] In like manner, the degree of antagonism and conflict between classes has varied at different stages in the development. Nevertheless, it is the basic contradiction between classes, generalized as class conflict, that typifies the development of capitalism. Class conflict permeates the whole of capitalist development, represented in the contradiction between those who own property and those who do not, and by those who oppress and those who are oppressed.[8] All past history that involves the development of capitalism is the history of class struggle.

Capitalism as a system of production based on the exploitation by the capitalist class that owns and controls the means of production is thus a dynamic system that goes through its own stages of development. In fact, capitalism is constantly transforming its forces and relations of production. As a result, the whole of capitalist society is constantly being altered—within the basic framework of capitalist political economy.

The Marxian view stresses the qualitative changes in social

organization and social relations, as well as (or in relation to) the quantitative changes in the economic system.[9] Capitalism transforms itself, affecting the social existence of all who live under it. This is the basic dynamic of capitalist development, an interdependence of production, the relations of production, and the social superstructure of institutions and ideas. "For it is a requirement of all social production that the relations which people enter into in carrying on production must be suitable to the type of production they are carrying on. Hence, it is a general law of economic development that the relations of production must necessarily be adapted to the character of the forces of production."[10]

As the preceding discussion indicates, analysis of the meaning of crime in the development of capitalism necessarily involves an investigation of the relation between the concrete stage of capitalist development and the social relations that correspond to that stage. This is not to argue that social relations and culture are an automatic (directly determined) product of the economic structure. After all, people may enter into relations of production in various ways in order to employ the given forces of production; and it is on the basis of these relations that they create further institutions and ideas. Because human social existence is in part a product of conscious activity and struggle, conscious life must be part of any analysis. Maurice Cornforth, in a discussion of historical materialism, describes the process:

> But ideas and institutions are not the automatic products of a given economic and class structure, but products of people's conscious activities and struggles. To explain the superstructure, these activities and struggles must be studied concretely, in their actual complex development. Therefore it is certainly not Marxism, just as it is certainly not science, to attempt to conclude from the specification of certain economic conditions what the form of the superstructure arising on that basis is going to be, or to deduce every detailed characteristic of the superstructure from some corresponding feature of the basis. On the contrary, we need to study how the superstructure actually develops in each society and in each epoch, by investigating the facts about that society and that epoch.[11]

Such is the task in our study of the meaning of crime in the development of capitalism.

In addition, the more developed the productive forces under capitalism, the greater the discrepancy between the productive forces and the capitalist relations of production. Capitalist development, with economic expansion being fundamental to capitalist economic development, exacerbates rather than mitigates the contradictions of capitalism.[12] Workers are further exploited, conditions of existence worsen, while the contradictions of capitalism increase. Capitalist development, in other words, creates the conditions for the transformation and abolition of capitalism, brought about in actuality by class struggle.

The history of capitalism can thus be traced according to the nature of capitalist development. The main contradictions of capitalism are concretely formed and manifested in each stage of development. The forms and intensity of exploitation are documented and understood in respect to the particular character of capitalism in each period. How crime—the control of crime and criminality—plays its part in each stage of capitalist development is our concern in any investigation of the meaning of crime.

The periods of capitalist development, for our purposes, differ according to the ways in which labor is appropriated. Capitalism, as distinct from other modes of production, has gone through periods that utilize various methods of production and create social relations in association with these productive forms. Each new development in capitalism, conditioned by the preceding historical processes, brings about its own particular forms of capitalist economy and social reality—and related problems of human existence.

Any investigation of the meaning (and changing meanings) of crime in America, therefore, requires a delineation of the periods of economic development. The United States has developed gradually as a capitalist society. The nascent capitalist economy of the colonial period of American capitalism was, by and large, an economy of farming, shipping, and commerce. Nevertheless, throughout this period a class-divided society was being created. Already the contradictions of early capitalism were manifested in antagonisms between slaves and indentured servants, farmers, artisans, laborers, and mechanics on the one hand—and merchants, plantation owners, and a rising petty bourgeoisie on the other.[13] A plantation economy in the southern colonies required a mass importation of labor, black slaves from Africa. And as manufacturing increased, a growing population of laborers—yeoman farmers in the colonies and workers imported from European countries—crowded into the cities to supply labor for factories. The further development of capitalism in the United States only served to widen the gap—and increase the class conflict—between the vast working population and the rising capitalist class that owned and controlled the means of production.

The social and moral order that emerged from the development of capitalism in the period from 1790 to 1860, the period of early industrialization, was shaped by conditions of capitalist exploitation. A society increasingly devoid of religious concern, a society increasingly secular, gave primacy to the capitalistic values of acquisitiveness, competition, and the ability to justify exploitation. Conditions continued to deteriorate for the working population in the course of industrialization. As Jurgen Kuczynski has shown in his study of the historical statistics, the working day for laborers was lengthened during this period, women and children were drawn into the factories, and actual working conditions grew worse.[14] In the capitalist exploitation during this early period of industrialization, however, workers began to alter their traditional conceptions of work and formed a consciousness appropriate for a working class in an industrializing, capitalist society. Not only was a working class created in the course of capitalist development, but the workers developed a consciousness of themselves as workers sharing a common condition.[15]

The United States was fast becoming the greatest industrial power in the world. During the years 1860 to 1900, continually at the expense of the working class, production grew and the accumulation of capital among the capitalist class mounted. Conditions did not improve for the newly freed black workers, however; insufficient wages, poor housing conditions, low standards of health, and overcrowding in cities were the norm. Immigrant laborers and their families were exploited. Although there was some improvement in real wages during this period of capitalist development, health conditions grew worse, housing deteriorated, the accident rate in industry increased, and the gap between the capitalist class and the working class widened.[16] At the same time, and largely because of growing capitalist exploitation, workers intensified their struggle against capitalist conditions. The workers' chief weapon was the strike, and it was used frequently during the last years of the nineteenth century. In 1886, as the eight-hour day was taking hold, there were 1,572 strikes and lockouts, involving 610,024 employees, against 11,562 establishments. With other actions, such as the slowdown and the boycott, workers were struggling against the particular social and moral order being created in the development of capitalism.

As capitalism developed beyond the industrial stage, becoming dominated by large corporations after 1900, the conditions of labor were affected even more adversely. Increasing technology served only to further alienate workers from the work process. Especially after World War I, with the coming of the economic depression, unemployment among workers increased. Rising unemployment continued to plague advanced capitalism as the general economy moved from one crisis to another. Even before World War II, the life of the American worker showed the consequences of a decaying capitalist system: "The worker's life tends more and more to be composed of a short period of years, during which he produces with unprecedented intensity, and of a long period during which he works at a considerably reduced rate of speed, often interrupted by illness, and at a much lower wage."[17] The struggle between the capitalist and the working class grew in intensity during the postwar period. Yearly strikes now included millions of workers and involved a range of workers from industrial employees to white-collar and public-service employees. Class struggle and class consciousness have continued to intensify with the further advancement of capitalism, as capitalism has reached an advanced stage of development. During this period the state has expanded and increased its role in reproducing the capitalist system.

Certainly we are today in a stage of late, advanced capitalism in the United States. The current meaning of crime in America can be understood only in relation to the social and moral character of capitalism in the present era. Similarly, the meanings of crime at various times in the past have to be understood according to the particular stage of development. Only in the investigation of crime in the development of capitalism do we truly understand the meaning of crime. Concrete research can provide us with knowledge about the role of crime in the development of capitalism.

Domination and Repression

The capitalist system must continuously reproduce itself. This is accomplished in a variety of ways ranging from the establishment of ideological hegemony to the further exploitation of labor, from the creation of public policy to the coercive repression of the population. Most explicitly, it is the state that secures the capitalist order. Through various schemes and mechanisms, then, the capitalist class is able to dominate. And in the course of this domination, crimes are carried out. These crimes, committed by the capitalist class, the state, and the agents of the capitalist class and state, are crimes of domination.

Historically the capitalist state is a product of a political economy that depends on a division of classes. With the development of an economy based on the exploitation of one class by another, a political form was needed that would perpetuate that order. With the development of capitalism, with class divisions and class struggle, the state became necessary. A new stage of development, Frederick Engels observes, called for the creation of the state:

> Only one thing was wanting: an institution which not only secured the newly acquired riches of individuals against the communistic traditions of the gentile order, which not only sanctified the private property formerly so little valued, and declared this sanctification to be the highest purpose of all human society; but an institution which set the seal of general social recognition on each new method of acquiring property and thus amassing wealth at continually increased speed; an institution which perpetuated, not only this growing cleavage of society into classes, but also the right of the possessing class to exploit the non-possessing, and the rule of the former over the latter. And this institution came. The state was invented.[18]

The state thus arose to protect and promote the interests of the dominant class, the class that owns and controls the means of production. The state exists as a device for controlling the exploited class, the class that labors, for the benefit of the ruling class. Modern civilization, as epitomized in capitalist societies, is founded on the exploitation of one class by another. Moreover, the capitalist state is oppressive not only because it supports the interests of the dominant class, but also because it is responsible for the design of the whole system within which the capitalist ruling class dominates and the working class is dominated.[19] The capitalist system of production and exploitation is secured and reproduced by the capitalist state.

The coercive force of the state, embodied in law and legal repression, is the traditional means of maintaining the social and economic order. Contrary to conventional wisdom, law, instead of representing the community custom, is an instrument of the state that serves the interests of the developing capitalist class.[20] Law emerged with the rise of capitalism. As human labor became a commodity, human relations in general began to be the object of the commodity form. Human beings became subject to juridic regulation; the capitalist mode of production called forth its equivalent mode of regulation and control, the legal system.[21] And criminal law developed as the most appropriate form of control for capitalist society. Criminal law and legal repression continue to serve the interests of the capitalist class and the perpetuation of the capitalist system.

Through the legal system, then, the state forcefully protects its interests and those of the capitalist class. Crime control becomes the coercive means of checking threats to the existing social and economic order, threats that result from a system of oppression and exploitation. As a means of controlling the behavior of the exploited population, crime control is accomplished by a variety of methods, strategies, and institutions.[22] The state, especially through its legislative bodies, establishes official policies of crime control. The administrative branch of the state formulates and enforces crime-control policies, usually setting the design for the whole nation. Specific agencies of law enforcement, such as the Federal Bureau of Investigation and the recent Law Enforcement Assistance Administration, determine the nature of crime control. And the state is able through its Department of Justice officially to repress the 'dangerous' and 'subversive' elements of the population. Together, these state institutions attempt to rationalize the legal system by employing the advanced methods of science and technology. And whenever any changes are to be attempted to reduce the incidence of crime, rehabilitation of the individual or reform within the existing institutions is suggested.[23] To drastically alter the society and the crime-control establishment would be to alter beyond recognition the capitalist system.

Yet the coercive force of the state is but one means of maintaining the social and economic order. A more subtle reproductive mechanism of capitalist society is the perpetuation of the capitalist concept of reality, a nonviolent but equally repressive means of domination. As Alan Wolfe has shown, in the manipulation of consciousness the existing order is legitimized and secured:

> The most important reproductive mechanism which does not involve the use of state violence is consciousness-manipulation. The liberal state has an enormous amount of violence at its disposal, but it is often reluctant to use it. Violence may breed counter-violence, leading to instability. It may be far better to manipulate consciousness to such an extent that most people would never think of engaging in the kinds of action which could be repressed. The most perfectly repressive (though not violently

so) capitalist system, in other words, would not be a police state, but the complete opposite, one in which there were no police because there was nothing to police, everyone having accepted the legitimacy of that society and all its daily consequences.[24]

Those who rule in capitalist society—with the assistance of the state—not only accumulate capital at the expense of those who work but impose their ideology as well. Oppression and exploitation are legitimized by the expropriation of consciousness; since labor is expropriated, consciousness must also be expropriated.[25] In fact, the legitimacy of the capitalist order is maintained by controlling the consciousness of the population. A capitalist hegemony is established.

Thus, through its various reproductive mechanisms capitalism is able to maximize the possibility of control over citizens of the state. Ranging from control of production and distribution to manipulation of the mind, capitalism operates according to its own form of dictatorship. André Gorz writes:

> The dictatorship of capital is exercised not only on the production and distribution of wealth, but with equal force on the manner of producing, on the model of consumption, and on the manner of consuming, the manner of working, thinking, living. As much as over the workers, the factories, and the state, this dictatorship rules over the society's vision of the future, its ideology, its priorities and goals, over the way in which people experience and learn about themselves, their potentials, their relations with other people and with the rest of the world. This dictatorship is economic, political, cultural and psychological at the same time: it is total.[26]

Moreover, a society that depends on surplus labor for its existence must not only control that situation but also must cope with the problems that the economic system naturally creates. The capitalist state must therefore provide social services in the form of education, health, welfare, and rehabilitation programs to deal with problems that could otherwise be dealt with only by changing the capitalist system. These state services function as a repressive means of securing the capitalist order.

Capitalism systematically generates a *surplus population*, an unemployed sector of the working class either dependent on fluctuations in the economy or made obsolete by new technology. With the growth of the surplus population, pressures build up for the growth of the welfare system. The function of expanding welfare, with its host of services, is to control the surplus population politically. Moreover, as James O'Connor observes: "unable to gain employment in the monopoly industries by offering their laborpower at lower than going wage rates (and victimized by sexism and racism), and unemployed, underemployed, or employed at low wages in competitive industries, the surplus population increasingly becomes dependent on the state."[27] Only a new economic order could replace the need for a welfare state.

Repression through welfare is in part the history of capitalism. The kinds of services have varied with the development of different economic conditions. In the same way, relief policies have varied according to the specific tensions produced by unemployment and subsequent threats of disorder. As Frances Fox Piven and Richard A. Cloward write in their study of the modern welfare system:

> Relief arrangements are ancillary to economic arrangements. Their chief function is to regulate labor, and they do that in two general ways. First, when mass unemployment leads to outbreaks of turmoil, relief programs are ordinarily initiated or expanded to absorb and control enough of the unemployed to restore order; then, as turbulence subsides, the relief system contracts, expelling those who are needed to populate the labor market. Relief also performs a labor-regulating function in this shrunken state, however. Some of the aged, the disabled, the insane, and others who are of no use as workers are left on the relief rolls, and their treatment is so degrading and punitive as to instill in the laboring masses a fear of the fate that awaits them should they relax into beggary and pauperism. To demean and punish those who do not work is to exalt by contrast even the meanest labor at the meanest wages. These regulative functions of relief, and their periodic expansion and contraction, are made necessary by several strains toward instability inherent in capitalist economies.[28]

Control through welfare can never be a permanent solution for a system based on the appropriation of labor. As with all forms of control and manipulation in capitalist society, welfare cannot completely counter the basic contradictions of a capitalist political economy.

Although the capitalist state creates and manages the institutions of control (employing physical force and manipulation of consciousness), the basic contradictions of the capitalist order are such that this control is not absolute and, in the long run, is subject to defeat. Because of the contradictions of capitalism, the capitalist state is more weak than strong.[29] Eventually the capitalist state loses its legitimacy and no longer is able to perpetuate the ideology that capital accumulation for capitalists (at the expense of workers) is good for the nation or for human interests. The ability of the capitalist economic order to exist according to its own interests is eventually weakened.[30] The problem becomes especially acute in periods of economic crisis, periods that are unavoidable under capitalism.

In the course of reproducing the capitalist system, crimes are committed. One of the contradictions of capitalism is that some of its laws must be violated in order to secure the existing system.[31] The contradictions of capitalism produce their own sources of crime. Not only are these contradictions heightened during times of crisis, making for an increase in crimes of domination, but the nature of these crimes changes with the further development of capitalism.

The crimes of domination most characteristic of capitalist domination are those crimes that occur in the course of securing the existing economic order. These *crimes of economic domination* include the crimes committed by corporations, ranging from price fixing to pollution of the environment in order to protect and further capital accumulation. Also included are the economic crimes of individual businessmen and professionals. In addition, the crimes of the capitalist class and the capitalist state are joined in organized crime. The more conventional criminal operations of organized crime are linked to the state in the present stage of capitalist development. The operations of organized crime and the criminal operations of the state are united in the attempt to assure the survival of the capitalist system.

Then there are the *crimes of government* committed by the elected and appointed officials of the capitalist state. The Watergate crimes, carried out to perpetuate a particular governmental administration, are the most publicized instances of these crimes. There are also those offenses committed by the government against persons and groups who would seemingly threaten national security. Included here are the crimes of warfare and the political assassination of foreign and domestic leaders.

Crimes of domination also occur in the course of state control. These are the *crimes of control*. They include the felonies and misdemeanors that law-enforcement agents, especially the police, carry out in the name of the law, usually against persons accused of other violations. Violence and brutality have become a recognized part of police work. In addition to these crimes of control, there are crimes of a more subtle nature in which agents of the law violate the civil liberties of citizens, as in the various forms of surveillance, the use of provocateurs, and the illegal denial of due process.

Finally, many *social injuries* committed by the capitalist class and the capitalist state are not usually defined as criminal in the legal codes of the state.[32] These systematic actions, involving the denial of basic human rights (resulting in sexism, racism, and economic exploitation), are an integral part of capitalism and are important to its survival.

Underlying all the capitalist crimes is the appropriation of the surplus value created by labor. The working class has the right to possess the whole of this value. The worker creates a value several times greater than the labor power purchased by the capitalist. The excess value created by the worker over and above the value of labor power is the surplus value appropriated by the capitalist, being the source of accumulation of capital and expansion of production.

Domination and repression are basic to class struggle in the development of capitalism. The capitalist class and the state protect and promote the capitalist order by controlling those who do not own the means of production. The labor supply and the conditions for labor must be secured. Crime control and crimes of domination are necessary features and natural products of a capitalist political economy.

Accommodation and Resistance

The contradictions of developing capitalism heighten the level of class struggle and thereby increase (1) the need to dominate by the capitalist class and (2) the need to accommodate and resist by the classes exploited by capitalism, particularly the working class. Most of the behavior in response to domination, including actions of the oppressed defined as criminal by the capitalist class, is a product of the capitalist system of production. In the course of capitalist appropriation of labor, for the accumulation of capital, conditions are established that call for behaviors that may be defined as criminal by the capitalist state. These behaviors become eligible for crime control when they disturb or threaten in some way the capitalist order.[33]

Hence, the class that does not own or control the means of production must adapt to the conditions of capitalism. Accommodation and resistance to the conditions of capitalism are basic to the class struggle. The argument here is that action by people who do not own and control the means of production, those who are exploited and oppressed, is largely an accommodation or resistance to the conditions produced by capitalist production. Thus, criminality among the oppressed classes is action (conscious or otherwise) in relation to the capitalist order of exploitation and oppression. Crime, with its many historical variations, is an integral part of class struggle in the development of capitalism.

Following Marx and Engels' limited and brief discussion, criminals outside the capitalist class are usually viewed as being among the lumpenproletariat.[34] Accordingly, criminals of the oppressed classes are regarded as unproductive workers; they are parasitical in that they do not contribute to the production of goods, and they create a livelihood out of commodities produced by the working class.[35] Much criminal activity in the course of accommodation is an expression of false consciousness, an individualistic reaction to the forces of capitalist production.

Many crimes of accommodation are of this lumpen nature. Nevertheless, these actions occur within the context of capitalist oppression, stemming from the existing system of production. Much criminal behavior is of a parasitical nature, including burglary, robbery, drug dealing, and hustling of various sorts.[36] These are *predatory crimes*. The behavior, although pursued out of the need to survive, is a reproduction of the capitalist system. The crimes are nevertheless antagonistic to the capitalist order. Most police activity is directed against these crimes.

In addition to predatory crimes there are *personal crimes*, which are usually directed against members of the same class. These are the conventional criminal acts of murder, assault, and rape. They are pursued by those who are already brutalized by the conditions of capitalism. These actions occur in immediate situations that are themselves the result of more basic accommodations to capitalism.

Aside from these lumpen crimes, actions are carried out, largely by the working class, that are in resistance to the capitalist system. These actions, sometimes directed against the work situation, are direct reflections of the alienation of labor—a struggle, conscious or unconscious, against the exploitation of the life and activity of the worker. For example, workers may engage in concrete political actions against their employers:

> On the assembly lines of the American automobile industry, this
> revolt extends as far as clandestine acts of sabotage against a
> product (the automobile body) which appears to the worker as the
> detestable materialization of the social uselessness and individual
> absurdity of his toil. Along the same lines is the less extreme and
> more complex example of miners fighting with admirable perse-
> verance against the closing of the mines where they are exploited
> under inferior human and economic conditions—but who, individ-
> ually, have no difficulty in recognizing that even if the coal they
> produced were not so bad and so expensive, their job, under the
> prevailing conditions, would still be abominable.[37]

These defensive actions by workers are likely to become even
more politically motivated and organized in the future. For built
into the capitalist economy is the contradiction that increased economic growth necessitates the kind of labor that further alienates
workers from their needs. Further economic expansion can bring
with it only an increase in crimes of resistance. For the purpose of
class struggle, leading to socialist revolution, a Marxist analysis of
crime gives attention to *crimes of resistance*, committed primarily
by members of the working class.

The effects of the capitalist mode of production for the worker
are all-inclusive, going far beyond the workplace. The worker can
no longer be at home anyplace in the everyday world. The alienation experienced in the workplace now represents the condition of
the worker in all other areas of life. Ownership and control of life in
general have been surrendered to alien hands.[38] The production of
life itself is alienated under capitalism. Furthermore, the natural
productive process, of which work is central, has become restricted
in the stages of capitalist accumulation. The increasing alienation
of work, as Harry Braverman notes,

> consists in the narrowing of the base of productive labor upon
> which the economy rests, to the point where an ever smaller por-
> tion of society labors to maintain all of it, while the remainder is
> drafted, at lower rates of pay and even more demeaning conditions
> of labor, into the unproductive economy of capitalism. And finally,
> it consists in the misery of unemployment and of outright pauper-
> ization, which are aspects of the reserve army of labor created by
> capital more or less automatically in the accumulation process.[39]

Moreover, large numbers of workers under advanced capitalism become expendable. For the capitalist the problem becomes

that of the kind and size of labor force necessary to maximize production and realize surplus value. The physical well-being and spiritual needs of the worker are not the concern; rather, capitalism requires an 'industrial reserve army' that can be called into action when necessary and relieved when no longer needed—but that is always available. Marx observed in *Capital*:

> But if a surplus laboring population is a necessary product of accumulation or of the development of wealth on a capitalist basis, this surplus population becomes, conversely, the lever of capitalist accumulation, nay, a condition of existence of the capitalist mode of production. It forms a disposable industrial reserve army that belongs to capital quite as absolutely as if the latter had bred it at its own cost. Independently of the limits of the actual increase of population, it creates, for the changing needs of the self-expansion of capital, a mass of human material always ready for exploitation.[40]

Under these conditions, "the labor force consists of two parts, the employed and the unemployed, with a gray area in between, containing the part-time or sporadically employed. Furthermore, all these categories of workers and potential workers continuously expand or contract with technological change, the ups and downs of the business cycle, and the vagaries of the market, all inherent characteristics of capitalist production."[41] Many workers are further exploited by being relegated to the degradations and uncertainties of a reserve army of labor.

For the unemployed, as well as for those who are always uncertain about their employment, this life condition has its personal and social consequences. Basic human needs are thwarted when the life-giving activity of work is lost or curtailed. This form of alienation gives rise to a multiplicity of psychosocial maladjustments and psychic disorders.[42] In addition, unemployment means the loss of personal and family income. Choices, opportunities, and even life maintenance are jeopardized. For many people, the appropriate reaction consists not only of mental disturbance but also of outright acts of personal and social destruction.

Although the statistical evidence can never show conclusively the relation between unemployment and crime, largely because such statistics are politically constructed in the beginning to obscure the failings of a capitalist economy, there is sufficient observation to recognize the obvious fact that unemployment produces criminality. Crimes of economic gain increase whenever the jobless seek ways to maintain themselves and their families. Crimes of violence rise when the problems of life are further exacerbated by the loss of life-supporting activity. Anger and frustration at a world that punishes rather than supports produce their own forms of destruction. Permanent unemployment—and the acceptance of that condition—can result in a form of life where criminality is an appropriate and consistent response.

Hence, crime under capitalism has become a response to the conditions of life.[43] Nearly all crimes among the working class in capitalist society are actually a means of survival, an attempt to exist in a society where survival is not assured by other, collective means. Crime is inevitable under capitalist conditions.

Yet, understanding crime as a reaction to capitalist conditions, whether as acts of frustration or means of survival, is only one side of the picture. The other side involves the problematics of the consciousness of criminality in capitalist society.[44] The history of the working class is in large part one of rebellion against the conditions of capitalist production, as well as against the conditions of life resulting from work under capitalism. Class struggle involves, after all, a continuous war between two dialectically opposed interests: on one hand, capital accumulation for the benefit of a non-working minority class that owns and controls the means of production and, on the other hand, control and ownership of production by those who actually labor. Since the capitalist state regulates this struggle, the institutions and laws of the social order are intended to assure the victory of the capitalist class over the working class. Yet the working class constantly struggles against the capitalist class, as shown in the long history of labor battles against the conditions of capitalist production.[45] The resistance continues as long as there is need for class struggle; that is, as long as capitalism exists.

With the instruments of force and coercion on the side of the capitalist class, much of the activity in the working-class struggle is defined as criminal. Indeed, according to the legal codes, whether in simply acting to relieve the injustices of capitalism or in taking action against the existence of class oppression, actions against the interests of the state are crimes. With an emerging consciousness that the state represses those who attempt to tip the scales in favor of the working class, working-class people engage in actions against the state and the capitalist class. This is crime that is politically conscious.

Crimes of accommodation and resistance thus range from unconscious reactions to exploitation, to conscious acts of survival within the capitalist system, to politically conscious acts of rebellion. These criminal actions, moreover, not only cover the range of meaning but actually evolve or progress from unconscious reaction to political rebellion. Finally, the crimes may eventually reach the ultimate stage of conscious political action—revolt. In revolt, criminal actions are not only against the system but are also an attempt to overthrow it.

The movement toward a socialist society can occur only with political consciousness on the part of those oppressed by capitalist society. The alternative to capitalism cannot be willed into being but requires the conscious activity of those who seek new conditions of existence. Political consciousness develops in an awareness of the alienation suffered under capitalism. The contradiction of capitalism—the disparity between actuality and human possibility— makes large portions of the population ready to act in ways that will bring about a new existence. When people become conscious of the extent to which they are dehumanized under the capitalist mode of production, when people realize the source and nature of their alienation, they become active in a movement to build a new society. Many of the actions taken result in behaviors defined as criminal by the capitalist state.

Crime in Capitalist Society

An understanding of crime, as developed here, begins with an analysis of the political economy of capitalism. The class struggle endemic to capitalism is characterized by a dialectic between domination and accommodation. Those who own and control the means of production, the capitalist class, attempt to secure the existing order through various forms of domination, especially crime control by the capitalist state. Those who do not own and control the means of production, especially the working class, accommodate to and resist the capitalist domination in various ways.

Crime is related to this process. Crime control and criminality (consisting of the crimes of domination and the crimes of accommodation) are understood in terms of the conditions resulting from the capitalist appropriation of labor. Variations in the nature and amount of crime occur in the course of developing capitalism. Each stage in the development of capitalism is characterized by a particular pattern of crime. The meaning and changing meanings of crime are found in the development of capitalism.

What can be expected in the further development of capitalism? The contradictions and related crises of a capitalist political economy are now a permanent feature of advanced capitalism. Further economic development along capitalist lines will solve none of the internal contradictions of the capitalist mode of production.[46] The capitalist state must therefore increasingly utilize its resources—its various control and repressive mechanisms—to maintain the capitalist order. The dialectic between oppression by the capitalist class and the daily struggle of survival by the oppressed will continue—and at a quickened pace.

The only lasting solution to the crisis of capitalism is socialism. Under late, advanced capitalism, socialism will be achieved in the struggle of all people who are oppressed by the capitalist mode of production, namely, the workers and all elements of the surplus population. An alliance of the oppressed must take place.[47] Given the objective conditions of a crisis in advanced capitalism, and the conditions for an alliance of the oppressed, a mass socialist movement can be formed, cutting across all divisions in the working class.

The objective of our analysis is to promote a further questioning of the capitalist system, leading to a deeper understanding of the consequences of capitalist development. The essential meaning of crime in the development of capitalism is the need for a socialist society. And as the preceding discussion indicates, in moving toward the socialist alternative, our study of crime is necessarily based on a social and moral analysis of capitalist society. Crime is essentially a product of the material and spiritual contradictions of capitalism. Crime can be a force in development when it becomes a part of the class struggle, increasing political consciousness. But we must continue to concentrate on the capitalist system itself. Our understanding is furthered as we critically investigate the nature, sources, and consequences of the development of capitalism.

As we engage in this work we realize the prophetic goal of socialism. The socialist struggle requires a religious consciousness as much as a class consciousness. The transition to socialism is both political and religious. And, ultimately, the religious goal transcends concrete societies. The prophetic expectation speaks finally to that which is infinite and eternal.

EIGHT

Myth and the Art of Criminology

The sun rises on the other side of town. I will watch it move high into the sky, and then I will begin another day—*ON THE ROAD AGAIN. I JUST CAN'T WAIT TO GET ON THE ROAD AGAIN.* I have decided to spend much of the summer alone traveling the roads of DeKalb County. A small grant from the university to photograph the changes that are taking place in this rural county will justify my travels along these country roads. The roads will lead only to the edges of the county, but travel even of this proportion is a journey of eternal consequence. *ON THE ROAD AGAIN—GOIN' PLACES THAT I'VE NEVER BEEN—SEEIN' THINGS THAT I MAY NEVER SEE AGAIN.* I have spent my life traveling.

In the white car—as on a great white steed—I drive out of town along a road that crosses a gently rolling prairie. Large white cumulus clouds float high over the horizon. This is a good day to be photographing. What I am looking for is not yet clear. A discovery of some kind, a way of making sense of this wandering journey.

I put on dark sunglasses and turn on the radio to WSQR— "Northern Illinois' Country Connection." I place the K2 yellow filter on my 35 mm camera. The land is already taking on a heightened look. Merle Haggard sings his current country song *"Someday When Things Are Good I'm Goin' To Leave You."* This is the country I left years ago and have returned to at this time in my life. Maybe I will be able to see anew. There is always the possibility of rebirth—of an awakening.

I turn onto one of the many dirt roads in the county. *TRAVELIN'*

Original source: Address delivered upon receiving the Edwin H. Sutherland Award, American Society of Criminology, Cincinnati, November 1984. Published in *Legal Studies Forum* 9:3 (1985): 291–299.

WITH THE RODEO IS THE ONLY LIFE I KNOW. A large yellow dog dashes from the farmyard. *YOU'RE THE TOUGHEST COWBOY IN TOWN.* Holding the wheel with one hand, I grab the camera and shoot the dog in motion. *I'VE ALWAYS BEEN A TRAVELIN' COWBOY—NOW THERE'S NO PLACE LEFT TO GO.* The dog gives up the chase. I wish I had tried to settle down. Why this longing of the heart?

The bright sun in the dark blue sky shines through the clouds and casts large shadows over the fields. I think about the news I have received in the morning mail: I have been given the Edwin Sutherland Award. I am pleased that others have thought I am worthy of this award. I also wonder about the meaning of the award at this point in my life—and wonder where I will go from here. And what will I say if I am asked to speak at the award ceremony? Earlier this year, when Eddie Arnold received a country music award, he simply said that he was grateful to be honored by his peers, and that he never wanted accolades, he just wanted to sing his songs. More is expected of a criminologist; we are dealers in words and myths of great elaboration. I will keep notes this summer as I drive along these country roads.

LOOKIN' FOR LOVE IN ALL THE WRONG PLACES. From the fields the smell of clover in blossom flows through the car window. On this late June afternoon, red-winged blackbirds perch on the fence in the lowland. Turning off County Line Road, I stop and rest in a country cemetery. The names of Irish families are carved on the headstones. In this quiet place I lie peacefully in the grass. I would be willing to give up much in this life. The farmland stretches out on all sides. Back in the car, the radio plays "*Someday Soon I'll Be Just One More Memory.*"

After all these years, we continue to give our highest respects to Edwin Sutherland. The award in his name is to honor him. He is still our model of what it is to be a criminologist; he gives direction to our work. While I was writing *The Social Reality of Crime*, Sutherland was my guide. At an earlier time, he had taken the conventional knowledge of criminology and reformulated it into a new theory. I, too, would attempt to reformulate a body of thought into a theory that expressed the needs of the time. It was the point of view that was important. Emily Dickinson's line of poetry caught the form: "Tell the Truth but tell it slant." Years later I would be informed by an Eastern philosophy that cautioned me not to cling to established images, to the known. As I now photograph the landscape, I look through the camera's viewfinder and see the world in another way. I see through the edge of the light that falls from the sun.

Why does Sutherland continue to hold our imagination? We certainly do not seek to emulate his methods and theories. His major work relied heavily on newspaper clippings; there are questions today about his sampling; and his theory is now commonplace. No, it is for another reason that we look to Sutherland: because we have made him our spiritual leader. Sutherland is our myth of the criminologist. The myth of Sutherland is our reference for the creation of our own personal and collective identities. We look up the side of the mountain to find our own likeness in the Great Stone Face. Each intellectual field, even in these modern times, has a mythology, and Edwin Sutherland is an important part of ours.

Our connection to a larger world is still through myth. Our contemporary myths are models for human behavior and, for this reason, give meaning and value to our lives. Rather than being falsehoods—as we tend to conceive of 'myths' in our modern usage—myths are the true stories of our existence. We have not outgrown our need for myth. Our myths may look different from those of traditional times, but our lives are still connected to the universe through the reality of myth.

Of late I have taken to looking at what is very near in my search for the ultimate. How to live daily with faith in a meaningful existence is the contemporary concern. We are seekers in a world where the traditional answers are no longer convincing. We are travelers who desire to reach beyond the material rationalism of the modern age. The sights and sounds along the road have a double meaning. They suggest that we are indeed in the world, but not of it. The traveler is a gnostic—an artist and a theologian— delving into the mysteries held by the land. I travel along these roads to know their secrets, and in so knowing to become part of the landscape.

North of DeKalb and east of Sycamore, I turn onto Old State Road. Parked next to the milkhouse is a public school bus that has been converted into a church-school bus. Printed in large letters on the back of the bus is *Luke 14:23*. As soon as I get home I look up the passage in the Bible. It is the parable Jesus told at the great banquet: "Then the master told his servant, 'Go out to the roads and country lanes and make them come in, so that my house may be full.'" There are many, including this traveler, who are on a mission of sacred purpose.

The myth which grounds my life is that of the traveler. It is the myth we all share—however consciously or unconsciously—in the struggle of our lives. As we have been reminded by Joseph

Campbell, the "hero on the journey" is one of the oldest and most pervasive myths in human cultures. The journey is filled with passages; leaving the threshold of home, the hero journeys through an unfamiliar world filled with strangely intimate forces, many of which are threatening and put the traveler to the test, some giving aid and sustenance. A triumph is possible, represented by the gaining of knowledge and understanding. If the traveler is successful, he or she is able to return home.

The myth of the stages of life places each person in a larger perspective as part of the total image of humanity. No matter how limited is each life, that life is an integral part of the totality of the culture. And in the richest of cultures, myths shared intimately and communally give direction and meaning to the journey of life. In the enlargement of vision made possible by the myth of the journey, the life of each person is supported and enhanced. A relation of the person to the cosmos is established. The myth of life as a journey—as a pilgrim's progress—informs my travels on these country roads.

As I travel one of the roads in the northwest corner of the county, Willie Nelson sings, *"I'll be leavin' in the mornin' for a place I hope to find—all the places must be better than the ones I leave behind."* I stop to read the few lines I have written on a piece of paper and carry in my billfold, words from a poem by T.S. Eliot: "We shall not cease from exploration / And the end of all our exploring / Will be to arrive where we started / And know the place for the first time." Travel may not always be away from home. There might be a road that would take me toward home.

Our travel—our journey toward home—is a journey through the modern era and an attempt to go beyond it. Below the ruins of modernism, we seek an underground tradition that allows the esoteric realm to enter into our daily lives. Taped inside my camera bag are the lines from a poem by Loren Eiseley:

> We sit before a microscope, or watch the Pleiades, but we
> belong to an old craft, wizards who loved
> the living world, loved mystery, kept talking birds
> close to their shoulders, never solved a thing
> but lived lives close to where solutions were
> and did not want them,
> preferred mystery.

Our travel is like that of the seventeenth-century Japanese poet Bashō, who set out near the end of his life on a two-and-a-half year journey to an unexplored territory. On a "narrow road to the deep north," Bashō cast away his possessions and worldly attachments, and cast away his own self. A hundred and fifty years later, in Denmark, Søren Kierkegaard examined the journey of the soul and the condition of the grasping self, of the typically Western self that refuses to become part of what is beyond itself. A "sickness unto death" is the despair we humans experience when we fail to become part of the otherness of the world. All is impermanent—including ourselves. A Zen poem ends with the line, "Change rules the world forever." We travel in eternity, in all the mystery of the universe, and we travel to lose ourselves to the world. Only then do we come home.

The silver maples planted long ago line the driveway of the farm and lead back to the vacant house. Rows of corn run to the edge of the old foundation. High-voltage power lines carrying nuclear-generated electricity to Chicago cut through the backyard. The post-and-beam structure of the barn is exposed like the bony skeleton of a giant mastodon. I stop and photograph the abandoned farmyard and sit for a while beside the house.

What if I am asked to make a connection between my summer travels and criminology? What do myth and life's journey have to do with crime? I would say something like this:

First, 'crime' is one of the predominant myths of our contemporary culture. It ranks with or above baseball and football—the sporting myths of play and competition. Whereas the ancient Greeks had their myths of the gods in the heavens and of heroic figures flying too close to the sun, we have our daily stories of crime which speak to us of our human nature and our relationship to authority. The life course in Greece was guided by the myth of the traveler Odysseus—a myth that suggested the trials of the human journey. In the myth of crime, we today are cautioned in a particular way; we are told about the character of the social world in which we must travel. In the daily stories of crime, we measure our existence.

And we as criminologists are an integral part of the myth. There are those who are the subjects of the myth: the public and the large part of the public that is defined as criminal at any time. There is the apparatus—the reifying structure—of the myth: the police, the courts, the prisons, and all the functionaries of these institutions. And, not least, are the storytellers: the newspaper reporters, the social critics, the preachers, and the criminologists. As high priests of the myth, we criminologists tell the story in detail and make it appropriate for the time and place. We all are part of the myth, whether we are conservative criminologists, liberal or radical criminologists, sociobiological criminologists or Marxist criminologists.

The question for us, then, is this: In what way do we choose to tell the story? The way we describe the myth is important, important because we are engaged in the highest of callings—mythology and travel into the depth of human and spiritual realms. *BE CAREFUL WHAT YOU'RE DREAMIN'—SOON YOUR DREAMS WILL BE DREAMIN' YOU.*

Second, thought of such kind necessarily leads us beyond the traditional boundaries of criminology. *MAMMAS, DON'T LET YOUR BABIES GROW UP TO BE* . . . criminologists. I will be asked, "Do you still do criminology?" What I am doing at the moment is asking other questions, but the asking is still about what it is to be human and how we can live a decent life in this world. *JUSTICE, SWEET JUSTICE, YOU TRAVEL SO SLOW.* This does not seem to be the time to construct more theories about the causes of crime. Why is it that we know so much about crime, and know it in so many different ways, and yet there still is so much crime? That is the problem for us now. And the problem necessarily takes us someplace beyond criminology. We are engaged in a theology of the lower range, in the highest of realms, in an understanding of the mysteries of everyday life. Our source is the popular culture of the age. We move from Karl Marx to Willie Nelson, but none of the former is lost—it is a part of us. Crime is a homelessness in the world—physically and spiritually. We will eliminate crime only when we find a way to travel home—only when we can be at home in this world of universal consequence. *IF I EVER FIND A PLACE I WANT TO BE, I THINK I'LL STAY. I THINK I'LL STAY.*

And third, is it possible to go beyond the myth of crime—that is, to go beyond the reality of crime? If crime is the dominant myth and reality of the age, and if the age is far from what may be possible, might we not envision a time and a place when and where we could live by some other means and thereby have a different life? It is not that we are lacking in knowledge about crime or anything else—but that we do not know how to transcend that knowledge. Krishnamurti tells us, rightly and wisely, that our lives are conditioned by a knowledge that enslaves us. As criminologists we tend to do little more than explicate, elaborate, and synthesize the obvious. When will we cease to name and begin to live—to live life first hand? Our task, it seems to me, is to see things exactly as they are and to live our lives accordingly. And to see things as they are requires an openness and an awareness—a mindfulness—that comes with a new practice, a practice that involves not only collective struggle, but also personal stillness. This is a practice that is unclouded by conventional thought, by the illusion of self, by the mythology of crime. This is a journey to the sacred, to that part of our humanity that is beyond all thought—to that part of us that is, in Zen terms, 'nothing.' With awareness we may go beyond myth to a new creation—to a world, among other things, free from crime. We are traveling into a new territory.

It is time to head back to town. The road stretches on, but it is getting late. I pass another grain elevator, one of the old ones on the line of the Chicago & Northwestern Railroad. SOMETIMES IT'S HEAVEN AND SOMETIMES IT'S HELL—AND SOMETIMES I DON'T EVEN KNOW. A red-tailed hawk watches from high on a telephone pole. The evening sun gently moves toward the far horizon. Beauty is all around and there is no need at the moment to know anything else.

As I drive into town the country version of the evangelical hymn is playing on the radio: AMAZING GRACE, HOW SWEET THE SOUND THAT SAVED A WRETCH LIKE ME. I ONCE WAS LOST, BUT NOW AM FOUND, WAS BLIND, BUT NOW I SEE. We struggle against the separation from all things. We seek to be a part of the world. Each day is a journey and the journey is toward home—the journey is home. I will stop at Sullivan's for a beer and a sandwich. And if I linger awhile, the band will come and the dancing will begin. We can sing some songs and dance the dance together. GEE, AIN'T IT FUNNY HOW TIME JUST SLIPS AWAY.

References

Bachelard, Gaston. *The Poetics of Space*. Trans. Maria Jolas. Boston: Beacon Press, 1969.

Bashō. *The Narrow Road to the Deep North and Other Travel Sketches*. Trans. Nobuyuki Yuasa. New York: Penguin Books, 1966.

Campbell, Joseph. *The Hero with a Thousand Faces*. Princeton: Princeton University Press, 1968.

Eiseley, Loren. "In the Red Sunset on Another Hill." *The Innocent Assassins*. New York: Charles Scribner's Sons, 1973.

Eliade, Mircea. *Myth and Reality*. Trans. Willard R. Trask. New York: Harper and Row, 1963.

Goldstein, Joseph. *The Experience of Insight*. Boulder: Shambhala, 1976.

Hamilton, Edith. *Mythology*. New York: New American Library, 1969.

Kierkegaard, Søren. *The Sickness Unto Death*. Ed. and Trans. Howard V. Hong and Edna H. Hong. Princeton: Princeton University Press, 1980.

Krishnamurti, J. *Freedom from the Known*. New York: Harper and Row, 1969.

MacIntyre, Alasdair. *After Virtue: A Study in Moral Theory*. Notre Dame: University of Notre Dame, 1981.

May, Rollo. "Myths and Culture: Their Death and Transformation." *Cross Currents* 33 (Spring 1983): 1–7.

Meinig, D. W., ed. *The Interpretation of Ordinary Landscapes: Geographical Essays*. New York: Oxford University Press, 1979.

Nishitani, Keiji. *Religion and Nothingness*. Trans. Jan Van Bragt. Berkeley: University of California Press, 1982.

Pirsig, Robert M. *Zen and the Art of Motorcycle Maintenance*. New York: William Merrow, 1974.

Quinney, Richard. *The Social Reality of Crime*. Boston: Little, Brown, 1970.

Sutherland, Edwin H. *Principles of Criminology*. 4th edition. Philadelphia: J. B. Lippincott, 1947.

NINE

The Way of Peace:
On Crime, Suffering, and Service

Let us begin with a fundamental realization: no amount of thinking and no amount of public policy have brought us any closer to understanding and solving the problem of crime. The more we have reacted to crime, the farther we have removed ourselves from any understanding and any reduction of the problem. In recent years, we have floundered desperately in reformulating the law, punishing the offender, and quantifying our knowledge. Yet this country remains one of the most crime-ridden nations. In spite of all its wealth, economic development, and scientific advances, this country has one of the worst crime records in the world.

With such realization, we return once again—as if starting anew—to the subject of crime, a subject that remains one of our most critical indicators of the state of our personal and collective being. If what is to be said seems outrageous and heretical, it is only because it is necessarily outside the conventional wisdom both of our understanding of the problem and of our attempt to solve it. Only by entering another world—yet one that is very simple and ultimately true—can we become aware of our own condition.

A few elementary observations serve as the basis for our understanding. (1) Thought of the Western rational mode is conditional, limiting knowledge to what is already known. (2) The truth of reality is emptiness; all that is real is beyond human conception. (3) Each life is a spiritual journey into the unknown and the

---

Original source: Chapter 1 in Harold E. Pepinsky and Richard Quinney (eds.), *Criminology as Peacemaking.* Bloomington: Indiana University Press, 1991. An earlier version appeared in *The Quest* 1:2(1988): 66–75.

unknowable, beyond the egocentric self. (4) Human existence is characterized by suffering; crime is suffering; and the sources of suffering are within each of us. (5) Through love and compassion, beyond the egocentric self, we can end suffering and live in peace, personally and collectively. (6) The ending of suffering can be attained in a quieting of the mind and an opening of the heart, in being aware. (7) Crime can be ended only with the ending of suffering, only when there is peace—through the love and compassion found in awareness. (8) Understanding, service, justice: all these flow naturally from love and compassion, from mindful attention to the reality of all that is, here and now. (9) A *criminology of peacemaking*, the nonviolent criminology of compassion and service, seeks to end suffering and thereby eliminate crime. Let us elaborate on this understanding.

Awareness of Human Suffering

Suffering is the condition of our existence. The forms of suffering are all around us. In our personal lives, there are tensions and anxieties. Each day we experience the physical pains in our bodies and the psychological hurts in our hearts and minds. Our interpersonal relations often are carried out in violence of one kind or another, if only in the withholding of what might be offered. We have created societies that are filled with the sufferings of poverty, hunger, homelessness, pollution, and destruction of the environment. Globally, nations are at war and threaten not only one another, but all of earthly life, with nuclear destruction. All these human problems, or forms of suffering, are a result of how we have lived our lives, moment by moment, day by day. The threat of nuclear war began as suffering on a very personal level and elevated gradually and systematically to the collective condition (see Walsh, 1984). The forms of suffering are symptoms of the sufferings within each of us.

If the social and global sufferings ever are to be ended, we must deal with the suffering of personal existence. What is involved, finally, is no less than the transformation of human behavior. Political and economic solutions without this transformation inevitably fail. The solution is very near to us. There is no shortcut to the ending of suffering.

Our suffering, then, and our ending of this suffering, begins in the human mind. The *Dhammapada*, the ancient text of Buddhism, states: "All that we are is a result of what we have thought" (1936:3). We act out of our thoughts, and we create social worlds out of these thoughts. Being human, we have constructed webs of meaning; and with these shared meanings we have constructed our interpersonal relations, our social structures, and our societies. All is a result of what we have thought.

The reconstruction of our existence—the ending of suffering—thus begins by giving attention to the mind. It is this mind, a modern mind that is busy and scattered, that creates its own suffering. To be able to observe the mind as it is, to be able to see clearly with the mind, we begin with what must seem at first a paradox: letting go. The author of A Gradual Awakening observes: "In letting go of who we imagine ourselves to be, letting go of our thinking, our attempt to control the world, we come upon our natural being which has been waiting patiently all these years for us to come home" (Levine, 1979:39). This open state of mind is what one Zen master calls a "beginner's mind." He (Suzuki, 1970:21) writes: "If your mind is empty, it is always ready for anything; it is open to everything. In the beginner's mind there are many possibilities; in the expert's mind there are few." We are ready to see things as they really are—beyond concepts and theories—when we have no thought of achievement, no thought of self. When our mind is open and thus compassionate toward all things, it is boundless in its understanding.

Without empty mind—without mindfulness—we are attached to our ideas, our thoughts, our mental constructions; and we take these productions to be reality itself. Many of our concepts are so deeply ingrained in our minds, in our education, and in our culture, that we forget that they completely condition our perceptions of reality (see Krishnamurti, 1975). In attachment to these mental productions, we are chained in the cave, observing merely the shadows of appearance on the wall before us. Awareness is a breaking of the chains of conditioned thought and a viewing of the reality beyond the shadows.

Without awareness, we humans are bound to the suffering caused by a grasping mind. Being attached to our thoughts, we take the thoughts to be our true selves. The mind that is attached to its own thoughts is the mind of a self-centered and possessive being. All conditioned and attached thought arises from the discursive mind of the egocentric self. That is why the sacred texts of the esoteric traditions, such as the wisdom literature of early Hinduism as found in the Upanishads and the Bhagavad Gita, suggest that truth can be known only through union with Brahman, through that which is beyond the ego-self and its attempt at purely rational thought. In contemplation and meditation, we can see the essence of all things as they rise and pass away.

The higher wisdom, the awareness of reality, can be attained only with the loss of the conditioned ego and with the realization of the transcendental Self. In other words, the essence of our existence is the interpenetration of ourselves with all things. In *Samadhi*, a treatise on self-development in Zen Buddhism, Mike Sayama (1986:12) writes: "The task before us is no longer to differentiate from nature and develop the ego, but transcend the ego and realize true Self that is one with the universe." Only then can one be at home. Peace and harmony come with the awareness of the oneness of all things and the transcendence of this small self to the wholeness of reality. All of this is to be found outside of the abstracting interpretations of the rational mind.

As we mature, we move beyond the rational and linear mode of thought to a more intuitive and transcendent mode. We lose the grasping and craving self of the individualized ego and find ourselves in the realm of the universal Self. It is not natural—it is unhealthy—for the academic and the intellectual (sociologist, criminologist) to continue strictly in the rational mode of speculative and dualistic thought as he or she matures, although this is the approved and rewarded form for the modern academic. To continue solely in the rational mode of thought is retrogressive for the maturing person, and for a discipline as well.

The author of *Samadhi* concludes: "At the most mature level of human being, a person realizes the true self which is one with the universe and experiences a meaning beyond question and articulation. Such a person transcends anxiety, is fearless and is moved by compassion" (Sayama, 1986:98). Rather than a life primarily of acquisition and scholarly production, life now demands an inner awakening, a spiritual development. One no longer clings to rationality and the ego as the final realities; one is not trapped in the world of interpretive abstractions taking form according to attachments of an egocentric existence. Once we have mastered rationality and moved to the possibilities of perennial wisdom, we can begin to live in compassionate oneness with all that is; we can begin to understand the world by being fully aware of it.

The truth is that no amount of theorizing and rational thinking can tell us much about reality. To enter into the essential realm requires a mind that is unattached and compassionate. In a book on perennial wisdom, Aldous Huxley (1970:x) writes: "It is a fact, con-firmed and re-confirmed during two or three thousand years of reli-gious history, that the ultimate Reality is not clearly and immedi-ately apprehended, except by those who have made themselves loving, pure in heart and poor in spirit." When we allow the higher Self to dwell in the depth of the particular self—when the egocen-tric, rational self is lost—we can attend to the unknown and unknowable mysteries of the world.

And the final expression of this realization may not be in more talk and more words, but in silence. Saint John of the Cross observed, "For whereas speaking distracts, silence and work collect thoughts and strengthen the spirit" (quoted in Huxley, 1970:218). With the wisdom gained by awareness, there may be no further need to talk and to write discursively. One then practices what is realized—with attention and silence, in charity and humility, in the service of others.

Right Understanding

The way to awareness, and thus the ending of suffering, begins with right understanding. An understanding of the true nature of reality involves the recognition that everything is imper-manent, that nothing remains the same, that within the flux of reality is the fact that every action brings a certain result. For instance, whenever our actions are motivated by greed, hatred, or delusion, the inevitable result is suffering. All of this occurs within a reality that is beyond the abstractions of a grasping and craving mind.

The true reality, beyond human conception, is what Zen Bud-dhism refers to as *Sunyata*: nothingness, emptiness, the void. In a recognition of the fullness of the unnamable, of emptiness, we may begin to see clearly and compassionately the concrete reality of our existence. With this understanding, as Alan Watts (1957:125) notes, we are "at the point where there is nothing further to seek, nothing to be gained." When we are empty—within the emptiness of all—we are in the realm of ultimate reality.

Beyond Western scientism, there is liberated action freed of the separation of ourselves from the world. Watts (1957:131) quotes a Zen line: "Only when you have no thing in your mind and no mind in things are you vacant and spiritual, empty and marvelous." This takes us beyond the products of Western thought, beyond the malaise and destruction that have resulted from being separated from the ineffable reality of our existence. By a "dropping off of body and mind," as Keiji Nishitani (1982) of the Kyoto School of Japanese Zen terms it, we allow ourselves to live in the wonder of absolute nothingness. We return to a home—we arrive at the "home-ground"—where all things are in harmony with what they actually are and ought to be. It is a "coming home with empty hands," and each being has found its place among all other things. But let us beware. Even this talk takes us into the place of mental abstractions, the place where we again lose touch with reality.

It is the presumed objectivity and rationality of modern science that we hope to avoid in a new criminology. We hope to avoid the personal and social consequences of positive science because, as one humanistic philosopher (Skolimowski, 1986:306) has noted, the mind trained in objective science "over a number of years becomes cold, dry, uncaring, always atomized, cutting, analyzing. This kind of mind has lost the capacity for empathy, compassion, love." Our mode of thinking affects the way we live, and in the meantime we have not gotten any closer to understanding. We seek a mind that, instead of producing conflict and violence, heals—a compassionate mind rather than an objective mind. The compassionate mind is found beyond the boundaries of Western scientific rationality.

Being on the simple path of right understanding, we create thought, words, and deeds that will end our suffering. The forest monk Achaan Chah writes: "Only when our words and deeds come from kindness can we quiet the mind and open the heart" (1985:50). Our work is not only to grow in wisdom and compassion but also to help others in their suffering. This takes place not necessarily in further theoretical work, but in moment-by-moment, day-by-day, step-by-step awareness of what actually is. We are on a wandering path to emptiness, to an awareness of the fullness and wholeness of all things.

That we criminologists are to be engaged in spiritual work in order to eliminate crime may require further reflection. To be fully human presupposes the development within oneself of a quality of being that transcends material existence. It is a quality that is not acquired automatically, but one that develops slowly and needs to be tended carefully. Through inner work, we forge a link between the profane and the sacred. Indeed, all of life becomes filled with the sacred. Such a quality within each of us assures a life of growing wisdom, compassion, and service.

Nothing any longer is profane, nothing is devoid of the transcendent dimension. The simplest actions, from eating and walking to talking and working, have a sacramental character signifying something beyond themselves. Our lives are within a realm that demands a spiritual as well as material existence. This is why the great religious traditions continue to emphasize a constant discipline of recollection, meditation, study, prayer, contemplation, and at least some measure of solitude and retirement. The Trappist monk Thomas Merton thus writes: "If the salvation of society depends, in the long run, on the moral and spiritual health of individuals, the subject of contemplation becomes a vastly important one, since contemplation is one of the indications of spiritual maturity. It is closely allied to sanctity. You cannot save the world merely with a system. You cannot have peace without charity" (1979:8). Seeing the truth, in contemplation and meditation, sets us on a path that promotes a humane and peaceful existence. Such an existence is a reality which we can attain only in a life lived in the depth of the sacred. A life devoted to criminology cannot avoid the importance of this truth. Care has to be given to the inner life of each of us.

This life of giving attention to spiritual matters, of going beyond the self to all that is in the world, is a socially committed life. The contemplative life is not self-indulgent, for social issues cannot be faced appropriately without inner spiritual preparation (see Merton, 1962). Oppression in the world is caused by selves that are not spiritually aware, by those who live by greed, fear, egoism, and the craving for power over others. As Jacob Needleman (1980:212–19) observes in *Lost Christianity*, the "outer" world is not out there, and the "inner" world is not solely one of personal emotions and thoughts. Both are of the same space, in interpenetration of everything. The objective is a compassionate living of each moment with all other beings—for the ending of suffering.

Compassion and Service

We are all of us interrelated—and "not just people, but animals too, and stones, clouds, trees" (Aitken, 1984:10). Those who are enlightened in the service of others, the *Bodhisattvas* of the world, realize fully the reality of the interpenetration of all things. By experiencing the ephemeral and transparent nature of reality, by being aware of the oneness of all things, we can know the potential of peace and harmony.

Were there complete perfection and unity, there would be no suffering. Suffering has arisen out of disunity and separation from the embracing totality, and it can be ended only with the return of all sentient beings to a condition of wholeness. We have fallen from the grace of wholeness into a separation from one another and from the ground of all being, a separation that is assured by craving and grasping selves, by selves that are really an illusion. If human beings were constantly and consciously in a proper relationship with the sacred and with the natural and social environment, there would be only as much suffering as creation makes inevitable (see Huxley, 1970:233–34). But our own created reality is one of separation, and therefore one of suffering.

Thus the healing of separation is necessary if suffering is to be ended. To begin to end suffering, we must be aware of the causes of suffering within ourselves and search for the reasons that make us suffer. The Tibetan Buddhist master Rinpoche Kalu says that the suffering we experience in the world "is caused by the six afflictions—ignorance, desire, pride, anger, jealousy, and greed" (Kalu, 1987:13). The most hopeful way to attain world peace, to end global suffering, he adds, is by developing within ourselves compassion and loving-kindness toward others.

In the practice of loving-kindness, what Buddhists call *metta*, there is developed the feeling of caring and connectedness. From within, thoughts of goodwill and benevolence are extended outward, embracing all others in an increasingly wider circle. In compassion, the suffering of others is recognized out of one's own suffering, and the suffering is shared. Jack Kornfield (1985:63) writes: "Compassion is the tender readiness of the heart to respond to one's own or another's pain without grief or resentment or aversion. It is the wish to dissipate suffering. Compassion embraces those experiencing sorrow, and eliminates cruelty from the mind." Looking directly at suffering, both the suffering in the world and the suffering in our own hearts and minds, we love others (as ourselves) and act in compassion to end suffering—to heal separation.

We begin our practice, then, by being aware of the ways in which suffering is manifested in each of us. "The more conscious we are in dealing with our own suffering, the more sensitive we will be in treating the pain of others" (Dass and Gorman, 1985:86). Our responsibility is to do what we can to alleviate the concrete conditions of human suffering. "We work to provide food for the hungry, shelter for the homeless, health care for the sick and feeble, protection for the threatened and vulnerable, schooling for the unedu-

cated, freedom for the oppressed" (Dass and Gorman, 1985:87).
When we acknowledge what is and act as witnesses in this shared
reality, without attachment and judgment, we open ourselves to all
suffering. Acting out of compassion, without thinking of ourselves
as doers, we are witnesses to what must be done.

The path to the ending of suffering is through compassion
rather than through the theories of science and the calculations of
conditioned thought. Our sufferings are, in fact, exacerbated by science and thought. The discoveries necessary for dealing with suffering are within our being.

The truth that relieves suffering lies in the concrete moment
of our awareness, an awareness that frees us from conditioned
judgments, creates loving-kindness within us, and allows us to realize the absolute emptiness of all phenomena.

As long as there is suffering in this world, each of us suffers.
We cannot end our suffering without ending the suffering of all others. In being witnesses to the concrete reality, and in attempting to
heal the separation between ourselves and true being (the ground
of all existence), we necessarily suffer with all others. But now we
are fully aware of the suffering and realize how it can be eliminated. With awareness and compassion, we are ready to act.

The Way of Peace and Social Justice

From the inner understanding of our own suffering, we are
prepared to act in a way of peace. As in Mahatma Gandhi's philosophy of *Satyagraha*, truth force, social action comes out of the
informed heart, out of the clear and enlightened mind. The source
of social action is within the human heart that has come to understand fully its own suffering and therefore the suffering of others.
If human actions are not rooted in compassion, these actions will
not contribute to a peaceful and compassionate world. "If we cannot
move beyond inner discord, how can we help find a way to social
harmony? If we ourselves cannot know peace, be peaceful, how will
our acts disarm hatred and violence?" (Dass and Gorman,
1985:165). The means cannot be different from the ends; peace can
come only out of peace. "There is no way to peace," said A. J. Muste.
"Peace is the way."

In other words, without *inner* peace in each of us, without
peace of mind and heart, there can be no *social* peace between people and no peace in societies, nations, and in the world. To be explic-

itly engaged in this process, of bringing about peace on all levels, of joining ends and means, is to be engaged in *peacemaking* (Musto, 1986:8–9). In peacemaking, we attend to the ultimate purpose of our science—to heal the separation between all things and to live harmoniously in a state of unconditional love.

The radical nature of peacemaking is clear: No less is involved than the transformation of our human being. We will indeed be engaged in action, but action will come out of our transformed being. Rather than attempting to create a good society first, and then trying to make ourselves better human beings, we have to work on the two simultaneously. The inner and the outer are the same. The human transformation in relation to action is described by Thich Nhat Hanh, the Vietnamese Buddhist peace activist, as a realization that begins in the human heart and mind:

> To realize does not only mean to act. First of all, realization con-
> notes transforming oneself. This transformation creates a har-
> mony between oneself and nature, between one's own joy and the
> joy of others. Once a person gets in touch with the source of under-
> standing and compassion, this transformation is accomplished.
> When this transformation is present, all one's actions will carry
> the same nature and effect—protecting and building life with
> understanding and compassion. If one wishes to share joy and
> happiness with others, one should have joy and happiness within
> oneself. If one wishes to transmit serenity, first one should realize
> it oneself. Without a sane and peaceful mind, one's actions could
> only create more trouble and destruction in the world. (Hanh,
> 1985:2; also see Hanh, 1987)

The transformation of ourselves and the world becomes our constant practice, here and now.

The practice is, in the true sense, spiritual and religious. In Buddhist terms, we become enlightened in the practice; and in Christianity, the transformation involves an inner conversion—a new age coming in both cases only when we have made ourselves ready. As a commentator (Musto, 1986:251) on the Catholic peace tradition writes, "Peace is not so much political revolution as personal conversion; it is not individual human ego and power at stake, but God's will to peace that only humans can accomplish on earth, as they are the recipients of God's gift and challenge to peace."

And there can be no peace without justice. This is the biblical command. A good social life—one based on equality, with the elimination of poverty, racism, sexism, and violence of all kinds—is a

peaceful existence. The Old Testament's Isaiah (32:17) states: "Justice will bring about peace, right will produce calm and security." Peace, the result of all the benefits of the covenant, is granted to those who fulfill the covenant by living in justice. "Peace and justice," Ronald Musto (1986:13) observes, "are thus inextricably bound: cause and effect, journey and goal." By living the covenant—by creating justice—there is peace. The peacemakers are truly "the children of God."

All of this is to say, to us as criminologists, that crime is suffering and that the ending of crime is possible only with the ending of suffering. And the ending both of suffering and of crime, which is the establishing of justice, can come only out of peace, out of a peace that is spiritually grounded in our very being. To eliminate crime—to end the construction and perpetuation of an existence that makes crime possible—requires a transformation of our human being. We as human beings must *be* peace if we are to live in a world free of crime, in a world of peace.

In recent years, we have seen several attempts at peacemaking in criminology. There have been writings and some programs employing conflict resolution, mediation, reconciliation, abolition, and humanistic action (see, for example, Abel, 1982; Currie, 1985; Pepinsky, 1988; Tifft and Sullivan, 1980; Sullivan, 1980). They offer the concrete beginnings of a *criminology of peacemaking*, a criminology that seeks to end suffering and thereby eliminate crime. It is a criminology that is based necessarily on human transformation in the achievement of peace and justice. Human transformation takes place as we change our social, economic, and political structure. And the message is clear: without peace within us and in our actions, there can be no peace in our results. Peace is the way.

We are fully aware by now that the criminal justice system in this country is founded on violence. It is a system that assumes that violence can be overcome by violence, evil by evil. Criminal justice at home and warfare abroad are of the same principle of violence. This principle sadly dominates much of our criminology. Fortunately, more and more criminologists are realizing that this principle is fundamentally incompatible with a faith that seeks to express itself in compassion, forgiveness, and love. When we recognize that the criminal justice system is the moral equivalent of the war machine, we realize that resistance to one goes hand-in-hand with resistance to the other.

The resistance must be in compassion and love, not in terms of the violence that is being resisted. A definition of "nonviolence" by a recent resister (Taylor, 1986:1) is appropriate: "Nonviolence is a method of struggling for human liberation that resists and refuses to cooperate with evil or injustice, while trying to show goodwill to all opponents encountered in the struggle, and being willing to take suffering on oneself, rather than inflicting it on others." We are back again to the internal source of our actions: Action is the form the essence of our being takes. Thich Nhat Hanh, whose thoughts follow that same definition of nonviolence, writes:

> The chain reaction of love is the essential nature of the struggle. The usual way to generate force is to create anger, desire, and fear in people. Hatred, desire, and fear are sources of energy. But a nonviolent struggle cannot use these dangerous sources of energy, for they destroy both the people taking part in the struggle and the aim of the struggle itself. Nonviolent struggle must be nurtured by love and compassion. (Quoted in Taylor, 1986:2)

When our hearts are filled with love and our minds with willingness to serve, we will know what has to be done and how it is to be done. Such is the basis of a *nonviolent criminology*.

We begin, then, by attending to the direction of our innermost being, the being that is the whole of reality. Out of this source, all action follows. In the words of Lao-tzu, "No action is taken, and yet nothing is left undone" (1963:184). Everything is done out of compassion to help lessen the suffering of others.

Living in harmony with the truth, we do everything as an act of service. Criminology can be no less than this, a part of the reality of all that is—a way of peace.

References

Abel, Richard L. *The Politics of Informal Justice*. Vol. 1. New York: Academic Press, 1982.

Aitken, Robert. *The Mind of Clover: Essays in Zen Buddhist Ethics*. San Francisco: North Point Press, 1984.

The Bhagavad-Gita. Tr. Juan Mascaro. New York: Penguin Books, 1962.

Chah, Achaan. *A Still Forest Pool*. Ed. Jack Kornfield and Paul Breiter. Wheaton: Theosophical Publishing House, 1985.

Currie, Elliott. *Confronting Crime: An American Challenge*. New York: Pantheon Books, 1985.

Dass, Ram and Paul Gorman. *How Can I Help? Stories and Reflections on Service*. New York: Alfred A. Knopf, 1985.

The Dhammapada. Tr. Irving Babbitt. New York: New Directions, 1936.

Goldstein, Joseph. *The Experience of Insight*. Boston: Shambhala, 1983.

Hanh, Thich Nhat. *Being Peace*. Berkeley: Parallax Press, 1987.

———. "Action and Compassion in the World." *Buddhist Peace Fellowship Newsletter* 7:3 (1985): 2.

Huxley, Aldous. *The Perennial Philosophy*. New York: Harper and Row, 1970 (1945).

Kalu, H. E. Rinpoche. "The Value of Retreat." *Buddhist Peace Fellowship Newsletter* 9 (Winter 1987): 13.

Kornfield, Jack. "The Buddhist Path and Social Responsibility." *ReVision* 8 (Summer-Fall 1985): 63–67.

Krishnamurti, J. *Freedom from the Known*. New York: Harper and Row, 1975.

Lao-tzu. *The Way of Lao Tzu*. Tr. Wing-Tsit Chan. Indianapolis: Bobbs-Merrill, 1963.

Levine, Stephen. *A Gradual Awakening*. Garden City: Anchor Books, 1979.

Merton, Thomas. *The Ascent to Truth*. New York: Harcourt Brace Jovanovich, 1979.

———. *New Seeds of Contemplation*. New York: New Directions, 1962.

Muste, A. J. *The World Task of Pacificism*. Wallingford, PA: Pendle Hill, 1942.

Musto, Ronald G. *The Catholic Peace Tradition*. Maryknoll, N.Y: Orbis Books, 1986.

Needleman, Jacob. *Lost Christianity: A Journey of Rediscovery*. New York: Bantam Books, 1980.

Nishitani, Keiji. *Religion and Nothingness*. Tr. Jan Van Bragt. Berkeley: University of California Press, 1982.

Pepinsky, Harold E. "Violence as Unresponsiveness." *Justice Quarterly* 5 (December 1988): 539–63.

Sayama, Mike. *Samadhi: Self Development in Zen, Swordsmanship, and Psychotherapy*. Albany: State University of New York Press, 1986.

Skolimowski, Henryk. "Life, Entropy and Education." *American Theosophist* 74 (1986): 305–10.

Sullivan, Dennis. *The Mask of Love: Corrections in America, Toward a Mutual Aid Alternative*. Port Washington, N.Y: Kennikat Press, 1980.

Suzuki, Shunryu. *Zen Mind, Beginner's Mind*. New York: Weatherhill, 1970.

Taylor, Richard. "What Are Nonviolent Tactics?" *Pledge of Resistance Newsletter* (Summer 1986): 1–2, 8.

Tifft, Larry and Dennis Sullivan. *The Struggle to Be Human: Crime, Criminology, and Anarchism*. Sanday, Orkney: Cienfuegos Press, 1980.

The Upanishads. Tr. Juan Mascaro. New York: Penguin Books, 1965.

Walsh, Roger. *Staying Alive: The Psychology of Human Survival*. Boston: Shambhala, 1984.

Watts, Alan W. *The Way of Zen*. New York: Pantheon Books, 1957.

TEN

Criminology as Moral Philosophy, Criminologist as Witness

I had decided to take the night train from Chicago to Albany. Riding the Lake Shore Limited, I would have time for needed silence and reflection. Leisurely thoughts, a few photographic shots on black and white film, and a couple hours of sleep along the way. The train slipped out of Union Station as the sun was setting and made its way along the shores of Lake Michigan, then over the Sandusky bridge and around the southern shore of Lake Erie to Buffalo, and by early morning we were riding through the Mohawk Valley. A day early, I would walk the once-familiar streets of Albany and prepare for a conference on "Justice Without Violence." The next day I would be part of a gathering of peacemaking criminologists and church-related workers on restorative justice.

For two and a half days, usually in formal sessions, we heard and talked about the subject of our life's work. As seems to be happening more of late, I listened, took notes in my notebook, but did not speak. For years we have been witnesses to the sufferings of others. We have sought ways, both structural and personal, to relieve some of the suffering associated with crime and criminal justice. And after such labors of mind and body, we too share the suffering. Being for others, as Dietrich Bonhoeffer termed it, we know that we share the common human condition of our time and place, and we suffer together (Bonhoeffer, 1971). Our gathering in Albany was first about suffering—the suffering of all of us. And this time I was to be a silent witness to the suffering. But a witness nevertheless.

Original source: *Contemporary Justice Review* 1:2, 3 (1998) 347–364.

A realization has been developing for some time, and the conference I was attending confirmed it: Whatever else we do as criminologists, we are engaged in a moral enterprise. Simply stated, our underlying questions are these: How are we human beings to live? Who are we, and of what are we capable? And how could things be different? The criminologist, although not likely educated as a moral philosopher, operates with an implicit moral philosophy, and is engaged in the construction of a moral philosophy.

The many and varied issues surrounding crime and criminal justice are ultimately about how we humans might live. And at the same time, what we criminologists are doing—in addition to the other things we think we are doing—is *witnessing* to all that is associated with crime and criminal justice. We are witnesses to the contemporary suffering brought about by poverty, exploitation, violence in its many forms, hate and greed, brutality, prejudice and inequality. And we are also witnesses—and as witnesses also promoters—of those things which finally alleviate suffering: compassion and loving-kindness. As witnesses, we are part of the process of changing the world. Witnessing is an active vocation, one that is grounded in a particular moral stance toward human existence.

There is, of course, more to consider. As Willie Nelson sings in his song cycle *Phases and Stages*, "Let me tell you some more."

Criminology as Moral Philosophy

Let us note the varieties of moral philosophy that inform contemporary criminology. We cannot delineate forms of moral philosophy that are exhaustive and mutually exclusive of one another. There are many dimensions to the phenomena of our attention, and there are many ways that the diverse phenomena overlap. Keep in mind, always, that in the grand reality everything happens at once. Only the human mind separates the world into discreet phenomena. Remembering this, I will go on to describe the moral philosophies I have known in the course of a career in criminology.

Conservative Moral Philosophy and the Established Order

Any criminology that favors the collective to the well-being of the individual (whether the individual is defined as criminal or not) is a conservative criminology. This is a criminology that is based on, and that fosters, a conservative moral philosophy. It is a criminology that values social order and seeks to preserve the existing order. Policies and programs are aimed at control and deterrence for the benefit of the established order. Rather than change the existing social and economic arrangements, solutions to criminal behavior are sought in controlling the individual.

I am not the criminologist to give a fair and sympathetic treatment to a conservatively grounded criminology, or to analyze the merits of the moral philosophy embodied in such a criminology. But this is a moral philosophy and a criminology of consequence, affecting the lives of whole populations. And it is conservative criminology that has guided much of criminological thought and criminal justice practice over the last thirty years.

Obviously, when it comes to moral philosophy, one cannot be impartial or relativistic. There are choices to be made, and these choices are translated into a particular criminology. In other words, we begin our inquiries with an implicit moral philosophy, and we advance a particular understanding of crime. This is what makes criminology a vital and relevant field of inquiry and practice.

Social Construction of Reality

The social constructionist prespective assumes that reality— our perception of reality—is a mental contstruction rather than a direct apprehension of the world. The social contructionist is interested not in the correspondence between "objective reality" and observation, but in the utility of observations in understanding our own multiple, subjective realities.

The constructs of the social scientist are thus founded upon the world created by social actors. Alfred Schutz conceptualized the problem: "The constructs of the social sciences are, so to speak, constructs of the second degree, that is, constructs of constructs made by the actors on the social scene, whose behavior the social scientist has to observe and explain in accordance with the procedural rules of his science" (Schutz, 1963:242). The world that is important to the social constructionist is the one created by human beings in interaction and communication with others. This *social reality* involves the social meanings and the products of the subjective world of everyday life (Berger and Luckmann, 1966).

The social constructionist mode of inquiry is a major advance over positivist thought in the crucial area of reflexivity. The social constructionist questions the process by which we know, instead of taking it for granted. The observer reflects upon the act of observation, using to advantage the social and personal character of observation.

It is often necessary to revise or reject the world as some social actors conceive it. Social constructionists give us the beginnings for examining multiple versions of reality, allowing us to transcend the official reality, and ultimately, our current existence. But they do not provide a yardstick for determining whether one reality is better than another.

The social constructionist perspective, however, has given new vitality to the study of crime. Departing significantly from positivist studies, social constructionists have exposed the problematic nature of legal order. Crime and other stigmatized behaviors are examined as categories created and imposed upon some persons by others (Becker, 1963). Crime exists because the society constructs and applies the label of crime. Criminal law, too, is not separate from society, but is itself a construction, created by those who are in power. The administration of justice is a human social activity that is constructed as various legal agents interpret and impose their order on those they select for processing. The social realtiy of crime is thus a process whereby conceptions of crime are constructed, criminal laws are established and administered, and behaviors are developed in relation to these definitions of crime (Quinney, 1970).

Judeo-Christian Theology and Prophetic Criticism

The roots of our contemporary world, in spite of secularity, are firmly anchored in the Judeo-Christian understanding of human existence and fulfillment. We have an image of our essential nature and the possibilities for our human existence. This essence, however, has become separated from the conditions of this world, contradicted by human existence. The separation between reality and essence can be overcome only by human action through the creative power of redemption. The modern historical consciousness, in other words, is derived from the historical thinking of the Judeo-Christian prophetic tradition (Quinney, 1980b:102–115).

Deeply rooted in the prophetic religious tradition is the urge toward justice in human affairs. This urge is seen as the will of divine origin operating in history, providing the source of inspiration to all prophets and revolutionaries. The identification of religion with political economy can be seen in the Hebrew prophets, who looked on all history as the divine law in human life. The highly ethical religion of the Old Testament prophets and the New

Testament Jesus sees human society from the perspective of a holy and just God who forgives human beings but also judges them. The prophetic soul is hopeful and optimistic in the "confidence that God will form a better society out of the ashes of the present world" (Dombrowski, 1936:26). The future in this world is built on the prophetic impulse that transcends this world.

Our prophetic heritage perceives the driving force of history as the struggle between justice and injustice. We the people—in a covenant with God—are responsible for the character of our lives and our society, for the pursuit of righteousness, justice, and mercy. The social and moral order is consequently rooted in the divine commandments; morality rests on divine command and concern.

Prophecy thus proclaims the divine concern for justice. The idea and belief that "God is justice" means the divine support and guidance for such human matters as the critique of conventional wisdom, the humanization of work, the democratization and social-ization of the economy, and the elimination of all forms of oppres-sion (Soelle, 1976). Material issues are conceived in terms of the transcendent, adding the necessary element that is missing in a strictly materialist (including Marxist) analysis. Prophetic justice is both sociological and theological. In fact, the dialectic of the the-ological and the sociological gives the prophetic its power as a cri-tique and an understanding of human society.

To the prophets of the Old Testament, injustice (whether in the form of crime and corruption or in the wretched condition of the poor) is not merely an injury to the welfare of the people but a threat to existence. Moral comprehension, in other words, is rooted in the depth of the divine. This is a sense of justice that goes far beyond our modern liberal and legalistic notions of justice. For the prophets, the worldly virtue of justice is founded on the under-standing that oppression on earth is an affront to God. Righteous-ness is not simply a value for the prophet; it is, as Abraham J. Hes-chel observes, "God's part of human life, God's stake in human history" (1962, vol. 1:198). The relation between human life and the divine is at stake when injustice occurs. Justice is more than a nor-mative idea; it is charged with the transcendent power of the infi-nite and the eternal, with the essence of divine revelation.

For the prophets, justice is a mighty stream, not merely a cat-egory or mechanical process. "The moralists discuss, suggest, coun-sel; the prophets proclaim, demand, insist" (Heschel, vol. 1:215). Prophetic justice is charged with the urgency of the divine presence in the world.

> Let justice roll down like waters,
> And righteousness like a mighty stream. (Amos 5:24)

In Heschel's phrase, "What ought to be, shall be!" Prophetic justice has a sense of urgency and depth.

According to the prophetic view, justice—or the lack of it—is a condition of the whole people. An individual's act expresses the moral state of the many.

> Above all, the prophets remind us of the moral state of a people: Few are guilty, but all are responsible. If we admit that the individual is in some measure conditioned or affected by the spirit of society, an individual's crime discloses society's corruption. In a community not indifferent to suffering, uncompromisingly impatient with cruelty and falsehood, continually concerned for God and every man, crime would be infrequent rather than common (Heschel, vol. 1:16).

Prophecy is directed to the whole world as well as to the inner spirit of the individual. And the purpose of prophecy—and of prophetic justice—is to revolutionize history.

We live in an era that tends to reject the claims of a religion-based prophetic theology. Heschel notes that "owing to a bias against any experience that eludes scientific inquiry, the claim of the prophets to divine inspiration was, as we have seen, *a priori* rejected" (vol. 2:192). A scientific rationality based entirely on empirical observation of this world excludes the prophetic critique of our existential estrangement from essence. History and its concrete conditions, accordingly, are bounded solely by time; there is little that would guide us beyond the mortality of our earthly selves. Which also means that an evaluation and judgment of our current situation are limited by the particular historical consciousness that comprehends nothing beyond itself. Not only have we silenced God, we have silenced ourselves before our own history.

The prophetic meaning of justice is in sharp contrast to the capitalist notion of justice. Distinct from capitalist justice, with its emphasis on human manipulation and control, prophetic justice is a form of address that calls human beings to an awareness of their historical responsibility and challenges them to act in ways that will change the existing human condition. Human fulfillment is found in the exercise of moral will in the struggle for a historical future. The pessimistic character of a deterministic and predictive materialism is overcome in the prophetic hope for a humane and spiritually filled existence.

The prophetic tradition, present also in the prophetic voice of Marxism (although in secular terms), can transform the world and open the future. Marxism and theology confront each other in ways that allow us to understand our existence and consider our essential nature. The human situation, no longer completely bounded by time, is "elevated into the eternal and the eternal becomes effective in the realm of time" (Tillich, 1971:91).

Marxist Analysis and Social Justice

The classic dichotomy about the meaning of justice dominates the discourse of contemporary social science and ethics (Quinney, 1980a:1–37). The dichotomy is found in the debate between Socrates and Thrasymachus chronicled by Plato in the first book of the *Republic*. When the question "What is justice?" is posed, Thrasymachus responds that "justice is the interest of the stronger," elaborating that what is regarded as just in a society is determined by the ruling elite acting in its own interest (Pitkin, 1972:169–192). Later Socrates gives his formulation of justice as "everyone having and doing what is appropriate to him," that is, people trying to do what is right.

Thrasymachus and Socrates are talking about two different problems. Whereas Thrasymachus is giving us a factual description of how justice actually operates, Socrates is telling us about what people think they are doing when they attend to that which is called "justice." There is justice as an ideal of goodness and justice in practice in everyday life. Justice as officially practiced in contemporary society is the justice of the capitalist state, and capitalist justice partakes of both the ideal and the practical. The question for us, then, given a Marxist understanding of the class and state character of capitalist justice, is, How do we attend to correct action and the creation of a better life?

The general concept of justice serves the larger purpose of providing a standard by which we judge concrete actions. We reflect critically upon the actions of the capitalist state, including the administration of criminal justice, because we have an idea of how things could be. Critical thought and its consequent actions are made possible because we transcend the conventional ideology of capitalism. Because we have a notion of something else, we refuse to accept capitalist justice either in theory or in practice. Critical thought, as Hannah Arendt (1971) has noted, allows us to interrupt all ordinary activity, entering into a different existence: "Thinking, the quest for meaning—rather than the scientist's thirst for knowledge for its own sake—can be felt to be 'unnatural,' as though men, when they begin to think, engage in some activity contrary to the human condition" (424). In talking and thinking about how things could be, we engage in thoughts and actions directed to the realization of a different life. Arendt adds that only with the desiring love of wisdom, beauty, and the like are we prepared with a kind of life that promotes a moral existence. Only when we are filled with what Socrates called 'eros,' a love that desires what is not, do we attempt to find what is good. Thinking and acting critically is thus political. In a collective effort, we change our way of life and alter the mode of social existence.

If any body of thought has a notion of truth and beauty, of how things could be, it is that of Marxism. In fact, Marxism is the philosophy of our time that takes as its primary focus the oppression inherent in capitalist society. Marxist analysis is historically specific and locates contemporary problems in the existing political economy. Marxist theory provides, most importantly, a form of thought that allows us to transcend in theory and in practice the oppression of the capitalist order.

Marx avoided the use of a justice terminology (McBride, 1975; Wood, 1972), steering away from justice-talk because he regarded it as "ideological twaddle," detracting from a critical analysis of the capitalist system as a whole. Both Marx and Engels were in fact highly critical of the use of the justice notion, employed as a means of mystifying the actual operation of capitalism. At the same time, they found a way to understand capitalism critically that carried with it a condemnation that goes beyond any legalistic notion of justice. Thus, Marxist analysis provides us with an understanding of the capitalist system, a vision of a different world, and a political life in struggling for that society.

According to Marx and Engels, the problem with the concept of justice, as it is used in capitalist society, is that it is fundamentally a juridical or legalistic concept. As such, the concept is restricted to rational standards by which laws, social institutions, and human actions are judged. This restricted analysis fails to grasp the material conditions of society. For Marx, society is to be understood in terms of productive forces and relations, with the state as an expression of the prevailing mode of production (Marx, 1970:19–23). To focus on the juridical nature of social reality is to misunderstand the material basis of reality. An analysis limited to legalistic questions of justice systematically excludes the important questions about capitalist society.

The critique of capitalism for Marx is provided in the very form of the capitalist system. Capitalism rests on the appropriation of labor power from the working class. Capital is accumulated by the capitalist class in the course of underpaying the workers for products made by their labor. The capitalist mode of production depends on 'surplus value,' on unpaid labor. Capitalism itself is a system of exploitation. The servitude of the wage laborer to capital is essential to the capitalist mode of production. Marx's condemnation of capitalism and the need for revolutionary action is based on the innate character of capitalism, on an understanding of capitalism as a whole and on its position in human history.

We have thus moved out of the classical dichotomy between value and fact. In a Marxist analysis, value and fact are integrated into a comprehensive scheme. Values are always attached to what we take to be facts, and facts cannot exist apart from values. In a Marxist analysis, the description of social reality is at the same time an evaluation. Nothing is "morally neutral" in such an understanding. The description contains within itself its own condemnation and, moreover, a call to do something about the condition. The critique is at once a description of the condition and the possibility for transforming it. All things exist in relation to one another—are one with the other.

The critical sense of justice will not disappear from philosophical and everyday discourse. That the terms "justice" and "social justice" continue to move us is an expression of their innate ability to join our present condition with an ultimate future.

Buddhism and the Way of Awareness

There is a mode of inquiry that assumes the critical mode but ultimately goes beyond it. This is the way of awareness (Quinney, 1988 and 1991). The way of awareness is essentially critical in that it sees things as they actually are, yet it goes beyond the critical mode of thought in its meditative character, requiring a quieting of the mind and an opening of the heart. Correct thought and action come out of such awareness. The way of awareness is the appropriate mode for the developing peace and social justice perspective in criminology.

Critical thought, especially as manifested in the way of awareness, seeks to avoid the personal and social consequences of what
modern science labels as "objective" and "rational." For, as one
humanistic philosopher has noted (Skolimowski, 1986), the mind
trained in such science "over a number of years becomes cold, dry,
uncaring, always atomized, cutting, analyzing. This kind of mind
has lost the capacity for empathy, compassion, love" (306). The
"objective" mode of thinking affects the way people live, and in the
meantime prevents them from getting any closer to understanding.
The way of awareness seeks a mind that, instead of producing conflict and violence, heals—a compassionate mind rather than an
objective mind.

We humans—and this is what especially makes us human—
have constructed webs of significance within which we have suspended ourselves. The *Dhammapada* (1936), the ancient text of
Buddhism, thus states, "All that we are is a result of what we have
thought" (3). And it is our human nature not only to be suspended
in webs of significance but to try to understand them, to search for
their meaning. We attempt to remove ourselves from the world of
everyday life in order to understand it in a new light. The human
mind is a busy and insatiable creation, craving always what is not.

Thus we come to the realization that rational thought alone
cannot answer the important existential questions of being human,
of being human in relation to the whole world. Cultivation of the
vital energy of the universe, rather than mere intellectual speculation, is the way to self-realization and to an understanding of our
shared existence. The way is simple, perhaps too simple and acces-
sible for the rational, complex academic mind to comprehend readily.

Without awareness—without mindfulness—we are unknowingly attached to our thoughts, taking these productions to be reality itself. Many of our concepts are so deeply ingrained in our
minds, in our culture, and in our education, that we forget that they
completely condition our perceptions of reality. In unconscious
attachment to these mental productions, we are chained in the
cave, observing merely the shadows of appearance on the walls
before us. Awareness is a breaking of the chains of conditioned
thought and a viewing of reality beyond the shadows. With awareness, we use concepts without being a slave to them, knowing that
they convey a conventional reality.

We begin by being aware of the ways in which suffering is
manifested. Our responsibility is to do what we can to alleviate the

concrete conditions of human suffering. "We work to provide food for the hungry, shelter for the homeless, health care for the sick and feeble, protection for the threatened and vulnerable, schooling for the uneducated, freedom for the oppressed" (Dass and Gorman, 1985:87). When we acknowledge what is and act as witnesses in this shared reality, without attachment and judgment, we open ourselves to all suffering. Acting out of compassion, without thinking of ourselves as doers, we are witnesses to what must be done.

As long as there is suffering in the world, each of us suffers. We cannot end our suffering without ending the suffering of all others. In being witnesses to the concrete reality, and in attempting to heal the separation between ourselves and true being (the ground of all existence), we necessarily suffer with all others. But now we are fully aware of the suffering and realize how it can be eliminated. With awareness and compassion, we are ready to act.

Awareness places us in the proper position to know the world, to pursue *a criminology with awareness*. Ultimately, only through awareness—beyond conditioned thought—can we understand reality as it truly is. We then begin to live in a way that takes us beyond the problems of contemporary existence, beyond the problem of crime. We would not leave society, not withdraw from fellowship with others; rather we would renounce the appearances of reality in order to live a life of love, and compassion, and union with all beings. We would be part of the process of creating a world without crime.

Socialist Humanism and Peacemaking Criminology

Social action comes out of the informed heart, out of the clear and enlightened mind. We act with an understanding of our own suffering and the suffering of others. If human actions are not rooted in compassion, these actions will not contribute to a compassionate and peaceful world. "If we cannot move beyond inner discord, how can we help find a way to social harmony? If we ourselves cannot know peace, be peaceful, how will our acts disarm hatred and violence?" (Dass and Gorman, 1985:185). The means cannot be different from the ends; peace can come only out of peace. "There is no way to peace," said A. J. Muste (1942). "Peace is the way."

As in Mahatma Gandhi's *satyagraha*, the truth is revealed in the course of action. And, in turn, it is truth as presently conceived that guides our action. Gandhi's Hindu and Jainist based concept of *satyagraha* was derived from the Sanskrit word *Sat* for "it is" or "what is," things as they are. *Graha* is "to grasp," to be firm. "Truth force" is the common translation of *satyagraha*. Gandhi often spoke of his inner voice, a still small voice that would be revealed in the preparedness of silence (Erikson, 1969:410–423).

Truthful action, for Gandhi, was guided by the idea of *ahimsa*, the refusal to do harm. Oppression of all kinds is to be actively resisted, but without causing harm to others. In *An Autobiography: The Story of My Experiments with Truth* (1957), Gandhi describes *ahimsa* as the refusal to do harm (349). Moreover, compassion and self-restraint grow in the effort not to harm.

Gandhi's insistence upon the truth is firmly within the tradition of socialist humanism. As Kevin Anderson (1991) has shown in his essay on Gandhian and Marxist humanism, both are radical rejections of Western capitalist civilization (14–29). Both posit a future society free of alienation, and both share a confidence that human liberation is on the immediate historical agenda. In reconstructing criminology, we are informed by a socialist humanism (Quinney, 1995).

In his 1965 collection of essays, *Socialist Humanism*, Erich Fromm included an essay on Gandhi by the Gandhian scholar and former secretary to Gandhi, N. K. Bose. In this essay, titled "Gandhi: Humanist and Socialist," Bose (1965) describes the *satyagrahi*, the one who practices *satyagraha*, as a person who lives "according to his own lights," one who opposes (does not cooperate with) what seems wrong, but also one who "attempts to accept whatever may be right and just" in the view of the opponent. Bose continues: "There is neither victory nor defeat, but an agreement to which both parties willingly subscribe, while institutions or practices proven wrong are destroyed during the conflict" (99). A humane society is created in the course of individual and collective struggle.

To be remembered, all the while, is the single objective of peace. Whatever the technique, whatever the philosophy or theory, the movement toward peace is the only true test of any thought or action. Erich Fromm spent a lifetime working in the movements for peace. He was a cofounder of SANE, an organization that sought to end the nuclear arms race and the war in Vietnam. Late in his life, Fromm worked on behalf of the 1968 presidential nomination campaign of Senator Eugene McCarthy. During the campaign, Fromm (1994) wrote: "America stands today at the crossroads: It can go in the direction of continued war and violence, and further bureaucratization and automatization of man, or it can go in the direction of life, peace, and political and spiritual renewal." His call was to "walk the way toward life" (96).

Our response to all that is human is for life, not death. What would a Gandhian philosophy of existence offer a criminologist, or any member of society, in reaction to crime? To work for the creation of a new society, certainly. But, immediately, the reaction would be neither one of hate for the offender, nor a cry for punishment and death. Punishment is not the way of peace. In a reading of Gandhi, and a commentary on punishment, Erik Erikson writes the following:

> Gandhi reminds us that, since we can not possibly know the absolute truth, we are "therefore not competent to punish"—a most essential reminder, since man when tempted to violence always parades as another's policeman, convincing himself that whatever he is doing to another, that other "has it coming to him." Whoever acts on such righteousness, however, implicates himself in a mixture of pride and guilt which undermines his position psychologically and ethically. Against this typical cycle, Gandhi claimed that only the voluntary acceptance of self-suffering can reveal the truth latent in a conflict—and in the opponent (412–413).

Responses to crime that are fueled by hate, rather than generated by love, are necessarily punitive. Such responses are a form of violence that can only beget further violence. Much of what is called "criminal justice" is a violent reaction to, or anticipation of, crime. The criminal justice system, with all of its procedures, is a form of *negative peace*, its purpose being to deter or process acts of crime through the threat and application of force.

Positive peace, on the other hand, is something other than the deterrence or punishment of crime. Positive peace is more than merely the absence of crime and violence—and of war. "It refers to a condition of society in which exploitation is minimized or eliminated altogether, and in which there is neither overt violence nor the more subtle phenomenon of structural violence" (Barash, 1991:8). Positive peace demands that attention be given to all those things, most of them structured in the society, that cause crime, that happen before crime occurs. Positive peace exists when the sources of crime—including poverty, inequality, racism, and alienation—are not present. There can be no peace—no positive peace— without social justice. Without social justice and without peace (personal and social), there is crime. And there is, as well, the violence of criminal justice.

The negative peacemaking of criminal justice keeps things as they are. Social policies and programs that are positive in nature—that focus on positive peacemaking—create something new. They eliminate the structural sources of violence and crime. A critical, peacemaking criminology is a form of positive peace.

Socialist humanism gives attention to everyday existence, to love and compassion, and to social justice. Its efforts are exerted not so much out of resistance, as in an affirmation of what we know about human existence. The way is simply that of peace in everyday life.

Criminologist as Witness

Upon reviewing the preceding account, I am struck by the apocalyptic vision embodied in much of Western moral philosophy. The notion that there is an ultimate destiny, that history is moving in the direction of fulfillment, and that the better world—the new kingdom—will come with the catastrophic collapse of the old order. Such a notion provides an imperative to make a better world, but at the same time promotes a judgment that impedes the humane living of daily life.

In contrast, Eastern thought, Buddhism particularly, identifies historical change with increasing individual awareness. As individuals transform their limited selves into an identification with the larger world, a more compassionate and humane existence is created. And in our own Western version of this mode of thought, Existentialism, the focus is on the living of everyday life. If attention is given to everyday life, the result cannot be other than the creation of a better world. Criminology—as moral philosophy—cannot help but be a part of the major thoughts and trends of the age.

But now I need to return to my thesis that criminology is, in addition to anything else, a stance for the witnessing of contemporary history. And that being witnesses, we criminologists occupy an important place in this history. What is more, witnessing is an active endeavor, not a passive observation. I was criticized by a colleague and long-time friend, shortly after my trip to Albany, for advocating what seemed to him an inactive role for the criminologist. In a session on "War and Peace," devoted specifically to terrorism and state-sponsored crime, at the annual meeting of the

American Sociological Association held in Toronto, I advanced the position that the criminologist is witness to the important events of the time—the atrocities, the injustices, the many forms of violence, and the sufferings of many people. The idea—the reality—that the witness is an engaged participant apparently needs to be elaborated. Our current sensibility posits action in a limited and materialistic way. I make the case that bearing witness is active participation in the most ultimate sense.

Criminologists, for instruction on the bearing of witness, can become familiar with the many kinds of witnessing that are evident in a host of sources. Journalists, photographers, artists, social scientists, and many other writers report the sufferings throughout the world. For example, there are recent books on bearing witness to the Holocaust (Feingold, 1995), to sexual abuse (Morris, 1994), to AIDS (Kayal, 1993), and to the atrocities that took place in the course of Yugoslavia's disintegration (Rohde, 1997). There are the many books by photographers who have documented various aspects of the human condition (Blom, 1984; Goldin, 1996; Modotti, 1995; Richards, 1994; Salgado, 1993; Vishiac, 1993; Yamahata, 1995).

Begin now to read the books by social scientists in the light of being a witness. Your list will rapidly develop, and you will appreciate both new and older works in a new way. Then begin to see your own work—written or otherwise—as the work of bearing witness. You may even begin to consider anew what is to be done as a witness in our times—a witness to our sufferings, and to our joys.

The witness, obviously, is not a neutral observer, as the rigid materialist dichotomy of active agent and passive observer might suggest. The witness first has to be where the suffering is taking place. And once being there, the witness is moved by conscience to observe and to make the report. An Armenian poet (Siamanto, 1996) writes of the German woman who witnessed a mass killing nearly a century ago:

> This thing I'm telling you about,
> I saw with my own eyes.
> From my window of hell
> I clenched my teeth
> and watched the town of Bardez turn
> into a heap of ashes (Siamanto, 1996:41).

Even in the quiet of the monastery, witness is being borne. Alexander Pushkin, in his story "Boris Godunov," written in verse

form and completed in 1825, has the monk Primen speak of his witnessing the history of Czarist Russia. Writing by lamplight (as can
be seen in Mussorgsky's opera), Primen makes a final entry
(Pushkin,1918):

> One more, the final record, and my annals
> Are ended, and fulfilled the duty laid
> By God on me a sinner. Not in vain
> Hath God appointed me for many years
> A witness, teaching me the art of letters;
> A day will come when some laborious monk
> Will bring to light my zealous, nameless toil,
> Kindle, as I, his lamp, and from the parchment
> Shaking the dust of ages will transcribe
> My true narrations (14).

As the last lines portend, someday the report will be found,
and perhaps it will be valued and of use. But even in witnessing,
one cannot hope for anything beyond the act of witnessing. As the
ancient Vedic text instructs in the *Bhagavad Gita* (1985:34–36), "do
not to the results be attached." We are to get on with what is to be
done, following the conscience of the witness.

All of this is to illustrate, and to argue, that witnessing is
itself an act. The witness is appropriately placed—makes certain to
be in the right place at the right time—and actively observes and
(oftentimes) records and reports what is being witnessed. If other
actions more physical in nature follow, they follow because first
there has been the witnessing. Without prior witnessing, there will
be no subsequent action that is wise and appropriate. Witnesses act
with clarity and purpose because they have the awareness and conscience of a witness. Ready and with open mind, the witness truly
sees what is happening, and knows what further action is to be
taken. Without witnessing, any action is unfocused, confused, and
little more than a chasing of the wind.

There is plenty for the criminologist to witness. Make your
own list of what we as criminologists should be witnessing. My
own current witnessing is to the kinds of suffering and violence
that are a systematic and structured part of contemporary existence. In fact, the largest portion of violence is structured and is
generated by, or committed by, governments, corporations, the
military, and agents of the law.

The war at home is against the poor. It is a war that is waged to maintain inequality so that the rich can maintain their position. Whole populations are being held hostage in poverty, sickness, addiction, brutality against one another, and they remain unemployed (or underemployed) and uneducated. Prisons are overflowing, and prison construction and operation are growing industries. The rich not only create the war, to secure their position, but also profit from the war. In our own nonviolent actions and protests, founded on witnessing, we take our stand. Which side are you on? is still the relevant question.

Directly associated with the war on the poor—the war to keep a minority of the population rich—is capital punishment. The death penalty—state-sponsored murder—is the final resort of a violent and greedy minority. That so many, the majority of the population when polled, support the practice of capital punishment is all the more reason that witnesses (criminologists) are needed to expose, to analyze, to protest, to bear witness. Someday, I am certain, historians will note that the United States was one of the last nations to continue to violate the most basic of human rights—the right to life. It was one of the last nations to systematically violate the rights of its own citizens.

In a critical essay titled "Reflections on the Guillotine," Albert Camus (1960) presented and discussed the many reasons offered for capital punishment and provided a rationale for abolishing it. Capital punishment is useless and harmful, he noted, and it besmirches the society that uses it. He wrote:

> It is a penalty, to be sure, a frightful torture, both physical and moral, but it provides no sure example except a demoralizing one. It punishes, but it forestalls nothing; indeed, it may even arouse the impulse to murder (197).

It is time to realize that there is no longer any defense for the death penalty. What is needed to achieve the abolition of capital punishment is a change in heart and mind, a spiritual and mental change.

I am certain capital punishment will eventually be abolished, but only when those who seemingly benefit from capital punishment, the minority known simply as the rich and the powerful, have lost their authority, have lost at least their authority to deny the basic human right of life.

As criminologists for the abolition of the death penalty, we are witnesses to life itself, and are a part of the movement to abolish capital punishment. For years, many criminologists have been arguing for the abolition of the death penalty (Bohm, 1991; Radelet, 1989; Zimring and Hawkins, 1986). We will continue to be witnesses to capital punishment until it is abolished. We cannot do otherwise.

To conclude my essay: Everything we do as criminologists is grounded in a moral philosophy. Whatever we think and do, our criminology is the advancement of one moral philosophy or another. And each moral philosophy generates its own kind of witnessing—in the events to be witnessed and in the form of the witnessing. The work in criminology that is historically important is the work that is informed by a moral philosophy. As witnesses, we are on the side of life. A reverence for all life. Such is the way of peace.

References

Anderson, Kevin. "Radical Criminology and the Overcoming of Alienation: Perspectives from Marxian and Gandhian Humanism." In Harold E. Pepinsky and Richard Quinney (eds.) *Criminology as Peacemaking*. Bloomington: Indiana University Press, 1991, pp. 14–29.

Arendt, Hannah. "Thinking and Moral Considerations," *Social Research* 38 (Autumn 1971):417–446.

Barash, David P. *Introduction to Peace Studies*. Belmont, CA: Wadsworth, 1991.

Becker, Howard. *Outsiders: Studies in the Sociology of Deviance*. New York: Free Press, 1963.

Berger, Peter L. and Thomas Luckmann. *The Social Construction of Reality*. Garden City, NY: Doubleday, 1966.

The Bhagavad Gita. translated by Eknath Easwaran. Petaluma: Nilgiri Press, 1985.

Blom, Gertrude. *Gertrude Blom—Bearing Witness*, Alex Harris and Margaret Sartor, eds. Chapel Hill: University of North Carolina Press, 1984.

Bohm, Robert M., ed. *The Death Penalty in America: Current Research*. Cincinnati: Anderson, 1991.

Bonhoeffer, Dietrich. *Letters and Papers From Prison*. Edited by Eberhard Bethage. New York: Macmillan, 1971.

Bose, Nirmal Kumar. "Gandhi: Humanist and Socialist." In Erich Fromm (ed.) *Socialist Humanism*. Garden City, NY: Doubleday, 1965, pp. 98–106.

Camus, Albert. "Reflections on the Guillotine." *Resistance, Rebellion, and Death*, translated by Justin O'Brien. New York: Random House, 1960, pp. 175–234.

Dass, Ram and Paul Gorman. *How Can I Help? Stories and Reflections on Service*. New York: Alfred A. Knopf, 1985.

The Dhammapada. Translated by Irving Babbitt. New York: New Directions, 1936.

Dombrowski, James. *The Early Days of Christian Socialism in America*. New York: Columbia University Press, 1936.

Erikson, Erik H. *Gandhi's Truth: On the Origins of Militant Nonviolence*. New York: W.W. Norton, 1969.

Feingold, Henry L. *Bearing Witness: How America and Its Jews Responded to the Holocaust*. Syracuse: Syracuse University Press, 1995.

Fromm, Erich. *On Being Human*. New York: Continuum, 1994.

Gandhi, Mohandas K. *An Autobiography: The Story of My Experiments with Truth*. Translated by Mahedeu Desai. Boston: Beacon Press, 1957.

Goldin, Nan. *I'll Be Your Mirror*. Zurick: Scalo Verlag, 1996.

Heschel, Abraham J. *The Prophets*, Vols. 1 and 2. New York: Harper and Row, 1962.

Kayal, Philip M. *Bearing Witness: Gay Men's Health Crisis and the Politics of AIDS*. Boulder: Westview, 1993.

McBride, William Leon. "The Concept of Justice in Marx, Engels, and Others." *Ethics* 85 (April 1975):204–218.

Marx, Karl. *A Contribution to the Criticque of Political Economy*. Maurice Dobb, ed. New York: International Publishers, 1970.

Modotti, Tina. *Tina Modotti: Photographs*. Sarah M. Lowe, ed. New York: Harry N. Abrams, 1995.

Morris, Celia. *Bearing Witness: Sexual Harrassment and Beyond—Every Woman's Story*. Boston: Little, Brown, 1994.

Muste, A. J. *The World Task of Pacificism*. Wallingford, PA: Pendle Hill, 1942.

Pitkin, Hanna F. *Wittgenstein and Justice*. Berkeley: University of California Press, 1972.

Pushkin, Alexander. *Boris Godunov*, translated by Alfred Hayes. New York: Dutton, 1918.

Quinney, Richard. *The Social Reality of Crime*. Boston: Little, Brown, 1970.

——. *Class, State, and Crime*, Second edition. New York: Longman, 1980.

——. *Providence: The Reconstruction of Social and Moral Order*. New York: Longman, 1980.

——. "Beyond the Interpretive: The Way of Awareness." *Sociological Inquiry* 58 (Winter 1988):101–116.

——. "The Way of Peace: On Crime, Suffering, and Service." In Harold E. Pepinsky and Richard Quinney (eds.), *Criminology as Peacemaking*. Bloomington: Indiana University Press, 1991, pp. 3–13.

——. "Socialist Humanism and the Problem of Crime: Thinking about Erich Fromm in the Development of Critical/Peacemaking Criminology." *Crime, Law and Social Change* 23 (November 2, 1995):147–156.

Radelet, Michael L., ed. *Facing the Death Penalty: Essays on a Cruel and Unusual Punishment*. Philadelphia: Temple University Press, 1989.

Richards, Eugene. *Cocaine True, Cocaine Blue*. New York: Aperature, 1994.

Rohde, David. *Endgame: The Betrayal and Fall of Srebrenica: Europe's Worst Massacre Since World War II*. New York: Farrar, Strauss and Giroux, 1997.

Salgado, Sebastiao. *Workers*. New York: Aperature, 1993.

Schutz, Alfred. *"Concept and Theory Formation in the Social Sciences."* In Maurice Nathanson (ed.), *Philosophy of the Social Sciences*. New York: Random House, 1963, pp. 231–249.

Siamanto. *Bloody News From My Friend*, translated by Peter Balakian and Nevart Yaghlian. Detroit: Wayne State University, 1996.

Skolimowski, Henryk. "Life, Entropy and Education." *The American Theosophist* 74 (October 1986):304–310.

Soelle, Dorothee. Review of *Marx and the Bible* by José Miranda, *Union Seminary Quarterly Review* 32 (Fall 1976):49–53.

Tillich, Paul. *Political Expectation*. New York: Harper and Row, 1971.

Vishiac, Roman. *To Give Them Light: The Legacy of Roman Vishiac*. Marion Wiesel, ed. New York: Simon and Schuster, 1993.

Wood, Allen W. "The Marxian Critique of Justice." *Philosophy and Public Affairs* 1 (Spring 1972): 244–282.

Yamahata, Yosuke. *Nagasaki Journey: the Photographs of Yosuke Yamahata*, edited by Rupurt Jenkins. San Francisco: Pomegranate, 1995.

Zimring, Franklin and Gordon Hawkins. *Capital Punishment and the American Agenda*. Cambridge: Cambridge University Press, 1986.

Part II. Reflecting

ELEVEN

Journey to a Far Place: The Way of Autobiographical Reflection

The telephone call came late in the afternoon—"Dad is gone."
A hurried packing, a taxi ride from the Greenwich Village apart-
ment to Kennedy International, and the flight to Wisconsin. On a
snowy and windy night in November, we drove the sixty miles west
from Milwaukee's Billy Mitchell airfield to the farm. Another
return out of need—neither the first nor last. My mother stood
waiting in the darkness halfway between the house and the barn.

A night of uncertain sleep, awakening with feelings unformed.
Arrangements made in the daylight: selecting the cufflinks from
the top bureau drawer for the shirt he will be buried in; the talk
with the Methodist minister about details for the funeral service;
the confrontation with the mortician. I was told by the undertaker's
son at the public viewing that it would be healthy for me to pay my
respects to the body in the open casket—that psychological studies
indicated the importance of this last ritual. My desire was to
remember my father as he was alive, not letting go of the need to
know him and to be understood by him. Talking to the farm neighbors that I had not seen for years, I remained in one corner of the
large room until the lights went out.

The next day, gray at noon, we rode slowly through the streets
of Delavan to the Spring Grove cemetery where my grandparents
and great-grandparents were buried. Looking out the car window
into the light snow, I began wondering about my own journey. Since
that time, autobiographical reflection about this journey called life
has affected all my life and work.

Original source: *Humanity and Society* 8:2 (1984): 182–198.

Life as a Journey

The "hero on the journey" is one of the oldest and most pervasive myths in human cultures. In his study of the mythological
adventures of the hero, Joseph Campbell (1968) traces the rites of
passage in the myth—separation, initiation, and return. Leaving
the threshold of home, the hero journeys through an unfamiliar
world, filled with strangely intimate forces, some of which threaten
him and put him to the test, some giving him aid and sustenance.
A triumph is possible, represented by the gaining of knowledge, a
union with the creator, and the expansion of consciousness. If the
adventure is successful, the hero is able to return home.

The myth of the stages of life places each person in a larger
perspective, as part of the total image of humanity. No matter how
limited is each life, that life is an integral part of the totality of the
culture. Each person is connected to the common language, social
interaction, and cultural myth. And in the richest of cultures,
myths shared intimately and communally give direction and meaning to the journey of each life. In the enlargement of vision made
possible by the myth of the journey, the life of each person is
enhanced, enriched, and supported. A relation of the person to the
cosmos is established.

In other cultures, most notably in the "advanced" cultures,
such as our twentieth-century secular culture, directions for the
journey are not as concisely contained in myth. There is less communal sharing of ceremonies around the passages of life. Our wandering in the world is not tied explicitly to an essential meaning of
the journey. Each journey, for each individual, tends to be an original and idiosyncratic adventure. Our wanderings lack unity, and
one adventure along the way is not intimately related to another.
Without the shared symbols of a humane culture, we are left to find
life's course on our own. We tend not to know who we are and where
we are going. Yet we still look for a sign, shared to whatever extent,
that will give meaning to our lives.

The image of fife as journey and pilgrimage has a universal
quality that has served human needs in a variety of cultures. As we
exhaust the possibilities of the secular culture, and as we find ourselves removed from a traditional Judeo-Christian religious tradition, the infusion into life of the transcendent and the universal
dimension of the life course may be the quality demanded of the age.

The metaphysic for everyday life that we are necessarily creating will likely incorporate the transcendent meaning of human

life in the process of its development. To what end we should live is a question that will not go away. It is a subversive question that makes us question our contemporary existence. In living our lives intentionally and in an ultimate way we are moved to actions of transformation, reconstructing our lives as well as changing the social and moral order.

The image of life as a journey—as a pilgrim's progress—informs many religious lives. Traveling through life, as travel of any kind, is a way of living. Bashō, the seventeenth century Japanese wanderer, took to the open road in the spirit of the Buddha, noting, "With no home 'twixt heaven and earth; travelers two," meaning "Homeless I wander, in the company of God" (Bashō, 1980:12). At the same time, the son of an English tinsmith, John Bunyan, was writing of the pilgrim's journey, of one greatly distressed, who at the beginning of the journey cries out, "What shall I do to be saved?" (Bunyan, 1964:18). That the journey of life, through time and space, should be of ultimate purpose is the message of the traveler.

To consider one's life in an autobiographical reflection is in the same tradition as the religious journey. As with the prophets of the Old Testament, but likely with less assurance of divine revelation, the modern traveler is placing a life in the context of something greater than itself. One's life is given meaning by the relation of that life to the needs of the human community and to the nature of the whole world. And in the course of autobiographical reflection one is prompted to a higher calling in the life that remains. In prophetic autobiography, as one literary critic (Couser, 1979:3) has termed this form of writing, one interprets one's own history and the history of the community in the light of God's will; the prophetic autobiographer serves "as a representative of his community—as a reformer of its ethos, articulator of its highest ideals, interpreter of its history, and activist in the service of its best interests." In an awareness of the divine, the transcendent, the prophetic autobiographer attends to the needs of contemporary existence—to the concerns of love and beauty and justice.

Life lived consciously as a journey is a life lived deliberately. With the awareness of the human need to intend life's journey, Henry David Thoreau built his cabin and lived in the woods for two years—in the solitude of nature—to contemplate and intensify the meaning of life. In his Walden journal, he wrote (1973:90): "I went to the woods because I wished to live deliberately, to front only the essential facts of life, and see if I could not learn what it had to teach, and not, when I came to die, discover that I had not lived." Completing his "experiment" after experiencing all of the seasons, Thoreau observed (1973:323–324) that he had met "with a success unexpected in common hours," and that through such experience "new, universal, and more liberal laws" are established around one, and that one comes to "live with the license of a higher order of beings." In the intense experience of contemplation, in a reflection upon nature, a foundation for a truly meaningful human existence was found.

Through autobiographical reflection, then, we come finally to the pilgrimage. Driven by the desire for satisfactions that are not supplied in a mundane existence devoid of the transcendent, we seek now to live deliberately in relation to a larger meaning in the universe. As the monk in moments of silence realizes, life becomes a journey into the unknown (Malits, 1980:21–52). Although the infinite realms of mystery remain, characterizing the essence of the world, we seek a form that permits us once again to entertain a meaning in the world. Our true home, I am suggesting, is found in the search for a place in the world. Home is where there is meaning—in this place, here and now.

We are thus entering into a new narrative world as we enter the world of autobiographical reflection. As with all ventures into a new world, through language, metaphor, and the narrative, we are in the process of redescribing reality. The world becomes transformed; or, in a different imagery, we come to regain that which was lost in another way of telling the story.

Autobiographical Reflection

For American writers in particular, the story is one of setting forth and returning. Moreover, as a student of American culture (Gunn, 1980:5) has observed, "The typical American adventurer eventually discovers that the only realm of authentic human existence is a kind of spiritual no place in-between, a territory which can only be described and encompassed in the energized forms of art." Autobiographical reflection allows the narrator to move in time and through space, tracing a life from an early time to a later one, and interpreting that life as it involves a wandering across a geographical landscape.

My life, upon reflection, embodies the same mythology shared by other American writers. There is the leaving of home, a leave-taking that is for the gaining of distance, for the development of a larger perspective. At the same time, more prominent now than

ever, there is the desire for a return to home. The act of writing—
in the form of autobiographical reflection—is a means of traveling
over the landscape, through time. The hope is that in the travel, in
the tension of being in-between, a return can be made. What the
return will look like is part of the journey.

Reflective writing in such a mode is a homecoming. It is a
homecoming that is not a return to to the past but an understanding of the process of becoming. The past self which we seek—in a
place and time of origin—is an unfinished self (Winquist,
1978:9–11). Homecoming is never completed because there is
always the possibility that awaits further development. The return,
the homecoming, becomes a story that is prophetic in direction and
mythic in form. It is a tale of the search for a life that transcends—
but is made possible by—daily existence. Autobiographical reflection is a process of renewal, and of re-creation.

In attempting to live life as a myth, and in re-creating that life
as a myth, we understand our lives as filled with prophetic intent,
instead of being shaped retrospectively for a certain effect. Placing
our lives into a metaphysic greater than our single lives, we elevate
our story to the level of universal myth. The facts of reality emerge
and are comprehended in the context of myth. The transcendent
and true quality of our existence is realized in life lived and understood autobiographically as mythical. Autobiographical reflection is
by its very mode the elevation of life and the narrative to the level
of the universal. Without myth, our lives are disconnected from the
source of our natural being.

The autobiographical narrative is grounded necessarily in
concrete historical reality. Autobiographical reflection makes possible, in fact, the coming into consciousness of history. The autobiographical narrative is the form this consciousness takes. The subject of autobiographical writing is in part the self, a self becoming
conscious of itself in and as history. In the self-examination of autobiography there is the interaction of the private self with the
greater public and historical reality. The self is grasped in the context of history, and history is made conscious in the writing of autobiography. Both the author and history are reborn in the process of
autobiographical reflection.

The re-creation of history—the coming into consciousness of
history—creatively involves a transcendence of the past, an elevation of time into the perspective of meaning. The mythical situation
naturally exists in the act of autobiographical writing. On the art of
autobiography, Mutlu Blasing (1977:3) thus observes: "Due to the

discrepancy in autobiography between the time of the action and the time of the narration, a fictional situation already exists, since the experiencing 'I' is being created out of the memory and within the conceptual framework of the recording 'I'." A transcendence of some 'objective' past is the natural product of autobiographical writing. In the re-creation of the past a true expression of reality is found, a myth of meaning is created.

My past as known in autobiographical reflection—in the context of history—is a reconstruction based on what I have become. I know what I was at an earlier age on the knowledge of what I am now (see Erikson, 1969:97–102). And in the dialectic of past and present, the crises at each point of my life are shaped by my resolutions of crises at former times. Thus, the way I recall—and do not recall—has much to do with my own particular development (Erikson, 1979). We are now in the territory of the meaning of memory in autobiographical reflection.

"Memory is a kind of accomplishment," writes William Carlos Williams (1963:77), "a sort of renewal." He adds in the same lines that memory is "even an initiation, since the spaces it opens are new places inhabited by hordes heretofore unrealized." With the new objective of consciously reconsidering my life in time and history, I remember part of that which has become lost to me. The problem now is not the full recall of the past, for the past cannot be recalled fully, nor is such recall desired. I recall, instead, that which assists in interpreting what I have become. On the basis of what I have become, and the placement of this interpretation in a framework of meaning, I speak to the human and collective need for ultimate understanding.

The remembered past is a reality. Hamlin Garland (1928:378), finally speaking about his recall of a Midwest life, said, "Some say it is all an illusion, this world of memory, or imagination, but to me the remembered past is more and more the reality." I also return to the Midwest on the wings of memory, on the gift of a dream that permits a return. I come to dwell again in the world, in a place where I can find some rest in the search for a home.

The impulse to write autobiographically, then, is not so much the need completely and objectively to understand the past as it is to live fully in the present and to prepare for the future. My own autobiographical reflection (Quinney, work in progress) is not a story about the past but a consideration of what is yet to be. It is the next step of my life. And as such, autobiography is subversive as a literary form, "for there is no way of knowing beforehand what shape the account must finally take or under what guise it may contrive to present itself (Gray, 1981:71). Anything—recollections, poetry, confessions, letters—and in any narrative mode that will allow us to find our place in the world is part of the autobiographical form. In the act of writing, the autobiographer is making a dwelling place. Some rest is found in the telling of the story. My life at this moment depends on the telling. I write to save my life.

Yet a journey into the unknown or the forgotten is an uneasy rest. We are taken into the forest, into the darkness of our lives. Much of the journey is likely to be a night journey—a descent into the primitive and unconscious sources of our personal and collective being (see Conrad, 1950). I am now looking for the hidden self, and in that self I am looking into the depths of our humanity. I am looking for the noise that rings out from the moment of our origin. I am trying to find the underside of our collective conscience and our structured existence—all that comes out of the primordial and deeply held past.

The reconsideration of our past, especially our childhood, draws us into the depths of our human being. Gaston Bachelard (1971:124) has written that "in our reveries toward childhood, all the archetypes which link man to the world, which provide a poetic harmony between man and the universe, are, in some sort, revitalized." Autobiographers in reflecting on the original existence of childhood and youth open themselves to the world and become immersed in the world. As a dreamer, the autobiographer suspends time in reverence for the world. In the reverie of poetic flight our place in the cosmos is opened up to us. We are born again into the cosmos as we gain reverie toward the past.

Autobiographical reflection—in the solitary realm of reverie—may bring back to our lives what never actually took place. Reverie is a looking forward to a reunion with the universe in a reflection on what could have been. Bachelard (1971:112) writes: "In reverie we re-enter into contact with possibilities which destiny has not been able to make use of." The paradox of our reverie toward childhood is that the past once thought dead—or the past never fully realized in reality—has a future. We now have access to a harmony with the universe, to a life lived in the possibility of its destiny.

We are engaged in a regeneration. Our lives are being placed in historical consciousness and in the consciousness of the universe. My life is sought in the search for something beyond that life. In the loss of self in a larger universe there is re-creation, deliverance, and a redemption. Life lived and life yet to be lived are elevated to the symbolic, the mythical, and the eternal, to the metaphysical grounding of all natural existence. Rather than an egotistic withdrawal from reality—as usually portrayed in the Narcissus myth—the conscious reconsideration of one's life is a movement toward oneness with the universe. Only when Narcissus was unable to gain a clear image of himself in the fountain did he plunge into the water and drown himself.

A relentless self-scrutiny led Thoreau to Walden Pond. The reflection in the water of Walden Pond provided Thoreau with the mirror for a rediscovery of the self, and the meaning of that self in the whole of the world. But as Blasing (1977:9) has pointed out, a paradox in the conscious act of self-discovery is a heightening of the sense of separation from the world: "In Thoreau's world, the bond between the ego and the universe has already been severed, and his attempted return to the state of oneness must necessarily be stained with self-consciousness." Knowing ourselves as human beings separates us from the original union, but without the conscious search we are not fulfilling a part of our nature as human beings. The demand for wholeness is thereby increased (Blasing, 1977:10):

> In the act of searching for and trying to recapture the wholeness of childhood or of youth, however, the author becomes at the same time conscious artist and various fictional selves—from narrator to hero. The act of writing, then, which necessarily splinters the self, itself increases the demand for wholeness.

Autobiographical reflection separates us but makes possible a regaining of a harmony with the natural world.

Autobiography, among all other things, is the anticipation of death. It is the entertainment of my own death. Yet in connecting our lives to a transcendent meaning in the universe we are attempting to overcome death—to reconcile it, to give it meaning (see Quinney, 1982). In the finiteness of historical time and a life in that time we are attending to the eternal.

I return to the landscape of the Midwest to find my reflection in the universe. I am looking for a reflection that will lead to an understanding in the ultimate sense, an understanding that is observed in the Gnostic Gospel of Thomas (Robinson, 1977:118): "Whoever finds the interpretation of these sayings will not experience death." My story is an attempt to discover what is real in the journey toward home. Autobiographical reflection is a preparation of the soul for a unity with the world.

The Transcendent Narrative

Autobiographical reflection in the prophetic mode is a form of religious inquiry. It is a narrative of the search for meaning in the realm of ultimate concerns. The fundamental aim of the narrative is that of allowing us to dwell in the world, to find a home. In modern times the autobiographical narrative releases us from the profane and strives toward the transcendent meaning of our existence.

The narrative that reflects on the human condition is itself a phenomenon of transcendent quality. The narrative is a fact of modern cultures, translating what is known or apprehended in specific cultures to the telling. It is, as Hayden White (1980:5) reminds us, "the fashioning of human experience into a form assimilable to structures of meaning that are generally human rather than culture-specific." Taking the substance of existence in a specific culture, the narrative within the culture transports the inhabitants to realms beyond the culture. The narrative is by its very nature mythic; it is a form of transcendence.

Storytelling is as ancient as the language it uses; storytelling emerged out of the need to speak and to understand. Storytelling secures and increases our consciousness and extends the reality of our experiences. In the telling of the story we reflect back upon our selves and entertain what we could become. In a covenant with others in the culture, we gather around the campfire to tell tales, bearing witness to what we are, what we were, and what we are yet to be. As Ursula Le Guin (1980:198) tells us, as of old we huddle about the campfire in our own time to confirm our existence, "to take actions that prevent our dissolution into the surroundings." Telling the story, we attend to our place in the cosmos.

Storytelling—the writing, reading, and the speaking of the narrative—takes us into the landscape of possibility. The mundane facts of this world are transformed to a level beyond themselves, to the level of meaning. We are now in the realm of what will be, in the prophetic realm of the true meaning of our personal and collective being. Embodied in the contemporary narrative, whether in fiction or nonfiction, is a metaphysic, a yearning for the metaphysical in everyday life. The narrative is, in our own time, the vehicle for transcendence. In a time that the transcendent is denied in most other realms, the narrative provides us with the gift of transcendence.

The narrative, then, is a modern form of myth, the escape from time-present and the interpretation of concrete historical events in terms of what has already happened and what will be.

The narrative, as with mythic forms in other cultures, presents a sacred history; it relates an event to a meaning beyond that event. In the last analysis, Mircea Eliade (1963:141) notes, the "world reveals itself as language" in the narrative. Through the language of the narrative the world is apprehended and made significant. The myths in our contemporary culture are not so much in the language of gods and spirits, but are tales of the meaning of the mysterious in everyday life.

In the narrative, the modern human being is able to regain the transcendent experience. When we are reading and when we are writing we are "escaping from time.'" The function of literary expression is connected to that of mythology. This is evident in the reading of the modern novel, as Eliade (1963:192) indicates:

> To be sure, the time that one "lives" when reading a novel is not the time that a member of a traditional society recovers when he listens to a myth. But in both cases alike, one "escapes" from historical and personal time and is submerged in a time that is fabulous and transhistorical.

As long as we are engaged in the narrative form—in its writing and reading—we are immersed in our own mythological endeavor. In the narrative we are renewing our access to the world and we are finding a meaning in a world that transcends our own concrete historical lives.

We thus come to the narrative in the search for the meaning of our existence. In the writing and the reading of the literary text we are addressing questions that have traditionally been raised in religious texts and rituals. At a time in which the metaphysical is excluded from most realms of modern enterprise, literature provides us with the satisfactions and consolations formerly gathered in religious faith. As a consequence, those involved in the literary form "have come to place increasingly heavy demand upon literature, asking it to perform a redemptive function once reserved for religion alone (Gunn, 1979:71). In the quest for value and meaning, the reading and writing of the narrative gain the ultimacy of religious experience. The writing for reflection in particular—for me as for others—is a religious act. In the telling of the story I am in quest of transcendent meaning.

When we enter into autobiographical reflection we are engaging in the mythic equivalent of dwelling in a world of meaning. In a creative enterprise that is different from the scientific reporting of the outward facts of history, we are gaining conscious contact with the deeper meaning of our history. Where once we looked to the myths communicated in the tales of a community, we now look to the interior lives of those who communicate through their writing the meaning of our place in the world. "The mythogenetic zone today," notes Joseph Campbell (1976:93) "is the individual in contact with his own interior life, communicating through his art with those 'out there.'" The secrets of the world are known today in the narrative.

That the narrative may be a part of the creation of a shared tradition in an emerging age is our hope. We moderns no longer believe in the collective and sacred symbolism that once provided the metaphysical foundation for traditional cultures. What we moderns—or post-moderns—have is an interpretive understanding of the world. And in the understanding provided in the narrative we seek to hear again. The modern desire and possibility contained in language and the narrative are poetically observed by Paul Ricoeur (1969:349): "It is not regret for the sunken Atlantides that animates us, but hope for a recreation of language. Beyond the desert of criticism, we wish to be called again."

The understanding that is known through the narrative is both a disclosure and a creation. In the telling of the story we attempt simultaneously to hear the word of the universe and to speak and act in a way that will make the world anew. There is a re-creation of the transcendent out of the transcendent that is given; the creative word spoken at the beginning of time is disclosed and becomes the source for constructing a social existence in our time. We are reminded that "all proper human speech is prophecy in which the eternal word sounds forth" (Meagher, 1978:292). The narrative in our time is part of the process that allows us to know the universe. Our daily reflections are of ultimate consequence. The wanderer is able to return home when blessed in the journey from home. In the mythologies that pervade human cultures, the one who travels from home—as we all must—returns home when the sacred meaning of life is found, when the father-creator is accepted, or when the proper relation to the universe has been established (Campbell, 1968:246). The final work of the wanderer is that of the return. If the wanderer has not yet received these blessings, the journey away from home must continue. A home in the world still awaits the traveler

Where is the home that we seek? It is most often symbolized as being in the land of our birth. We are ourselves when we are surrounded by the landscape of our origins, by our native soil. Yet our home also is symbolized by a psychological and existential placement in the world that is not necessarily related to the place of our birth. Return to home we must, but where is this home—in the land or in our head? Or is the home in a union of place and mind, of place and soul? Home is where we finally are called. It is the place where we become lost and in so losing ourselves find ourselves and give ourselves to the world. The human journey is toward home.

We of the Midwest, especially we of the Midwest, wonder about and are bothered by the quest for home. Still firmly within the frontier experience of the midwestern pioneer—our lives within the grasp of the ancestral past—we need a home, but we fear the hidden meaning of home. To return home, we think, is to deny that part of us which is essential to our quest onward across the frontier. We continue to dream of home, yet we have the fear of our pioneer ancestors; we fear the permanence and stability that may come with the return home. "You can't go home again" is an expression that "is a warning to the individual that society, the hometown, the cozy rural smalltown community, can destroy all freedom" (Robertson, 1980:220). This cultural psychology recreates our uprootedness in each generation; it promises to make us wanderers in the world.

But there is another way to think about our return home. Returning home is itself an active process of regeneration. "Homecoming," a student of American religious culture (Winquist, 1978:9) writes, "is not a return to the past but it is a becoming into the future. The natural self with which we seek a reunion is an unfinished self." Homecoming is a dynamic part of our lives. To the extent that we allow it to exist, homecoming is the dimension of possibility that awaits our living. Homecoming is our future. I tell a tale of my homecoming as a part of my becoming human. The story is the ancient and eternal myth of the wanderer who in venturing out must return from the journey. The return is the necessary extension of the journey.

Certainly I cannot recover the special magic of a remembered childhood in the Midwest. Such a recovery is necessarily of the imagination, serving its own useful purpose. The magic is of a former time as Hamlin Garland (1979:67) well knew:

> It all lies in the unchanging realm of the past—this land of my childhood. Its charm, its strange dominion cannot return save in the poet's reminiscent dream. No money, no railway train can take us back to it. It did not in truth exist—it was a magical world, born

of the vibrant union of youth and firelight, of music and the voice of moaning winds—a union which can never come again to you or me, father, uncle, brother, till the coulee meadows bloom unscarred of spade or plow.

It was a childhood well lived—and beautifully and creatively recalled. But not one that can be recovered in a return home.

Further to the west, at a later time, another son of the frontier remembered a childhood. Looking back, Loren Eiseley (1973:113–14) wrote:

Through the night mist on the mountain I see far away a light in a farmhouse window on the plain, the mist mellowing it until it glows yellow as the kerosene lamps of my boyhood by which I first studied, the lamp of home far away in the mist.

Eiseley concluded, "I have rushed like a moth through time toward the light in the kitchen."

Wright Morris, a writer of the territory west of the Mississippi, is concerned with the problem of how to return to the home place and "come to terms with that past in a way that does not cripple, but rather nurtures the imagination" (Neinstein, 1979:122). He worries about a regional literature that is "strangling in the death grip of nostalgia for a past that is largely mythic and definitely over." In a confrontation with the present reality of the region, Morris hopes that there may be an imaginative repossession of the landscape, free of nostalgia. Hoped for, in the return, is the realization of an authentic relationship with the home place. In the return we are not to ride what Morris calls the Dead Wagon, living by outmoded myths, especially the myth of the frontier, the myth of inexhaustible resources, and the myth of our own national youth.

I suppose that most of us are unprepared for the world—coming from the home place. We have our times of being uncomfortable in the world, of being confused by it. Wright Morris (especially 1948, 1973) is suggesting that we should not become destroyed by a path that leads backward to a mythic past but, rather, we must live forward. Creative connections can be made with the past, connections that demythologize a past that never was. The home place is thereby transformed in the return. Going home can be, and should be, something that takes us forward, that takes us to what could be, rather than backward to something that never was. With such consciousness—aware of itself—we can return home to find our place in the world. The landscape of the home place gives us the foundation for our future living.

We return home to reappropriate our sense of who we are. In the landscape of the home place we recognize ourselves; we recognize ourselves in a way that we never have before. The return home provides us with a dwelling place for our emerging life. At home we can become ourselves, in relation to the universe. The home, as in the house described by Gaston Bachelard (1969:6), "shelters daydreaming, the house protects the dreamer, the house allows one to dream in peace." The dwelling place of home remains with us for all time, promoting our dreaming and living in the present. In the place we call home, we put down our roots, we love others and the world there, we become a part of the universe there; it is there that we become human. Without these, we remain forever homesick.

The return journey home is a forward movement in time. We are not nomads as long as we are on the journey toward home. We have ceased to be wanderers once we have started the journey home. Forever—as long as we remain centered in consciousness—we long to return home. The farm in Wisconsin forever furnishes me with an image of what is home. It is that visible place, that deeply loved place, that draws me home, that allows me to be on the journey toward home.

Preparations are being made. On a recent return to the farm in Wisconsin, I planted some trees down at the old place where the homestead house used to stand. I planted an apple tree in the aging orchard at the bottom of the sloping hill. Farther up the hill I have dug the holes where I will plant more trees when I visit the farm again.

A short time ago I awoke from a dream. My father was planting trees up the driveway to the farm. He was planting them for my return. On the top of the hill there is an old foundation that waits for the building of a house. Creator of all things, I do not know your name. I call you *home*. I begin to see now from the hill of a very old place.

References

Bachelard, Gaston. 1969. *The Poetics of Space.* Tr. Maria Jolas. Boston: Beacon Press.

———. 1971. *The Poetics of Reverie; Childhood, Language, and the Cosmos.* Tr. Daniel Russell. Boston: Beacon Press.

Bashō, Matsuo. 1980. *A Haiku Journey*. Tr. Dorothy Britton. New York: Kodansha International.

Blasing, Mutlu Konuk. 1977. *The Art of Life: Studies in American Autobiographical Literature*. Austin: University of Texas Press.

Bunyan, John. 1964. *The Pilgrim's Progress*. New York: New American Library.

Campbell, Joseph. 1968. *The Hero with a Thousand Faces*. 2nd ed. Princeton: Princeton University Press.

———. 1976. *The Masks of God: Creative Mythology*. New York: Penguin Books.

Conrad, Joseph. 1950. *Heart of Darkness* and *The Secret Sharer*. New York: New American Library.

Couser, G. Thomas. 1979. *American Autobiography: The Prophetic Modes*. Amherst: University of Massachusetts Press.

Eiseley, Loren. 1973. "The Mist on the Mountain." In *The Innocent Assassins*, pp. 113–15. New York: Scribner's.

Eliade, Mircea. 1963. *Myth and Reality*. Tr. Willard R. Traak. New York: Harper & Row.

Erikson, Erik H. 1969. *Gandhi's Truth: On the Origins of Militant Nonviolence*. New York: Norton.

———. 1979. "Reflections on Dr. Borg's Life Cycle." In *Adulthood*, ed. Erik H. Erikson, pp. 1–31. New York: Norton.

Garland, Hamlin. 1928. *Back—Trailers from the Middle Border*. New York: Macmillan.

———. 1979. (*1917*). *A Son of the Middle Border*. Lincoln: University of Nebraska Press.

Gray, Rockwell. 1981. "Time Present and Time Past: The Ground of Autobiography." *Soundings* 64:52–74.

Gunn, Giles. 1979. *The Interpretation of Otherness: Literature, Religion, and the American Imagination*. New York: Oxford University Press.

———. 1980. "New World Metaphysics and the Religious Interpretation of American Writing." University Lecture in Religion. Arizona State University, Tempe.

Le Guin, Ursula K. 1980. "It Was a Dark and Stormy Night: Or, Why Are We Huddling about the Campfire? *Critical Inquiry* 7:191–99.

Malits, Elena. 1980. *The Solitary Explorer: Thomas Merton's Transforming Journey*. New York: Harper & Row.

Meagher, Robert E. 1978. *Augustine: An Introduction*. New York: New York University Press.

Morris, Wright. 1948. *The Home Place*. New York: Scribner's.

———. 1973. *A Life*. New York: Harper & Row.

Neinstein, Raymond L. 1979. "Wright Morris: The Metaphysics of Home." *Prairie Schooner* 53:121–54.

Quinney, Richard. 1982. "Nature of the World: Holistic Vision for Humanist Sociology." *Humanity and Society* 6:322–44.

———. 1991. *Journey to a Far Place*. Philadelphia: Temple University Press.

Ricoeur, Paul. 1969. *The Symbolism of Evil*. Tr. Emerson Buchanan. Boston: Beacon Press.

Robertson, James Oliver. 1980. *American Myth, American Reality*. New York: Hill and Wang.

Robinson, James M. 1977. "The Gospel of Thomas." In The Nag Hammadi Library, ed. James M. Robinson. Tr. Members of the Coptic Gnostic Library Project of the Institute for Antiquity and Christianity. New York: Harper & Row.

Thoreau, Henry D. 1973. *Walden*. Ed. J. Lyndon Shanley. Princeton: Princeton University Press.

White, Hayden. 1980. "The Value of Narrativity in the Representation of Reality." *Critical Inquiry* 7:5–27.

Williams, William Carlos. 1963. *Paterson*. New York: New Directions.

Winquist, Charles E. 1978. *Homecoming: Interpretation, Transformation and Individuation*. Missoula: Scholars Press.

TWELVE

Try to Make it Real, Compared to What?

To create a world. A reality. Poised between faith and reason and space and information. The end of a long winter. Signs of a new season. Five ways to make it real.

Consider This: Impermanence and Transformation

All things change. Nothing remains the same. There is no permanent substance to anything. Everything is in the process of becoming something else. Water to wine; wine to blood. Body to dust. Larva to butterfly. Once I was blind but now I see.

Always the possibility of a new awareness. A deconstruction, a revisualization, a renewal. The construction of an alternative reality. And in practice, transformation of the old reality.

Let us entertain impermanence, change, the alternatives. Even before the technology of virtual reality, we humans imagined being elsewhere. We are mystics by birth. The sublime imagination entertaining an infinity of possibilities. Michael Heim (1993:137) thus writes these lines in his book *The Metaphysics of Virtual Reality*:

> The final point of a virtual world is to dissolve the constraints of the anchored world so that we can lift anchor—not to drift aimlessly without point, but to explore anchorage in ever-new places and, perhaps, find our way back to experience the most primitive and powerful alternative embedded in the question posed by Leibniz: Why is there anything at all rather than nothing?

Original source: *Studies in Symbolic Interaction*, Vol. 19, Edited by Norman K. Denzin. Greenwich, CT: JAI Press, 1995, pp. 199–211.

233

All things change, this mind included. Only nothing—that is, nothing, no thing that this human mind can shape into being, remains the same. But now we are in the territory of the sacred texts. Of wisdom literature. In the *Bhagavad Gita* (1985:155). Arjuna says to Sri Krishna, "Changeless, you are what is and what is not, and beyond the duality of existence and nonexistence." Sri Krishna gently responds to Arjuna (157):

> It is extremely difficult to obtain the vision you have had; even the gods long always to see me in this aspect. Neither knowledge of the Vedas, nor austerity, nor charity, nor sacrifice can bring the vision you have seen. But through unfailing devotion, Arjuna, you can know me, see me, and attain union with me. Whoever makes me the supreme goal of all his work and acts without selfish attachment, who devotes himself to me completely and is free from ill will for any creature, enters into me.

In the flux of change, in the human world, in the world of duality, we mortals can cling to nothing. Cling to naught is our earthly epistemology.

Let us Consider This: What is Real?

What can we perceive as real? As really real. As actually existing. As ontologically real. Simply to ask is to realize that reality is existential. All human perception is subject to the lived experience. Some years ago, during that ontological shift of the 1960s, I sat in the cafés and I walked the streets of Greenwich Village. Daily, without ceasing. The song was playing then, as it is now this day on the CD player. Les McCann's "Compared to What." After 30 years, this song still speaks to me. Singing of the events of the time, hoping to understand, McCann sings, "Everybody now, try to make it real compared to what." He wails the lines: "The goddamn nation. . . ." "The president he's got his war. Folks don't know what it's for." "But I can't use it." "Where's my God, and where's my money?" "Goddamn it, try to make it real compared to what."

In those days, I was trying to make my own song. One result was a book I called *The Social Reality of Crime* (1970). Shortly after its publication, Taylor, Walton, and Young (1973:253), in their influential book *The New Criminology*, wrote about my efforts: "Many of Quinney's statements about a theoretical orientation to the social reality of crime seem to be the product more of the author's own existential *Angst* than they are the result of clear-headed theoretical analysis." I remain to this day pleased with their observation. For one thing, I am happy to be counted among the existentialists. Albert Camus, I think of you daily. ("Mother died today, or maybe it was yesterday." [1988]) And secondly, "clear-headed theoretical analysis," abstract and removed from everyday life, is not something to which I aspire.

My questioning of the conventional scientific enterprise took further attack from Robert Merton (1976:175), in his book *Sociological Ambivalence*. He wrote:

> Now, it is one thing to maintain, with Weber, Thomas, and the other giants of sociology, that to understand human action requires us to attend systematically to its subjective component: what people perceive, feel, believe, and want. But it is quite another thing to exaggerate this sound idea by maintaining that action is *nothing but* subjective. That extravagance leads to sociological Berkeleyanism (the allusion being, of course, to the English champion of philosophical idealism, not to an American geographic or academic place). Such total subjectivism conceives of social reality as consisting *only* in social definitions, perceptions, labels, beliefs, assumptions, or ideas, as expressed, for example, in full generality by the criminological theorist, Richard Quinney, when he writes that "We have no reason to believe in the objective existence of anything." A basic idea is distorted into error and a great injustice is visited upon W. I. Thomas whenever his theorem is thus exaggerated.

I still do not know if I am a total subjectivist, or even what that might be. But it does seem to me that the subjective/objective debate is as much ideological as it is a statement about what is real and how we can know reality. The problem goes beyond a debate over the subjective and the objective. The matter has something to do with the human mind's ability to think and to see beyond its own innate construction. How can we know for certain of the existence of anything, including existence itself? The mind is the grand piano which provides the space for the mice—our thoughts—to play. We humans cannot step outside of our existence. And we cannot know, in the larger scheme of things, or non-things, if the grand piano is other than a dream. The dream of a cosmic dreamer. Why not?

It is not for us to know that which cannot be known. To seek such knowledge is not to be human. The simple teaching of Buddhism (Seung, 1982): "Only don't know." We have the mind to ask questions of the reality of our existence, universal and otherwise, but we do not have the capacity to answer with objectivity and certainty. (Camus [1955], again: "The absurd is the essential concept and the first truth.") Entirely reasonable, then, our perpetual ambivalence, our uncertainty, and our fear of life and death. Humility, mixed with wonder, makes more sense than the continuous pursuit of scientific knowledge.

We stand before the mystery of existence. Our understanding is in the recognition of our common inability to know for certain. Our fate, and our saving grace, is to be compassionate beings, in all humility. Whatever may be known is known in love. Not in manipulation and control, not in the advancement of a separate self and a career, but in the care for one another. That is reality enough.

Now Consider This: Truth and Existence

The really big problem. Truth. Of biblical proportions. Speaking to Pilate, Jesus said (at least this is what John says Jesus said), "My task is to bear witness to the truth. For this I was born; for this I came into the world, and all who are not deaf to the truth listen to my voice." To which Pilate asked of Jesus, "What is truth?" After this, according to Matthew, Pilate washed his hands of the whole matter.

This is but one of the human encounters with the idea of truth. Historical cultures—East and West—are filled with questions of truth. We thus lend our small voices to the great myth of human thought and existence: truth.

In these times, these postmodern times, the only approach to truth that makes sense is one that is existentially grounded. A notion of truth that is essentially intersubjective, sociological, experiential—existential. We remind ourselves, again and again, that any truth—as with all knowledge and understanding—occurs only in the context of personal existence.

Thus we welcome the publication of Jean-Paul Sartre's *Truth and Existence* (1992). Written in 1948, published posthumously in 1989, the English translation appeared in 1992. Sartre wrote the treatise after completing *Being and Nothingness* and before writing *Critique of Dialectical Reason*. The question for Sartre in this middle period was what can be known. The focus of the text is as much on ignorance as it is on truth. For Sartre, the existentialist, ignorance is an intentional act. And there is the moral question of avoiding the search for truth, as well as the moral question of bad faith, of not acting and taking responsibility when truth is known. Ignorance, as with truth, is relational and intersubjective—and of great consequence in human interaction.

To make a long story short, Sartre comes very close to arguing that an objective truth can be known directly through subjective intuition, his theory thus assuming a kind of absolute intuitionism. There is for Sartre the existence of truth, distinguishing his existential philosophy from a postmodern existentialism. Reality—the truth of reality—is self-evident and direct. Yet, truth is never simply given to us, but takes work and good intentions.

Our ontology of truth, as postmodern existentialists, is more relative than Sartre's. But Sartre already was moving in this direction as his text was being completed, and likely for this reason left the manuscript unpublished. *Truth and Existence* was abandoned because of its idealist ethics, as a "writer's ethics." A theory of truth abandoned because it was merely a "writer's conception of truth." Any truth, Sartre wrote, that is abstract and thus removed from the struggle of everyday life, is but a form of ignorance and bad faith. As such, Sartre (58) writes, "an *'idealist'* type of truth is created, i.e., truths that are statements about Being without contact with Being. Thus is created a kind of thought making truth the product of reasoning and of discourse that refuse intuition's fundamental revealing value." For the abstract person, knowledge replaces Being; the abstract person is one who is absent. Sartre (58) writes: "The abstract man thinks upon the thought of others, that is, on revelations that he does not bring about. He is like the mathematician who places himself at the level of complex formulas containing the operations to be undertaken, but who never carries out these operations. The abstract person *reasons* not because he does not see but *in order not to see*." Knowing everything while being ignorant of everything.

Sartre ends the posthumously published work with the call that will guide the rest of his life. I quote intact the last paragraph of *Truth and Existence* (80):

> Therefore we must make ourselves historical against a mystifying history, that is, historialize ourselves against historicity. This can be done only by clinging to the finitude of the lived experience as interiorization. It is not by attempting to transcend our age towards the eternal or towards a future of which we have no grasp that we will escape from historicity, on the contrary, it is by accepting to transcend ourselves only in and through this age, and by seeking in the age itself the concrete ends that we intend to propose to ourselves. If I know myself as, and want to be, part of my

age, I transcend it towards itself and not towards an age that has not yet arrived. I most certainly do not escape from historization, but it is a *minimal* historization: only of my age. By not pretending to be living with my grandchildren, I keep them from judging me by their standards. By giving them my act as a *proposition*, in order that they may do with it what they want, I escape the risk that they do with it something other than I wanted.

For us, in our times as well, our thoughts (committed to paper or to Internet) are fully within the context of our lived experience. Otherwise, we would merely possess a truth, an abstract truth, rather than live a truth (be a truth) that comes out of the struggle of our living and our knowing. The truth that comes from our own intersubjective struggle to be human—a truth however relative and lacking of the absolute—is the real truth. The reality, compared to what?—compared to a life not lived. Our writing, our thinking and our talking (as at the Stone Symposium) is an intimate part of the struggle for existence. We write and we talk in order to be present. Truth and reality may be the subject, but life is what is happening.

What Yet To Consider? The Thought of Interpretation

If, as social actors and cultural interpreters, our understanding of truth and reality is from within the confines of our personal and historical experience, how may we continue to explore and to investigate this world? That is, what happens when we realize that all thought is tentative and conditional, especially when our enterprise has assumed otherwise? When we finally realize that interpretive understanding is bound by what is understood in the first place?

We live, as Ricoeur (1969:351–352) observes, in the aura of the meaning we are inquiring after. He writes: "Hermeneutics proceeds from a prior understanding of the very thing that it tries to understand by interpreting it." (Again, the grand piano of our existence.) Rather than debilitating us, it seems to me, this realization is wonderfully liberating. A paradox, perhaps, that the more we are aware of our intellectual limitations, the more we realize what it is to be truly human. The reality test now is in how we live wholly—in spirit, in compassion with one another, in reconciliation with our unknowing, in releasement to mystery.

Just a few words to this realization as it applies to an interpretive sociology (for a larger discussion, see Quinney, 1988). In my own work, I have been helped by the writings and insights of Krishnamurti. Outside of Western thought, he has stressed the importance of achieving a freedom from preconceptions and a freedom from the conventional structures of the times (Powell, 1983). Although Krishnamurti does not use the term "hermeneutical circle," he has found a way to transcend the circle by posing the problem in a much different way. In a series of talks and books, Krishnamurti has repeatedly observed that we cannot arrive at understanding through creeds and dogmas (including scientism) and philosophical inquiry. Only through an awareness of the mind—beyond intellectual analysis and interpretation—can we understand.

The essential awareness is a state of mind or consciousness that is described in the esoteric literature of Hinduism and Buddhism. Awareness is not a product of thought; it is unconditioned. When there is complete attention—in awareness—there is no separation between the observer and the observed (Krishnamurti, 1975:95–98). What can be observed exists only in the field of the observer's awareness. The presumed division between the observer and the observed, maintained in positive science, is an illusion. Thus one must be attentive to the mind of the observer, to one's own mind with its memories, stored-up knowledge, its likes and dislikes, all of its assumptions. The mind must be watched. "When this observation is clear," Krishnamurti (1977:307) asks, "isn't there then a freedom from the observer?"

Thought, Krishnamurti notes, derives from the experience and knowledge of the past. Thinking is bound by what was, rather than what actually is. "Therefore," he says, "when you try to understand activity in the present, with the past, which is thought, you don't understand it at all" (1976:272). Are we able, then, if thought distorts the present, to discover anything new, to understand what is? The answer for Krishnamurti is in an awakening which is above and beyond thought. With awareness of the actuality of thought, awareness of thought's limitation, in a quieting of the mind, thought becomes different in its operation.

The question raised by Krishnamurti is whether we can see the world and understand it without the distortion of images created by thought. Krishnamurti recognizes that many images are necessary and desirable, having a valuable protective function. However, we carry with us many other images from the past that distort what we perceive in the present, and these images hamper our relationships with others and the world. As with thought, the ending of images comes with observation and awareness, not in analysis and further discursive thinking and interpretation. We begin, in the stillness of observation and awareness, by understanding the processes by which thought and images are created.

The problem of knowing is how to uncondition the mind. In one of Krishnamurti's talks, he asks (1972:59): "Is it possible to be so intensely aware of conditioning that you see the truth of it?—not whether you like or dislike it, but the fact that you are conditioned and therefore have a mind incapable of freedom." If this conditioning can be observed, we realize that we are the product of the past, living and knowing secondhand, constantly viewing the present (what actually is) through past conditioning. The only possible way of breaking out of this conditioning is through awareness. Krishnamurti (1976:70–71) observes:

> So I must be aware of my conditioning, which means, I must be aware of it not only superficially, but at the deeper levels. That is, I must be aware totally. To be so aware, means that I am not trying to go beyond the conditioning, not trying to be free of the conditioning. I must see it as it actually is, not bring in another element, such as: wanting to be free of it, because that is an escape from actuality, I must be aware. What does that mean? To be aware of my conditioning totally, not partially, means my mind must be highly sensitive, mustn't it? Otherwise I can't be aware. To be sensitive means to observe everything very, very closely—the colors, the quality of people, all the things around me. I must be aware of what actually is without any choice. Can you do that?—not trying to interpret it, not trying to change it, not trying to go beyond it or trying to be free of it—just to be totally aware of it.

This means we also go beyond the language which has conditioned us. Interpretation in Western phenomenology is firmly grounded in language. Gadamer (1976:68) has written: "Language is the real medium of human being; if we only see it in the realm it alone fills out, the realm of common understanding, or every-replenished common agreement—a realm as indispensable to human life as the air we breathe." All interpretation, in the Western mind, takes place in the medium of language. For Krishnamurti, however, drawing from the esoteric tradition of the East, we can go beyond the conditioning of language to an understanding of reality. It is only when we look without the movement of language and thought that we transcend our conditioning.

In the process of true learning—learning that actively takes place in the present—we focus our attention on what is actually happening; we go beyond the accumulated knowledge of the past. With "intelligence," as Krishnamurti calls it, with the ability to be free from the known, we are in the present, observing things as they are in their actuality. Krishnamurti (1977:141) states: "Intelligence is the seeing of what is." This is awareness, observation relieved of the dead weight of the past or expectations of the future. And intelligence can exist only when there is a stillness of mind in a state of harmony. With such a mind we can see things as they are, being free to use knowledge and thought as we choose, without division, conflict, and conditioning.

Heuristically (see Butcher, 1986:48–49), then, we observe the true reality—come to "know" it—when we free ourselves of the conditionality of past thought and assumptions, when we become aware of ourselves and the world. Moreover, and most importantly, through the action that comes from awareness we can create a different world. We can transcend the destructive materialist rationality characteristic of Western thought and existence. We can act in good faith.

And Consider This, Always: In the End Is My Beginning

The *New York Times* reports the discovery of a tremendous pull on the Milky Way (which acts upon our solar system and the neighboring galaxies). The unexpected discovery, we are told, may force a revision of some basic notions about the universe. We are informed (Wilford 1994:A6): "What is tugging at these galaxies is not known, but it may be invisible matter clumped on much larger scales than can be readily explained by any current theory." Each new discovery, made possible by another theory and another method of observation and measurement, opens us to yet another unknown. We give names to our discoveries, and in the naming make things real. But beyond conditioned thought, we realize that all is story. The poet Muriel Rukeyser (quoted in Kornfield, 1993:324) said, "The universe is made of stories, not atoms." Or to say it another way, atoms are stories of our human comprehension of the universe. Even the universe, the idea of the universe, is a story we humans tell.

In the beginning was the word. We begin with words; we live with words, a life. And we end with the awareness that even words fail us in knowing the meaning of our existence. We are left with life itself, the living of this life. And the final expression of this realization may not be more words and more talk, but silence. The mystic Saint John of the Cross (quoted in Huxley, 1945:218) observed: "For whereas speaking distracts, silence and work collect thoughts and strengthen the spirit." With the wisdom gained by awareness there is less need to talk and to write discursively. One then practices what is realized, with charity and humility.

The modern intellectual paradox is that in all of our learning and complex analysis—including our attempts at interpretation— we obscure and perhaps completely miss the reality of the experience that we wish to understand. We have so filled our minds with assumptions, concepts, and methods that we have left little room for understanding. The subsequent paradox for us, as intellectuals steeped in the lore of social science, is that we must empty our minds before we can begin to understand.

Shunryu Suzuki, the contemporary descendent of the thirteenth-century Zen Master Dogen, has referred to this open state of mind as "beginner's mind." He has written: "If your mind is empty, it is always ready for anything; it is open to everything. In the beginner's mind there are many possibilities; in the expert's mind there are few" (1970:21). The goal of Zen practice is to develop beginner's mind. We can really learn something, Suzuki says, when we have no thought of achievement, no thought of self. When our mind is compassionate toward all things, it is boundless in its understanding.

Without empty mind—without mindfulness—we are attached to our ideas, our thoughts, our mental constructs, taking these productions to be reality itself. Many of our concepts are so deeply ingrained in our minds, in our culture, and in our education, that we forget that they completely condition our perceptions of reality. Awareness is a breaking of the chains of conditioned thought. We no longer take the concepts to be the reality.

In awareness we develop insight into the nature of the concepts we use to interpret what we think is reality. We discover our attachment to the concepts; and we then are able to move beyond the concepts to see the ways things are in the moment of their occurrence. It is this awareness that places us in the position to be in the world, to do what still might be called an interpretive sociology, a "sociology-with-awareness."

Sociology or no sociology, as human beings, as existential beings, we wait. We wait without expectation of anything. This is our postmodern being. In the end, I turn to the modernist poet, T. S. Eliot. In one of the poems of the *Four Quartets*, Eliot (1974) writes that in the end is the beginning. It is to such an end, such a beginning, that our lives are moving.

> We shall not cease from exploration
> And the end of all our exploring
> Will be to arrive where we started
> And know the place for the first time.

References

Bhagavad Gita. 1985. Translated by Eknath Easwaran. Petaluma, CA: Nilgiri Press.

Butcher, P. 1986. "The Phenomenological Psychology of J. Krishnamurti." *Journal of Transpersonal Psychology* 18: 35–50.

Camus, A. 1988 [1942]. *The Stranger*, translated by M. Ward. New York: Alfred A. Knopf.

———. 1955 [1942]. *The Myth of Sisyphus and Other Essays*, translated by J. O'Brien. New York: Alfred A. Knopf.

Eliot, T. S. 1974 [1963]. *Collected Poems*, 1909–1962. London: Faber and Faber.

Gadamer, H. G. 1976. *Philosophical Hermeneutics*, translated by D. E. Linge. Berkeley, CA: University of California Press.

Heim, M. 1993. *The Metaphysics of Virtual Reality*. New York: Oxford University Press.

Huxley, A. 1945. *The Perennial Philosophy*. New York: Harper and Row.

Kornfield, J. 1993. *A Path With Heart*. New York: Bantam Books.

Krishnamurti, J. 1977. *The Second Krishnamurti Reader*, edited by M. Lutyens. London: Penguin.

———. 1976. *The Awakening of Intelligence*. New York: Harper and Row.

———. 1975. *Freedom From the Known*. New York: Harper and Row.

———. 1972. *You Are the World*. New York: Harper and Row.

Merton, R. K. 1976. *Sociological Ambivalence*. New York: The Free Press.

Powell, R. 1983. *The Great Awakening: Reflections on Zen and Reality*. Wheaton: Theosophical Publishing House.

Quinney, R. 1988. "Beyond the Interpretive: The Way of Awareness." *Sociological Inquiry* 58: 101–116.

———. 1970. *The Social Reality of Crime*. Boston: Little, Brown.

Ricoeur, P. 1969. *The Symbolism of Evil*, translated by E. Buchanan. Boston: Beacon Press.

Sartre, J-P. 1992 [1948]. *Truth and Existence*, translated by A. Van den Hoven. Chicago: University of Chicago Press.

Seung, S. 1982. *Only Don't Know*. San Francisco: Four Seasons Foundation.

Suzuki, S. 1970. *Zen Mind, Beginner's Mind*. New York: Weatherhill.

Taylor, I., P. Walton, and J. Young. 1973. *The New Criminology*. London: Routledge & Kegan Paul.

Wilford, J. N. 1994. "Surprise, Milky Way Gets a Tug Way Out There." *New York Times* March 21, p. A6.

THIRTEEN

The Question of Crime:
Enlightenment in the Allegory of Oxherding

Let us consider anew the subject of our labor: the question of crime. And let us assume that the question of crime has something to do with the most basic truth: a truth that is in the realm of absolute reality, a truth on the nature of life and death and our place in the world of things.

We will consider crime as a koan in the Zen tradition. This is an inquiry that differs from our usual way of thinking about crime. The koan opens the intuitive mind; the koan takes us beyond linear sequential thought and moves us to an intimate and direct perception of the question. Internal dialogue is slowed down, and other senses—especially the visual—are awakened. The small self—the ego self—is forgotten as one becomes a part of the larger reality.

To study crime as a koan is to realize the true self. In realizing the true self, crime is understood in a way that has not been available to us in the Western mode of thinking and being. The question of crime is now inseparable from the question of who we are. Our study of crime (our criminology) is simultaneously a study of ourselves. We and the criminal are one and the same.

We may enter this realm by way of the allegory of oxherding. At least as early as the twelfth century, Chinese Buddhist monks were using the oxherding allegory as a training guide for the gradual achievemnet of enlightenment. By that time the search for the ox had been depicted in a series of woodblock pictures. In the middle of the twelfth century, the Zen master Kuo-an Shih-ÿuan drew a series of pictures and wrote comments on the ten stages of the

---

Original source: *Justice Professional* 11(1998): 35–46.

search for the ox. This version was brought to Japan by Japanese monks who had visited China. Later, in the early fifteenth century, a handscroll with ten ink paintings was made at Shōkoku-ji temple and attributed to the artist Shūban who lived at the temple.

In the allegory of the search for the ox, the ox has never been missing. To search for the ox is to find who we are originally. The criminologist, as an oxherd, searches for the meaning of crime and discovers what was present at the beginning. But now there is the enlightened realization, and there is a compassion in a return to the everyday world.

We would do well to consider the ten oxherding pictures in our criminology. We will, then, with the help of the drawings, trace the enlightenment of a criminologist. I will add a few words of commentary.

1. Searching for the Ox

The ox for which we must search is our own true nature. The first stage is the starting of the investigation. The student, as oxherd, has become interested in the phenomenon known as crime. The reasons for study, a study that may last a lifetime, are varied and mixed: to work for others, to know the causes of our actions, to make a career. The student travels through a maze of paradigms, theories, and research findings. Byways and crossways are confronted and transversed. Amusements abound. Eventually a course is found and a path in life becomes fixed. At this point, the criminologist realizes that something is missing. Doubts and uncertainties arise—perhaps there is a dark night of the soul. What is missing is a sense of who we are. At the same time, there are questions about the true meaning of crime and what is to be done. The criminologist continues to search for the ox.

1. Searching for the Ox

2. Seeing the Tracks

With the help of sacred texts and writings of great wisdom and inspiration, the oxherd finds the first traces of the ox. Footsteps are found in a snow-covered field. The footsteps, not ironically, are those of the observing participant. There is a glimmering, even within the confusion, that all things are related. Everything is composed of the same substance. The student of crime has some confidence that he or she is heading in the right direction.

2. Seeing the Tracks

3. Seeing the Ox

The student catches a glimpse of the ox. It is only the backside, the heels and the tail, but it is enough to convince us that there is an ox and that we have seen it. With the help of teachers, our eyes and our minds are properly directed. Our first research into crime yields an insight into the nature of the beast. There is a first awareness of the orgin of things, and a developing sense that we are part of what is being observed.

3. Seeing the Ox

4. Catching the Ox

At last the ox, after hiding in the wilderness, is discovered. But the ox is stubborn and hard to catch. To be tamed, the ox must first be caught. The oxherd is impatient and burns with desire and anger. The oxherd struggles with an undisciplined mind. The ox remains elusive, just as the crime that is to be understood and controlled remains elusive. The ox is caught under duress; violence begets violence. The mind of the oxherd is still unruly and separate from the object that is to be tamed.

4. Catching the Ox

5. Taming the Ox

Continuous effort—thought and practice—is required. False perceptions occur; the mind deceives itself. The oxherd keeps a firm hold on the cord as the ox is taken along the path and through pastures. Right thinking leads to the truth.

5. Taming the Ox

6. Riding Home on the Ox

The ox has been tamed. The oxherd will no longer lose the ox. Even when the reins go free, the ox walks quietly homeward with the oxherd peacefully on its back. The simple songs of children are played on the flute. The oxherd and the ox are one. The student has achieved maturity. The criminologist is on the path to a deeper understanding. A certain peace and an ease now prevail.

6. Riding Home on the Ox

7. The Ox Forgotten, the Self Alone

The oxherd is home. The seeker no longer needs the ox. The oxherd realizes that the ox is within the one who has been seeking. The ox—the need for the ox—has been transcended by the one truth, the oneness of all. Or, when we realize that the meaning is within each of us, the distinction between ourselves and the other (the criminal) is overcome. The criminologist is at home, in a new place. Beyond even Zen, abiding nowhere. Things happen as they may.

7. The Ox Forgotten, the Self Alone

8. The Ox and the Self Forgotten

Gone are both the ox and the oxherd. Confusion has disappeared and equanimity prevails. Even the idea of holiness—the Buddha—has vanished. Without dualism, the observed and the observer are one. No particular forms exist; circumstances appear only with the ego. All things—the ten thousand things—are joined in the great void of nothingness. Beyond naming:

> *The tao that can be told*
> *is not the eternal Tao.*
> *The name that can be named*
> *is not the eternal Name.*
> *The unnameable is the eternally real.*
> *Naming is the origin*
> *of all particular things.*
>
> (Lao Tzu)

The empty mind is clear of limitation. No crime and no crimelessness. Things are as they are. A time to practice this wisdom of absolute reality.

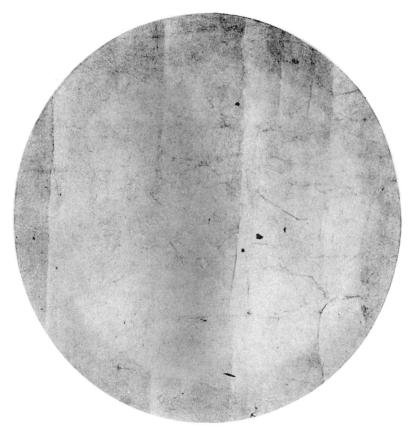

8. The Ox and the Self Forgotten

9. Returning to the Source

Mountains are mountains and rivers are rivers. No need to strive; all things change and nothing remains the same. Cling to naught. Sit in silence and watch things endlessly change. The one who once was a criminologist embraces all things—neither identifying with them nor striving for anything. An open heart and an open mind.

9. Returning to the Source

10. Entering the Marketplace with Helping Hands

Barefooted and naked of breast, I mingle with the
*   people of the world.*
My clothes are ragged and dust-laden and I am
*   ever blissful.*
I use no magic to extend my life;
Now, before me, the trees become alive.

                                    (Kuo-an Shih-ÿuan)

The enlightened, carefree one lives an ordinary life. A daily walk into town. A compassion toward all beings that comes with the ending of the ego. A helping hand. We are what we think and what we practice. Life is in the living. What more can be done? A great joy.

10. Entering the Marketplace with Helping Hands

Living in harmony with the truth portrayed in the allegory of oxherding, we will do the right thing. Whether we think of ourselves as criminologists, and perhaps we would do well not to think of ourselves as criminologists, our way is that of peace. And peace comes to the world only with the peace that we know and practice within ourselves. Selves—oxherd selves—that are of the world.

Notes

Chapter Two. The Social Reality of Crime

1. An earlier version of the theory of the social reality of crime was contained in a paper I presented at the 63rd annual meeting of the American Sociological Association, August 28, 1968. This chapter is a revision of my later paper, "The Social Reality of Crime," in Jack D. Douglas (ed.), *Crime and Justice in American Society* (Indianapolis: Bobbs-Merrill, 1970).

2. I have developed this position in *The Problem of Crime* (New York: Dodd, Mead, 1970), chap. 3.

3. For a discussion of the usage of causation in modern philosophy of science and in the physical sciences, see Percy W. Bridgman, "Determinism in Modern Science," in Sidney Hook (ed.), *Determinism and Freedom in the Age of Modern Science* (New York: Collier, 1961), pp. 57–75; Mario Bunge, *Causality: The Place of the Causal Principle in Modern Science* (New York: The World Publishing Co., 1963); Werner Heisenberg, *Physics and Philosophy: The Revolution in Modern Science* (New York: Harper & Row, 1958).

4. Alternatives in causal explanation in criminology have been suggested in Hermanus Bianchi, *Position and Subject Matter of Criminology: Inquiry Concerning Theoretical Criminology* (Amsterdam: North Holland, 1956); Nathaniel Cantor, "The Search for Causes of Crime," *Journal of Criminal Law, Criminology and Police Science*, 22 (March–April 1932), pp. 854–863; Peter Lejins, "Pragmatic Etiology of Delinquent Behavior," *Social Forces*, 29 (March 1951), pp. 317–321; David Matza, *Delinquency and Drift* (New York: John Wiley, 1964); Walter C. Reckless, Criminal Behavior (New York: McGraw-Hill, 1940). Acceptance of causal analysis in contemporary criminology is found in Travis Hirshi and Hanan C. Selvin, *Delinquency Research: An Appraisal of Analytic Methods* (New York: The Free Press, 1967).

5. Norwood Russell Hanson, *Patterns of Discovery* (Cambridge: Cambridge University Press, 1965), p. 64.

6. On the confusion between nominal and real constructs in general, see Robert Bierstedt, "Nominal and Real Definitions in Sociological Theory," in Llewellyn Gross (ed.), *Symposium in Sociological Theory* (Evanston, IL: Row, Peterson, 1959), pp. 121–144.

7. Alfred Schutz, "Concept and Theory Formation in the Social Sciences," in Maurice Nathanson (ed.), *Philosophy of the Social Sciences* (New York: Random House, 1963), p. 242.

8. George Casper Homans, "Contemporary Theory in Sociology," in Robert E. L. Faris (ed.), *Handbook of Modern Sociology* (Chicago: Rand McNally, 1964), pp. 951–977.

9. See Robert Brown, *Explanation in Social Science* (Chicago: Aldine, 1963); Morris R. Cohen and Ernest Nagel, *An Introduction to Logic and Scientific Method* (New York: Harcourt, Brace, 1934), pp. 197–222; Abraham Kaplan, *The Conduct of Inquiry: Methodology for the Behavioral Sciences* (San Francisco: Chandler Publishing Co., 1964), pp. 327–369.

10. David Miller, *Scientific Sociology: Theory and Method* (Englewood Cliffs, N.J.: Prentice-Hall, 1967), pp. 9–10.

11. For discussions of sequential theories, see Howard S. Becker, *Outsiders: Studies in the Sociology of Deviance* (New York: The Free Press of Glencoe, 1963), pp. 22–25; Clarence Schrag, "Elements of Theoretical Analysis in Sociology," in Llewellyn Gross (ed.), *Sociological Theory: Inquiries and Paradigms* (New York: Harper & Row, 1967), pp. 242–244.

12. See Robert A. Nisbet, *The Sociological Tradition* (New York: Basic Books, 1966); Reinhard Bendix and Bennett Berger, "Images of Society and Problems of Concept Formation in Sociology," in Gross, *Symposium on Sociological Theory*, pp. 92–118.

13. Howard Becker, *Systematic Sociology on the Basis of the Beziehungslehre and Gebildelehre of Leopold von Wiess* (New York: John Wiley & Sons, 1932).

14. Robert MacIver, *Social Causation* (New York: Ginn, 1942), p. 130.

15. Walter Buckley, "A Methodological Note," in Thomas J. Scheff, *Being Mentally Ill* (Chicago: Aldine, 1966), pp. 201–205.

16. Ralf Dahrendorf, *Class and Class Conflict in Industrial Society* (Stanford: Stanford University Press, 1959), pp. 161–162.

17. Ralf Dahrendorf, "Out of Utopia: Toward a Reorientation in Sociological Analysis," *American Journal of Sociology*, 67 (September 1958), p. 127.

18. Robin M. Williams, Jr., *American Society*, 2nd ed. (New York: Alfred A. Knopf, 1960), p. 375.

19. Lewis A. Coser, *The Functions of Social Conflict* (New York: The Free Press, 1956), p. 8.

20. Lewis A. Coser, "Social Conflict and the Theory of Social Change," *British Journal of Sociology*, 8 (September 1957), pp. 197–207.

21. Dahrendorf, *Class and Class Conflict in Industrial Society*, p. 208. The importance of conflict in society is also discussed in, among other works, George Simmel, *Conflict*, trans. Kurt H. Wolff (New York: The Free Press, 1955); Irving Louis Horowitz, "Consensus, Conflict and Cooperation: A Sociological Inventory," *Social Forces*, 41 (December 1962), pp. 177–188; Raymond W. Mack, "The Components of Social Conflict," *Social Problems*, 12 (Spring 1965), pp. 388–397.

22. Dahrendorf, *Class and Class Conflict in Industrial Society*, p. 165.

23. Max Weber, from *Max Weber: Essays in Sociology*, trans. H. H. Gerth and C. Wright Mills (New York: Oxford University Press, 1946); Hans Gerth and C. Wright Mills, *Character and Social Structure* (New York: Harcourt, Brace, 1953), especially pp. 192–273; C. Wright Mills, *The Power Elite* (New York: Oxford University Press, 1956); George Simmel, *The Sociology of George Simmel*, trans. Kurt H. Wolff (New York: The Free Press, 1950), pp. 181–186; Robert Bierstedt, "An Analysis of Social Power," *American Sociological Review*, 15 (December 1950), pp. 730–738.

24. David Easton, *The Political System* (New York: Alfred A. Knopf, 1953), p. 137. Similar ideas are found in Harold D. Lasswell, *Politics: Who Gets What, When, How* (New York: McGraw-Hill, 1936); Harold D. Lasswell and Abraham Kaplan, *Power and Society* (New Haven: Yale University Press, 1950).

25. Among the vast amount of literature on interest groups, see Donald C. Blaisdell, *American Democracy Under Pressure* (New York: Ronald Press, 1957); V. O. Key, Jr., *Politics, Parties, and Pressure Groups* (New York: Thomas Y. Crowell, 1959); Earl Latham, *Group Basis of Politics* (Ithaca, N.Y.: Cornell University Press, 1952); David Truman, *The Governmental Process* (New York: Alfred A. Knopf, 1951); Henry W. Ehrmann (ed.), *Interest Groups on Four Continents* (Pittsburgh: University of Pittsburgh Press, 1958); Henry A. Turner, "How Pressure Groups Operate," *Annals of the American Academy of Political and Social Science*, 319 (September 1958), pp. 63–72; Richard W. Gable, "Interest Groups as Policy Shapers," *Annals of the American Academy of Political and Social Science*, 319 (September 1958), pp. 84–93; Murray S. Stedman, "Pressure Groups and the American Tradition," *Annals of the American Academy of Political and Social Science*, 319 (September 1958), pp. 123–219. For documentation

on the influence of specific interest groups, see Robert Engler, *The Politics of Oil* (New York: Macmillan, 1961); Oliver Garceau, *The Political Life of the American Medical Association* (Cambridge: Harvard University Press, 1941); Charles M. Hardin, *The Politics of Agriculture: Soil Conservation and the Struggle for Power in Rural America* (New York: The Free Press of Glencoe, 1962); Grant McConnell, *Private Power and American Democracy* (New York: Alfred A. Knopf, 1966); Harry A. Millis and Royal E. Montgomery, *Organized Labor* (New York: McGraw-Hill, 1945); Warner Schilling, Paul Y. Hammond, and Glenn H. Snyder, *Strategy, Politics and Defense* (New York: Columbia University Press, 1962); William R. Willoughby, *The St. Lawrence Waterway: A Study in Politics and Diplomacy* (Madison: University of Wisconsin Press, 1961).

26. Truman, *The Governmental Process*, p. 322.

27. Evaluations of the pluralistic and power approaches are found in Peter Bachrach and Morton S. Baratz, "Two Faces of Power," *American Political Science Review*, 61 (December 1962), pp. 947–952; Thomas I. Cook, "The Political System: The Stubborn Search for a Science of Politics," *Journal of Philosophy*, 51 (February 1954), pp. 128–137; Charles S. Hyneman, *The Study of Politics* (Urbana: University of Illinois Press, 1959); William C. Mitchell, "Politics as the Allocation of Values: A Critique," *Ethics*, 71 (January 1961), pp. 79–89; Talcott Parsons, "The Distribution of Power in American Society," *World Politics*, 10 (October 1957), pp. 123–143; Charles Perrow, "The Sociological Perspective and Political Pluralism," *Social Research*, 31 (Winter 1964), pp. 411–422.

28. For essentially this aspect of human action see Peter Berger, *Invitation to Sociology: A Humanistic Perspective* (New York: Doubleday, 1963), chap. 6; Max Mark, "What Image of Man for Political Science?" *Western Political Quarterly*, 15 (December 1962), pp. 593–604; Dennis Wrong, "The Oversocialized Conception of Man in Modern Sociology," *American Sociological Review*, 26 (April 1961), pp. 183–193.

29. Tamotsu Shibutani, *Society and Personality: An Interactionist Approach to Social Psychology* (Englewood Cliffs, N.J.: Prentice-Hall, 1961), especially pp. 60, 91–94, 276–278. Also see S. F. Nadel, "Social Control and Self-Regulation," *Social Forces*, 31(March 1953), pp. 265–273.

30. Erving Goffman, *Asylums* (New York: Doubleday, 1961), pp. 318–320.

31. Richard A. Schermerhorn, "Man the Unfinished," *Sociological Quarterly*, 4 (Winter 1963), pp. 5–17; Gordon W. Allport, *Becoming: Basic Considerations for a Psychology of Personality* (New Haven: Yale University Press, 1955).

32. Herbert J. Muller, *The Uses of the Past* (New York: Oxford University Press, 1952), especially pp. 40–42.

33. Julian Huxley, *New Bottles for New Wines* (New York: Harper, 1957).

34. Florian Znaniecki, *Social Actions* (New York: Farrar and Rinehart, 1936); MacIver, *Social Causation*; S. F. Nadel, *Foundations of Social Anthropology* (New York: The Free Press, 1951); Talcott Parsons, *The Structure of Social Action* (New York: The Free Press, 1949); Howard Becker, *Through Values to Social Interpretation* (Durham: Duke University Press, 1950).

35. Max Weber, *The Theory of Social an Economic Organization*, trans. A. M. Henderson and Talcott Parsons (New York: The Free Press, 1947), p. 88.

36. Alfred Schutz, *The Problem of Social Reality: Collected Papers I* (The Hague: Martinus Nijhoff, 1962), p. 53.

37. See Peter L. Berger and Thomas Luckmann, *The Social Construction of Reality* (Garden City, N.Y.: Doubleday, 1966).

38. For earlier background material, see Richard Quinney, "A Conception of Man and Society for Criminology," *Sociological Quarterly*, 6 (Spring 1965), pp. 119–127; Quinney, "Crime in Political Perspective," *American Behavioral Scientist*, 8 (December 1964), pp. 19–22; Quinney, "Is Criminal Behavior Deviant Behavior?" *British Journal of Criminology*, 5 (April 1965), pp. 132–142.

39. See Jane R. Mercer, "Social System Perspective and Clinical Perspective: Frames of Reference for Understanding Career Patterns of Persons Labelled as Mentally Retarded," *Social Problems*, 13 (Summer 1966), pp. 18–34.

40. This perspective in the study of social deviance has been developed in Becker, *Outsiders*; Kai T. Erikson, "Notes on the Sociology of Deviance," *Social Problems*, 9 (Spring 1962), pp. 307–314; John I. Kitsuse, "Societal Reactions to Deviant Behavior: Problems of Theory and Method," *Social Problems*, 9 (Winter 1962), pp. 247–256. Also see Ronald L. Akers, "Problems in the Sociology of Deviance: Social Definitions and Behavior," *Social Forces*, 46 (June 1968), pp. 455–465; David J. Bordua, "Recent Trends: Deviant Behavior and Social Control," *Annals of the American Academy of Political and Social Science*, 369 (January 1967), pp. 149–163; Jack P. Gibbs, "Conceptions of Deviant Behavior: The Old and the New," *Pacific Sociological Review*, 9 (Spring 1966), pp. 9–14; Clarence R. Jeffery, "The Structure of American Criminological Thinking," *Journal of Criminal Law, Criminology and Police Science*, 46 (January–February 1956), pp. 658–672; Austin T. Turk, "Prospects for Theories of Criminal Behavior," *Journal of Criminal Law, Criminology and Police Science*, 55 (December 1964), pp. 454–461.

41. See Richard C. Fuller, "Morals and the Criminal Law," *Journal of Criminal Law, Criminology and Police Science*, 32 (March–April 1942), pp. 624–630; Thorsten Sellin, *Culture Conflict and Crime* (New York: Social Science Research Council, 1938), pp. 21–25; Clarence R. Jeffery, "Crime, Law and Social Structure," *Journal of Criminal Law, Criminology and Police Science*, 47 (November–December 1956), pp. 423–435; John J. Honigmann, "Value Conflict and Legislation," *Social Problems*, 7 (Summer 1959), pp. 34–40; George Rusche and Otto Kirchheimer, *Punishment and Social Structure* (New York: Columbia University Press, 1939); Roscoe Pound, *An Introduction to the Philosophy of Law* (New Haven: Yale University Press, 1922).

42. I am obviously indebted to the conflict formulation of George B. Vold, *Theoretical Criminology* (New York: Oxford University Press, 1958), especially pp. 203–242. A recent conflict approach to crime is found in Austin T. Turk, "Conflict and Criminality," *American Sociological Review*, 31 (June 1966), pp. 338–352.

43. Considerable support for this proposition is found in the following studies: William J. Chambliss, "A Sociological Analysis of the Law of Vagrancy," *Social Problems*, 12 (Summer 1964), pp. 66–77; Kai T. Erikson, *Wayward Puritans* (New York: John Wiley, 1966); Jerome Hall, *Theft, Law and Society*, 2nd ed. (Indianapolis: Bobbs-Merrill, 1952); Clarence R. Jeffery, "The Development of Crime in Early England," *Journal of Criminal Law, Criminology and Police Science*, 47 (March–April 1957), pp. 647–666; Alfred R. Lindesmith, *The Addict and the Law* (Bloomington: Indiana University Press, 1965); Rusche and Kirchheimer, *Punishment and Social Structure*; Andrew Sinclair, *Era of Excess: A Social History of the Prohibition Movement* (New York: Harper & Row, 1964); Edwin H. Sutherland, "The Sexual Psychopath Law," *Journal of Criminal Law, Criminology and Police Science*, 40 (January–February 1950), pp. 543–554.

44. Vold, *Theoretical Criminology*, p. 202. Also see Irving Louis Horowitz and Martin Liebowitz, "Social Deviance and Political Marginality: Toward a Redefinition of the Relation Between Sociology and Politics," *Social Problems*, 15 (Winter 1968), pp. 280–296.

45. See Michael Banton, *The Policeman and the Community* (London: Tavistock, 1964); Egon Bittner, "The Police on Skid-Row: A Study of Peace Keeping," *American Sociological Review*, 32 (October 1967), pp. 699–715; John P. Clark, "Isolation of the Police: A Comparison of the British and American Situations," *Journal of Criminal Law, Criminology and Police Science*, 56 (September 1965), pp. 307–319; Nathan Goldman, *The Differential Selection of Juvenile Offenders for Court Appearance* (New York: National Council on Crime and Delinquency, 1963); James Q. Wilson, *Varieties of Police Behavior* (Cambridge: Harvard University Press, 1968).

46. Abraham S. Blumberg, *Criminal Justice* (Chicago: Quadrangle Books, 1967); David J. Bordua and Albert J. Reiss, Jr., "Command, Control

and Charisma: Reflections on Police Bureaucracy," *American Journal of Sociology*, 72 (July 1966), pp. 68–76; Aaron V. Cicourel, *The Social Organization of Juvenile Justice* (New York: John Wiley, 1968); Arthur Niederhoffer, *Behind the Shield: The Police in Urban Society* (Garden City, N.Y.: Doubleday, 1961); Jerome H. Skolnick, *Justice Without Trial: Law Enforcement in Democratic Society* (New York: John Wiley, 1966); Arthur L. Stinchcombe, "Institutions of Privacy in the Determination of Police Administrative Practice," *American Journal of Sociology*, 69 (September 1963), pp. 150–160; David Sudnow, "Normal Crimes: Sociological Features of the Penal Code in a Public Defender Office," *Social Problems*, 12 (Winter 1965), pp. 255–276; William A. Westley, "Violence and the Police," *American Journal of Sociology*, 59 (July 1953), pp. 34–41; Arthur Lewis Wood, *Criminal Lawyer* (New Haven: College & University Press, 1967).

47. Turk, "Conflict and Criminality," p. 340. For research on the evaluation of suspects by policemen, see Irving Piliavin and Scott Briar, "Police Encounters with Juveniles," *American Journal of Sociology*, 70 (September 1964), pp. 206–214.

48. Assumed within the theory of the social reality of crime is Sutherland's theory of differential association. See Edwin H. Sutherland, *Principles of Criminology*, 4th ed. (Philadelphia: J. B. Lippincott, 1947). An analysis of the differential association theory is found in Melvin L. De Fleur and Richard Quinney, "A Reformulation of Sutherland's Differential Association Theory and a Strategy for Empirical Verification," *Journal of Research in Crime and Delinquency*, 3 (January 1966), pp. 1–22.

49. On the operant nature of criminally defined behavior, see Robert L. Burgess and Ronald L. Akers, "A Differential Association-Reinforcement Theory of Criminal Behavior," *Social Problems*, 14 (Fall 1966), pp. 128–147; C. R. Jeffery, "Criminal Behavior and Learning Theory," *Journal of Criminal Law, Criminology and Police Science*, 56 (September 1965), pp. 294–300.

50. A discussion of the part the person plays in manipulating the deviant defining situation is found in Judith Lorber, "Deviance as Performance: The Case of Illness," *Social Problems*, 14 (Winter 1967), pp. 302–310.

51. Edwin M. Lemert, *Human Deviance, Social Problems, and Social Control* (Englewood Cliffs, N.J.: Prentice-Hall, 1964), pp. 40–64; Edwin M. Lemert, *Social Pathology* (New York: McGraw-Hill, 1951), pp. 3–98. A related and earlier discussion is in Frank Tannenbaum, *Crime and the Community* (New York: Columbia University Press, 1938), pp. 3–81.

52. See Berger and Luckmann, *The Social Construction of Reality*. Relevant research on the diffusion of information is discussed in Everett M. Rogers, *Diffusion of Innovations* (New York: The Free Press of Glencoe, 1962).

53. Research on public conceptions of crime is only beginning. See Alexander L. Clark and Jack P. Gibbs, "Social Control: A Reformulation," *Social Problems*, 12 (Spring 1965), pp. 398–415; Thomas E. Dow, Jr., "The Role of Identification in Conditioning Public Attitude Toward the Offender," *Journal of Criminal Law, Criminology and Police Science*, 58 (March 1967), pp. 75–79; William P. Lentz, "Social Status and Attitudes Toward Delinquency Control," *Journal of Research in Crime and Delinquency*, 3 (July 1966), pp. 147–154; Jennie McIntyre, "Public Attitudes Toward Crime and Law Enforcement," *Annals of the American Academy of Political and Social Science*, 374 (November 1967), pp. 34–46; Anastassios D. Mylonas and Walter C. Reckless, "Prisoners' Attitudes Toward Law and Legal Institutions," *Journal of Criminal Law, Criminology and Police Science*, 54 (December 1963), pp. 479–484; Elizabeth A. Rooney and Don C. Gibbons, "Social Reactions to 'Crimes Without Victims'," *Social Problems*, 13 (Spring 1966), pp. 400–410.

Chapter Four. A Critical Philosophy of Legal Order

1. See A. R. Louch, *Explanation and Human Action* (Berkeley: University of California Press, 1969).

2. Martin Heidegger, *What Is a Thing?*, trans. W. B. Barton, Jr. and Vera Deutsch (Chicago: Henry Regnery Company, 1967), p. 46.

3. Ibid.

4. See John H. Schaar, "Legitimacy in the Modern State," in Philip Green and Sanford Levinson (eds.), *Power and the Community: Dissenting Essays in Political Science* (New York: Vintage Books, 1970), especially pp. 303–308.

5. For example, see the issues of the journal of the Law and Society Association, *Law and Society Review*.

6. Norval Morris and Gordon Hawkins, *The Honest Politician's Guide to Crime Control* (Chicago: University of Chicago Press, 1970).

7. See C. Ray Jeffery, "The Structure of American Criminological Thinking," *Journal of Criminal Law, Criminology and Police Science* 46 (January 1956), pp. 658–672.

8. For example, see most of the research studies collected in Richard Quinney (ed.), *Crime and Justice in Society* (Boston: Little, Brown and Company, 1969).

9. Alfred Schutz, "Concept and Theory Formation in the Social Sciences," in Maurice Nathanson (ed.), *Philosophy of the Social Sciences* (New York: Random House, 1963), p. 242.

10. See Alfred Schutz, *The Problem of Social Reality: Collected Papers I* (The Hague: Martinus Nijhoff, 1962); and Peter L. Berger and Thomas Luckmann, *The Social Construction of Reality* (Garden City, N.Y.: Doubleday, 1966).

11. Richard Lichtman, "Symbolic Interactionism and Social Reality: Some Marxist Queries," *Berkeley Journal of Sociology*, 15 (1970–71), pp. 75–94.

12. Howard S. Becker, *Outsiders: Studies in the Sociology of Deviance* (New York: The Free Press, 1963).

13. Aaron V. Cicourel, *The Social Organization of Juvenile Justice* (New York: John Wiley & Sons, 1968).

14. Richard Quinney, *The Social Reality of Crime* (Boston: Little, Brown, and Company, 1970).

15. See Quentin Lauer, *Phenomenology: Its Genesis and Prospect* (New York: Harper Torchbooks, 1965), pp. 1–2; and Pierre Thévenaz, *What is Phenomenology?* ed. James M. Edie (Chicago: Quadrangle Books, 1962), pp. 42–43.

16. Kant made this clear, and on this Husserl agreed. See Lauer, *Phenomenolgy*, p. 21.

17. This distinction is found in Immanuel Kant, *Critique of Pure Reason*, trans. Norman Kempt Smith (New York: Macmillan, 1929).

18. Martin Heidegger, *Discourse on Thinking*, trans. John M. Anderson and E. Hans Freund (New York: Harper & Row, 1966), p. 53.

19. Ibid.

20. Richard M. Zaner, *The Way of Phenomenology: Criticism as a Philosophical Discipline* (New York: Pegasus, 1970), p. 203.

21. See Zaner, *The Way of Phenomenology*, especially pp. 112–113, 117, 196, and 203.

22. Alan F. Blum, "Theorizing," in Jack D. Douglas (ed.), *Understanding Everyday Life: Toward the Reconstruction of Sociological Knowledge* (Chicago: Aldine, 1970), p. 305.

23. See Jurgen Habermas, *Knowledge and Human Interests*, trans. Jeremy J. Shapiro (Boston: Beacon Press, 1971), pp. 301–307.

24. Hannah Arendt, "Thinking and Moral Considerations," *Social Research*, 38 (Autumn 1971), pp. 417–446.

25. Ibid., p. 424.

26. Herbert Marcuse, *One-Dimensional Man* (Boston: Beacon Press, 1964), p. 9.

27. Jurgen Habermas, *Toward a Rational Society: Student Protest, Science, and Politics* (Boston: Beacon Press, 1970), pp. 81–121.

28. Herbert Marcuse, *Reason and Revolution* (Boston: Beacon Press, 1960), especially pp. vii–xiv and 3–29.

29. See, for example, Karl E. Klare, "The Critique of Everyday Life, Marxism, and the New Left," *Berkeley Journal of Sociology*, 16 (1971–72), pp. 15–45.

30. Horowitz writes in this regard: "There already exists, of course, a traditional corpus of Marxian theory which would logically form the starting point of any new analytical approach. But revision of the analytic tools and propositions of traditional Marxist theory is inevitable if the theory is to develop as an intellectual doctrine, and not degenerate into mere dogma. In principle, it may even be possible to create a theory which is 'Marxist' in the restricted sense urged here, but which has little surface relation to the traditional Marxist categories and conclusions. Nonetheless, at this historical juncture, the traditional Marxist paradigm is the only economic paradigm which is capable of analyzing capitalism as an historically specific, class-determined social formation. As such it provides an indispensable framework for understanding the development and crisis of the present social system and, as an intellectual outlook, would occupy a prime place in any scientific institution worthy of the name." David Horowitz, "Marxism and Its Place in Economic Science," *Berkeley Journal of Sociology*, 16 (1971–72), p. 57. Also see Jean-Paul Sartre, *Search for a Method*, trans. Hazel E. Barnes (New York: Alfred A. Knopf, 1963).

31. For example, Paul A. Baran and Paul M. Sweezy, *Monopoly Capitalism: An Essay on the American Economic and Social Order* (New York: Monthly Review Press, 1966).

Chapter Five. The Production of a Marxist Criminology

1. Karl Marx. *The Eighteenth Brumaire of Louis Bonaparte* (New York: International Publishers, 1963), p. 15.

2. See Fredric Jameson, *Marxism and Form: Twentieth-Century Dialectical Theories of Literature* (Princeton, NJ: Princeton University Press, 1971), pp. 38–46, 296–300.

3. The class structure in the United States, in relation to class struggle and the capitalist state, is analyzed in Richard Quinney, *Class, State, and Crime: On the Theory and Practice of Criminal Justice* (New York: Longman, 1977), pp. 63–105.

4. Theotonio Dos Santos, "The Concept of Social Class," *Science and Society* 34 (1970), pp. 166–193.

5. See Francesca Freedman, "The Internal Structure of the American Proletariat: A Marxist Analysis," *Socialist Revolution* 5 (October–December 1975): 41–83.

6. Nicos Poulantzas, *Classes in Contemporary Capitalism* (London: New Left Books, 1975); and Anthony Giddens, *The Class Structure of the Advanced Societies* (New York: Harper & Row, 1975). Also see Nicos Poulantzas, "On Social Classes," *New Left Review* 78 (March–April 1973): 27–54.

7. Freedman, *op. cit.,* p. 47.

8. The Marxist formulation of productive and unproductive labor is discussed at length in Ian Gough, "Marx's Theory of Productive and Unproductive Labour," *New Left Review* 76 (November–December 1972): 47–72.

9. Harry Braverman, *Labor and Monopoly Capital: The Degradation of Work in the Twentieth Century* (New York: Monthly Review Press, 1974).

10. On the increasing role of the state, in relation to class struggle, see David A. Gold, Clarence Y. H. Lo, and Erik Olin Wright, "Recent Developments in Marxist Theories of the Capitalist State, Part 2," *Monthly Review* 27 (1975): 36–71; Claus Offe, "Political Authority and Class Structures: An Analysis of Late Capitalist Societies," *International Journal of Sociology* 2 (Spring 1972): 73–108; and Gosta Esping-Andersen, Roger Friedland, and Erik Olin Wright, "Modes of Class Struggle and the Capitalist State," *Kapitalistate* 4–5 (1976): 186–220.

11. See James Farganis, "A Preface to Critical Theory," *Theory and Society* 2 (Winter 1975): 438–508; and Peter Laska, "A Note on Habermas and the Labor Theory of Value," *New German Critique* 1 (Fall 1974): 154–162.

12. See James O'Connor, "Productive and Unproductive Labor," *Politics and Society* 5:3 (1975): 297–336.

13. A detailed description of the working class hierarchy is provided in Judah Hill, *Class Analysis: United States in the 1970's* (Emeryville, CA: Class Analysis, 1975).

14. A similar analysis is found in Freedman, *op. cit.*, pp. 73–74; and O'Connor, *op. cit.*, pp. 303–305.

15. Regarding "contradictory class locations," I am following Erik Olin Wright, "Class Boundaries in Advanced Capitalist Societies," *New Left Review* 98 (1976): 3–41.

16. Ibid., p. 27. Also see the articles in *Synthesis: A Journal of Marxist-Leninist Debate* 1:1 (1976).

17. Fredric Jameson, *op. cit.*, pp. 367–368.

18. See George Lukács, *History and Class Consciousness: Studies in Marxist Dialectics*, trans. Rodney Livingstone (Cambridge, MA: MIT Press, 1971). Also Richard Lichtman, "Marx's Theory of Ideology," *Socialist Revolution* 5 (April 1975): 45–76; Joseph Femia, "Hegemony and Consciousness in the Thought of Antonio Gransci," *Political Studies* 23 (March 1975): 29–48; and Bertell Ollman, "Toward Class Consciousness Next Time: Marx and the Working Class," *Politics and Society* 3 (Fall 1972): 1–24.

19. See Terry Eagleton, *Marxism and Literary Criticism* (Berkeley: University of California Press, 1976): pp. 60–76.

20. Adolfo Sánchez Vázquez, *Art and Society: Essays in Marxist Aesthetics* (trans. Maro Riofrancos), (New York: Monthly Review Press, 1973): p. 61.

21. Ibid. p. 63.

22. Karl Marx, *The Grundrisse*, ed. David McLellan (New York: Harper & Row, 1971): pp. 132–143.

23. The realization that artistic and cultural productions are mediated by the capitalist socioeconomic structure, rather than being the exact reflections or correspondents of it, is the advance made in recent Marxist cultural theory. See Stanley Aronowitz, "Cuture and Politics," *Politics and Society* 6:3 (1976): 347–376.

24. Much of liberal (non-socialist, bourgeois) criminology is usable as we develop a socialist criminology. While most of its expressions (in form and content) are direct reflections of capitalism, they represent the decay and collapse of capitalist society at the end of the twentieth century. This social realism provides evidence and data on the hopelessness of the individual life under capitalism, the alienation of social life, and the repressive nature of social control. In bourgeois terms the daily existence of life under capitalism is realistically described. On the meaning and use of bourgeois writing, see Georg Lukács, *Realism in Our Time: Literature and the Class Struggle* (New York: Harper & Row, 1964).

25. Aronowitz, *op. cit.*, pp. 384–387.

26. Eagleton, *op. cit.*, p.65. Commenting on the Brechtian structure of the play, Eagleton continues: "Instead of appearing as a seamless whole, which suggests that its action is inexorably determined from the outset, the play presents itself as discontinuous, open-ended, internally contradictory, encouraging in the audience a 'complex seeing' which is alert to several conflicting possibilities at any particular point. The actors, instead of 'identifying' with their roles, are instructed to distance themselves from them, to make it clear that they are actors in a theatre rather than individuals in real life. They 'show' the characters they act (and show them-

selves showing them), rather than 'become' them; the Brechtian actor 'quotes' his part, communicates a critical reflection on it in the act of performance. He employs a set of gestures which convey the social relations of the character, and the historical conditions which makes him behave as he does; in speaking his lines he does not pretend ignorance of what comes next, for, in Brecht's aphorism, 'important is as important becomes'" (65).

27. Jameson, *op. cit.*, p. 340.

28. Ibid., p. 341.

29. See Mao Tse-tung, *On Practice* (New York: International Publishers, n.d.)

30. André Gorz, *Socialism and Revolution* (New York: Doubleday, 1973): pp. 170–174.

31. Dos Santos, *op. cit.*, p. 186.

32. Mao Tse-tung, *Where Do Correct Ideas Come From?* (Peking: Foreign Language Press, 1966). Also, on the role of intelletual workers, see Mao Tse-tung, *Speech at the Chinese Communist Party's National Conference on Propaganda Work* (Peking: Foreign Language Press, 1968).

33. Quoted in Wilhelm and Marion Pauck, *Paul Tillich: His Life and Thought* (New York: Harper & Row, 1976): front matter.

Chapter Seven. Crime and the Development of Capitalism

1.Paul Q. Hirst, "Marx and Engels on Law, Crime and Morality," *Economy and Society* 1 (February 1972): 28–56.

2. Karl Marx, *A Contribution to the Critique of Political Economy*, ed. M. Dobb (New York: International Publishers, 1970), pp. 20–21.

3. Paul Tillich, *Theology of Culture*, ed. Robert C. Kimball (New York: Oxford University Press, 1959), p. 198.

4. L. Afanasyev et al., *The Political Economy of Capitalism* (Moscow: Progress Publishers, 1974), p. 12.

5. E. P. Thompson, *The Making of the English Working Class* (New York: Random House, 1963), p. 9.

6. Maurice Dobbs, *Studies in the Development of Capitalism* (New York: International Publishers, 1963), p. 15.

7. Jurgen Kuczynski, *The Rise of the Working Class* (New York: McGraw-Hill, 1967).

8. Robert Heiss, *Engels, Kierkegaard, and Marx* (New York: Dell, 1957), p. 390.

9. Paul M. Sweezy, *The Theory of Capitalist Development* (New York: Monthly Review Press, 1968), pp. 92–95.

10. Maurice Cornforth, *Historical Materialism* (New York: International Publishers, 1962), p. 59.

11. Ibid., p. 91.

12. Erik Olin Wright, "Alternative Perspectives in the Marxist Theory of Accumulation and Crisis," *Insurgent Sociologist* 6 (Fall 1975): 5–39.

13. See Herbert Aptheker, *The Colonial Era* (New York: International Publishers, 1966), pp. 35–37.

14. Jurgen Kuczynski, *A Short History of Labour Conditions Under Industrial Capitalism in the United Stares of America, 1789–1946* (New York: Barnes & Noble, 1973), pp. 65–66. Also see Normal Ware, *The Industrial Worker, 1840–1860* (Boston: Houghton Mifflin, 1924).

15. See Gary Kulik, "Pawtucket Village and the Strike of 1824: The Origins of Class Conflict in Rhode Island." *Radical History Review* 17 (Spring 1978): 5–37.

16. Kuczynski, *A Short History of Labour Conditions Under Industrial Capitalism*, pp. 105–22. Also see Gabriel Kolko, *Main Currents in Modern American History* (New York: Harper & Row, 1976), pp. 1–99.

17. Kuczynski, *A Short History of Labour Conditions Under Industrial Capitalism*, pp. 171–172.

18. Frederick Engels, *The Origin of the Family, Private Property, and the State* (New York: International Publishers, 1942), p. 97.

19. David A. Gold, Clarence Y. H. Lo, and Erik Olin Wright, "Recent Developments in Marxist Theories of the State," *Monthly Review* 27 (November 1975): 36–51.

20. Stanley Diamond, "The Rule of Law Versus the Order of Custom," *Social Research* 38 (Spring 1971): 42–72; and Michael Tigar, with the assistance of Madeleine Levy, *Law and the Rise of Capitalism* (New York: Monthly Review Press, 1977).

21. E. B. Pashukanis, "The General Theory of Law and Marxism," in *Soviet Legal Philosophy*, trans. and ed. Hugh W. Babb (Cambridge. Mass.: Harvard University Press, 1951), pp. 111–225; and Isaac D. Balbus, "Commodity Form and Legal Form: An Essay on the 'Relative Autonomy' of the Law," *Law and Society Review* 11 (Winter 1977): 571–88. Discussions of Pashukanis are found in C. J. Arthur, "Towards a Materialist Theory of Law," *Critique* 7 (Winter 1976–77): 31–46; and Steve Redhead, "The Discrete Charm of Bourgeois Law: A Note on Pashukanis," *Critique* 9 (Spring–Summer 1978): 113–120.

22. See Richard Quinney, *Critique of Legal Order: Crime Control in Capitalist Society* (Boston: Little, Brown, 1974), pp. 95–135.

23. Alexander Liazos, "Class Oppression: The Functions of Juvenile Justice," *Insurgent Sociologist* 5 (Fall 1974): 2–24.

24. Alan Wolfe, "Political Repression and the Liberal State," *Monthly Review* 23 (December 1971): 20.

25. Alan Wolfe, "New Directions in the Marxist Theory of Politics," *Politics and Society* 4 (Winter 1974): 155–157.

26. André Gorz, *Strategy for Labor: A Radical Proposal*, tr. Martin A. Nicolaus and Victoria Ortiz (Boston: Beacon, 1967), pp. 131–132.

27. James O'Connor, *The Fiscal Crisis of the State* (New York: St. Martin's, 1973), p. 161.

28. Frances Fox Piven and Richard A. Cloward, *Regulating the Poor: The Functions of Public Welfare* (New York: Random House, 1971), pp. 3–4.

29. Wolfe, "New Directions in the Marxist Theory of Politics," p. 155.

30. See Stanley Aronowitz, "Law, Breakdown of Order, and Revolution," in *Law Against the People: Essays to Demystify Law, Order and the Courts*, ed. Robert Lefcourt (New York: Random House, 1971), pp. 150–182; and John H. Schaar, "Legitimacy in the Modern State," in *Power and Community: Dissenting Essays in Political Science*, ed. Philip Green and Sanford Levinson (New York: Random House, 1970), pp. 276–327.

31. See Richard Quinney, *Criminology* (2nd ed.; Boston: Little, Brown, 1979), pp. 163–261.

32. Tony Platt, "Prospects for a Radical Criminology in the United States," *Crime and Social Justice* 1 (Spring–Summer 1974): 2–10; and Herman and Julia Schwendinger, "Defenders of Order or Guardians of Human Rights?" *Issues in Criminology* 5 (Summer 1970): 123–157.

33. Steven Spitzer, "Toward a Marxian Theory of Deviance," *Social Problems* 22 (June 1975): 638–651.

34. Karl Marx and Frederick Engels, *The Communist Manifesto* (New York: International Publishers, 1965; original 1848), p. 20.

35. Hirst, "Marx and Engels on Law, Crime and Morality," pp. 49–52; Ian Taylor, Paul Walton, and Jock Young, *The New Criminology: For a Social Theory of Deviance* (London: Routledge & Kegan Paul, 1973), pp. 217–220.

36. Judah Hill, *Class Analysis: United States in the 1970's* (Emeryville, Calif.: Class Analysis, 1975), pp. 86–87.

37. Gorz, *Strategy for Labor*, pp. 57–58.

38. Karl Marx. *The Grundrisse*, ed. David McLellan (New York: Harper & Row, 1971), pp. 132–143.

39. Harry Braverman, "Work and Unemployment," *Monthly Review* 27 (June 1975): 30.

40. Karl Marx, *Capital*. vol. I (New York: International Publishers, 1967), p. 632.

41. Editors, "The Economic Crisis in Historical Perspective," *Monthly Review* 26 (June 1975): 2.

42. K. William Kapp, "Socio-Economic Effects of Law and High Employment," *Annals of the American Academy of Political and Social Science* 418 (March 1975): 60–71.

43. David M. Gordon, "Capitalism, Class, and Crime in America," *Crime and Delinquency* 19 (April 1973): 163–186.

44. Taylor, Walton, and Young, *The New Criminology*, pp. 220–221.

45. Sidney Lens, *The Labor Wars: From the Molly Maguires to the Sitdowns* (New York: Doubleday, 1973); Jeremy Brecher, *Strike!* (Greenwich, Conn.: Fawcett, 1972); Samuel Yellin, *American Labor Straggles* (New York: Russell, 1936); and Richard O. Boyer and Herbert M. Morais, *Labor's Untold Story* (New York: Cameron Associates, 1955).

46. Ernest Mandel, "The Industrial Cycle in Late Capitalism," *New Left Review* 90 (March–April 1975): 3–25.

47. O'Connor, *Fiscal Crisis of the State*, pp. 221–256.

Index

accommodation, 152, 164–69
Adler, H. M., 18
Adler, Mortimer J., 28–29
ahimsa (refusal to do harm), 204
Aitken, Robert, 185
Altgeld, Peter, 12
American Institute of Criminal Law and Criminology, 23
American Sociological Association, 207
analytic induction, 35
Anderson, Kevin, 204
animism, 6
L'Annee Sociologique (journal), 7
anomie, 32, 33
anthropological criminology, 16–17, 23. *See also* positivist mode
apocalyptic vision, 206. *See also* prophetic theology
Archives de L'Anthropologie (journal), 7
Arendt, Hannah, 104, 140, 200
Aristotle, 5
Arnold, Eddie, 172
art form: capitalist mediation of, 270n. 23; criminology compared to, 119–20; transcendence of, 120–21
Aschaffenburg, Gustav, 17
astronomy, discoveries in, 241

autobiographical reflection: concept and function of, 219–24; on journey home, 171–77; on life course, 217; as transcendent narrative, 221–30
awareness: conditioning removed in, 239–41, 242; divine call to, 198–99; effects of, 206; as endpoint, 241–43; of life as journey, 219–20; right understanding and, 183–85; self-scrutiny in, 224; of suffering, 180–83, 202–3; truth through, 239; way of, 201–3. *See also* mindfulness

Bachelard, Gaston, 223, 230
Barash, David P., 205
Bashō (poet), 174–75, 219
Beard, Charles A., 20
Beccaria, Cesare, 6–7, 136, 137
Becker, Gary S., 134
Becker, Howard, 74
beginner's mind, 181, 242
Belgium, crime statistics in, 7–8
Bentham, Jeremy, 136
Bhagavad Gita, 181–82, 208, 234
biological approach. *See* positivist mode
Blasing, Mutlu, 221–22, 224

.